Admirals of India

ADMIRALS OF INDIA

Col.(Retd.) M.K. Vats

PRASHANT PUBLISHING HOUSE
DELHI-110094

Published by :
Prashant Publishing House
C-34, 28 Foota Road, Gali No.-3,
West Karawal Nagar, Delhi-110094
Phone : 011-22963970, Mob. : 9810396373

Admirals of India

First Published 2012

ISBN 978-93-80565-30-9

PRINTED IN INDIA
Published by Mr. R.K. Jha M/s Prashant Publishing House and Published at **Dynamic Printers, Delhi**

Preface

About this time, i.e., at the beginning of the 1950s, in an appreciation of the future naval requirements for India and Pakistan, however, the Admiralty said that it was in the interest of the Commonwealth as a whole that India and Pakistan should maintain such naval forces as could be supported by their resources in material, manpower and finance and that the functions of these naval forces in war would primarily be to provide for the security of India and Pakistan including provision for harbour defence, minesweeping and coastal convoys, and, secondarily, to contribute to the overall security of the British Commonwealth. This would also include a share in the control of sea communications in the Indian Ocean, particularly in the Arabian Sea and the Bay of Bengal.

The Indian Navy is the naval branch of the armed forces of India. It currently has approximately 56,000 personnel on active duty, including 5,000 members of the naval aviation branch, 2,000 marine commandos and 1,000 Sagar Prahari Bal soldiers., making it the world's sixth largest navy. The Indian Navy currently operates more than 155 vessels, including the aircraft carrier INS *Viraat*, along with operational jet fighters.

The aims of this book is to provide our readers the latest research inputs on the Indian Admi ral, Naval Ships, Future of Indian Navy etc.

—Editor

Contents

1

Indian Navy Admirals

TALBOT SAVIGNAC HALL

Rear-Admiral John Talbot Savignac Hall, CIE (30 November 1896-21 January 1964) was a Royal Navy officer who later became the first post-Independence Commander-in-Chief and Chief of Naval Staff of the Indian Navy (then the Royal Indian Navy).

Life and Career

Hall was born in Kent, the third son of Dr. William Hamilton Hall, FSA. He was educated at Elstow School in Bedford and then served in the Royal Navy. In 1921, he was commissioned as a Lieutenant in the Royal Indian Maritime Component, and was promoted to Lieutenant-Commander in 1928. The following year, he became the Executive Officer on HMIS *Lawrence* a minesweeper and then transferred to another minesweeper, HMIS *Clive* in 1930.

In 1932, he was appointed commanding officer of the patrol boat HMIS *Baluchi*. He held this command until 1934. From February to July 1937, Hall was appointed Officer-in-Charge, Navy Office Section for the Defence Department (Navy Branch) of the Government of India. In April 1937, he was promoted to Commander. In 1938, he was appointed Staff Officer (Plans), Naval HQ, aboard HMIS *Dalhousie*. Hall was promoted to Commodore 2nd Class in December 1942, and appointed Chief of Staff to the Commander-in-Chief of the RIN. In January

1944, he was promoted to Captain and appointed a Companion of the Order of the Indian Empire. He was then appointed as the Senior Naval Staff Officer and RIN liaison officer to the India Office, serving in this capacity until 1946. Hall then commanded HMS *Achilles*. Upon Indian independence, he was selected to become the first post-Independence Commander-in-Chief of the Royal Indian Navy. Hall served for one year, when he was replaced by Admiral Edward Parry.

Afterwards, in his permanent rank of Captain, Hall commanded a destroyer squadron with HMIS *Delhi* (later INS *Delhi*) as his flagship. He retired from active duty in September 1950, with the rank of Rear-Admiral. From 1951 to 1959, he served as a civil defence officer for northeast Essex. Hall died in London in 1964, aged 67.

In 1933, he married Agnes Maud Shereen; the couple had one daughter and a son who died at a young age.

EDWARD PARRY (ROYAL NAVY OFFICER)

Admiral Sir William Edward Parry KCB (1893–1972) was an officer of the Royal Navy. During World War II, he served in the New Zealand Division commanding HMS *Achilles* at the Battle of the River Plate in December 1939. He assumed command of HMS *Renown* in 1943.

Parry was the second Chief of Naval Staff (Commander-in-Chief) of the Royal Indian Navy (14 August 1948-13 October 1951), replacing Rear Admiral John Talbot Savignac Hall who commanded (15 August 1947-14 August 1948). Parry was later replaced by Admiral Sir Charles Thomas Mark Pizey (13 October 1951-31 March 1955).

In the 1956 film *The Battle of the River Plate*, Parry was played by Jack Gwillim.

CHARLES PIZEY

Admiral Sir Charles Thomas Mark Pizey, GBE, CB, DSO & Bar, DL (17 June 1899-17 May 1993) was a Royal Navy officer who served as the last Commander-in-Chief and first Chief of Naval Staff of the Indian Navy from 1951 to 1955.

Early Life and Career

Pizey was born in Axbridge, Somerset, the son of the Rev. Charles Edward Pizey (?-1932), and Geraldine Fowle (1866-1949). He joined the Royal Navy in 1912 and served as a Midshipman aboard HMS *Conway* and HMS *Revenge* during the First World War. He was promoted to Lieutenant in 1920, and served on HMS *Danae* from 1921 to 1923. Pizey then served as a First Lieutenant, first aboard HMS *Violent* in the Atlantic Fleet from 1924 to 1925, and then aboard HMS *Winchelsea* in the Mediterranean from 1926 to 1927.

He was promoted to Lieutenant-Commander on 18 December 1928 and served from 1929 to 1930 as Flag Lieutenant-Commander to Vice-Admiral Sir W.A. Howard Kelly in the Mediterranean, aboard the battleship HMS *Revenge*. From 1930 to 1932 he commanded the destroyers HMS *Torrid* and HMS *Boreas*. He was promoted to Commander on 2 January 1934. From 1935 to 1937, he was the Executive Officer aboard HMS *Woolwich* in the Mediterranean, and then commanded the destroyer HMS *Fortune* in the Home Fleet from 1938 to 1939.

Second World War

In June 1939, Pizey was promoted to Captain. From 1939 to 1940, he commanded the heavy repair vessel HMS *Ausonia* as part of the Atlantic convoys. From 1940 to 1942, he commanded the destroyer HMS *Campbell* in the Channel and North Sea, seeing action against the German battleships *Gneisenau* and *Scharnhorst* as well as the heavy cruiser *Prinz Eugen*, for which he was appointed a Companion of the Bath on 27 March 1942 and was also appointed DSO and was mentioned in despatches. In July 1942, he was given the command of a destroyer depot ship, HMS *Tyne*, and served as a chief staff officer to a Rear-Admiral in charge of protecting Soviet convoys in the North Sea. For this service, he was awarded a bar to his DSO on 27 November 1942. In December 1943, Pizey was appointed Director of Operations Division (Home) for the Admiralty, commanding HMS *President*. He served in this capacity until the end of the war.

Postwar Career

In 1946, Pizey was appointed a Commodore and appointed as Chief of Staff to the Commander-in-Chief, Home Fleet, serving aboard HMS *Nelson*. He was promoted to Rear-Admiral in 1948 and served as Senior Naval Liaison Officer and Chief of UK Services Liaison Staff, Australia, aboard HMS *Terror* (RN base, Singapore). From 1950 to 1951, he served as Flag Officer Commanding, First Cruiser Squadron, aboard HMS *Liverpool*. On 30 November 1951, he was promoted to Vice-Admiral In October 1951, he replaced Admiral Edward Parry as the last Commander-in-Chief of the Indian Navy. He was knighted with the KBE in the Coronation Honours List of 1953, and promoted to Admiral the following year. In April 1955, Pizey became the first Chief of Naval Staff of the Indian Navy, which had replaced the former designation of Commander-in-Chief, Indian Navy. He was honoured with the Order of the People's Army of Yugoslavia that year upon Josip Broz Tito's state visit to India. Pizey was succeeded in his post by Vice-Admiral Stephen Hope Carlill in July 1955. From later that year he served as Commander-in-Chief, Plymouth. He was promoted to a GBE in the 1957 New Year Honours and retired in 1958. In 1962, he was appointed a Deputy Lieutenant of the County of Somerset.

Personal Life and Death

In 1928, Pizey married Phyllis May D'Angibau (27 November 1904-4 April 1993), the eldest daughter of Alfred D'Angibau (1865-1926), and Florence May D'Angibau (?-1947), formerly of Bournemouth; the couple had two daughters.

He died at Burnham-on-Sea, Somerset on 17 May 1993, a month short of 94.

STEPHEN HOPE CARLILL

Sir Stephen Hope Carlill, KBE, CB, DSO (23 December 1902-9 February 1996) was a Vice-Admiral who served as the last British Chief of Naval Staff of the Indian Navy from 1955 to 1958, when he was succeeded by Vice-Admiral Ram Dass Katari.

Early Life and Career

Carlill was born in Orpington, Kent, the son of Harold Flamenk Carlill (1875-1959), a civil servant, and Beatrice Newton Hope (d. 1924). He was educated at the Royal Naval colleges at Osborne and Dartmouth, and was commissioned as an Acting Sub-Lieutenant in 1923. From 1923 to 1926 he served aboard HMS Ramillies and was promoted to Lieutenant in 1925. In 1927 he served aboard the minelayer HMS Adventure. From 1928 to 1930, Carlill studied gunnery at the Royal Naval College, Greenwich and aboard HMS Excellent from 1929 to 1930. He served as 2nd Gunnery Officer on the cruiser HMS Norfolk in the Atlantic Fleet from 1930 to 1931.

From 1932 to 1935, he served as gunnery officer on the cruiser HMS Dunedin and as squadron gunnery officer for the New Zealand Station. Carlill was promoted to Lieutenant-Commander in 1933, and returned to Portsmouth from 1935 to 1936 to further study gunnery aboard HMS Excellent.

RAM DASS KATARI

Vice Admiral Ram Dass Katari was the First Chief of Naval Staff of the Indian Navy after India's Independence.

Biography

His vision for having a strong Naval tradition of Defence led to the establishment of a fighter navy in free India. He had designed an appropriate strategy for managing national security issues. The first Indian to become the Chief of the Naval Staff, he had the proud distinction of holding many 'firsts' in his academic and professional career.

That was Ram Dass Katari, who assumed charge as the Chief of the Naval Staff, on April 22, 1958. The senior-most Indian Officer of the Navy, Katari, was born in Chingleput (near Chennai) and spent his childhood and youth in Hyderabad. After completing his school and college studies, he joined the Training Ship *Dufferin* and stood first in the entrance examination.

He had the unique triple distinction of being the first cadet to join *Dufferin*, when this institution was founded in 1927, the first winner of the Viceroy's Gold Medal and the first Member representative ex-Cadets on the Governing Body of *Dufferin*. When World War II broke out, he was commissioned as a Sub-Lieutenant in the Royal Indian Navy Volunteer Reserve and served actively in Atlantic and Indian Oceans.

After the war, he was commissioned into the regular cadre of the Royal Indian Navy in the rank of Lieutenant Commander and was appointed as Commander of HMIS *Cauvery*, a frigate. Having specialised in anti-submarine warfare, Vice Admiral Katari was for a while instructor at the Anti-Submarine School. He also held important sea commands and was responsible for clearing the mines that had been laid near the Andaman and Nicobar Islands. When India gained Independence, he became the senior-most Indian Naval officer with the rank of a Commander. He subsequently took part in the Junagadh operations.

He was promoted to the rank of Captain in December 1948, about two months before he took over as Chief of Personnel at Naval HQ in Delhi. For about a year from December 1951, Katari was the Commanding Officer of a Destroyer Squadron and Commanding Officer of INS *Rajput*, the senior ship of the Squadron.

He attended a course at the Imperial Defence College in the UK in 1953. After his return to India he took over as the Deputy Chief of Naval Staff (DCNS) early in 1954 and was invested with the rank of Commodore. In the same year, he officiated as the Commander-in Chief of the Indian Navy, and was the first Indian Officer to do so.

In March 1956 he was promoted to the rank of Rear Admiral. After handing over to his successor at Naval HQ he went abroad on a study tour, returning to India in August 1956. In October, he took over as the Flag Officer Commanding the Fleet, a post that was until then held by British officers. He was promoted to the rank of Vice Admiral in April 1958 when he assumed the command of Indian Navy. During his tenure as the Chief of the Naval Staff, the Indian Navy saw a consolidation of its acquisitions, planned future growth and enhanced its training and operational effectiveness.

The operational effectiveness was amply demonstrated in the liberation of Goa from the Portuguese in December 1961. India's first aircraft-carrier, INS *Vikrant*, was commissioned during his tenure. He retired as CNS in April 1962 and two years later he was appointed as India's Ambassador to Burma, where he served with distinction for over five years.

Vice Admiral Katari has the unique triple distinction of being the first cadet to join the Training Ship Dufferin, when this institution was founded in 1927, to be first winner of the Viceroy's Gold Medal and to become the first Member representative Ex-Cadets on the Governing Body of the Dufferin. During World War II, he was active in service in the Atlantic and Indian Oceans and held a variety of appointments both afloat and ashore. Having specialized in anti-submarine warfare, he was for a while instructor in the Anti-Submarine School.

Subsequent to World War II, Vice Admiral Katari held important sea commands and was responsible for clearing the mines that had been laid near the Andaman & Nicobar Islands. Later, command of the naval forces that took part in the operation off the Kathiawar coast devolved upon him when he commanded INS *Kistna*. In the same ship, he also took the main body of ratings to the U.K. for India's first cruiser-INS *Delhi* and since the time she was taken over in July 1948 up to early 1949, he served as the commander of the Indian Navy's flagship.

He was promoted to the rank of Captain in December 1948, about two months before he took over as Chief of Personnel at Naval HQ. For about a year from December 1951, Vice Admiral Katari was the Commanding Officer of a Destroyer Squadron and Commanding Officer of INS *Rajput*, the senior ship of the Squadron.

He attended a course at the Imperial Defence College in the U.K. in 1953. After his return to India he took over as the Deputy Chief of Naval Staff (DCNS) early in 1954 and was constituted with the rank of Commodore. In the same year, he officiated as the Commander-in Chief of the Indian Navy, and was the first Indian Officer to do so.

In March 1956 he was promoted to the rank of Rear Admiral. After handing over to his successor at Naval HQ he went abroad on a study tour, returning to India in August 1956. Later in October of the same year, he took over as the Flag Officer Commanding the Fleet, a post which was until then held by British Officers. He was promoted to the rank of Vice Admiral in April 1958 when he assumed the command of Indian Navy.

ADHAR KUMAR CHATTERJI

Admiral AK Chatterji took over as the Chief of Naval Staff, Indian Navy, from Vice Admiral B.S. Soman on 4 March 1966. Adhar kumar Chatterji was born in 1914 and entered the Royal Indian Navy in 1933 as one of the first cadet-entry officers. He qualified as an anti-submarine specialist in the United Kingdom in 1940, and subsequently saw active service afloat in World War II in the Atlantic and Indian Ocean areas in various ships of the Royal and Royal Indian Navies.

In August 1947, Admiral Chatterji completed his staff course in the United Kingdom and on his return to India, was appointed Director of Naval Plan in Naval Headquarters. In June 1950, he assumed command of the flagship of the Indian fleet, I. N. S. Delhi (The erstwhile H. M. S. ACHILL of the Battle of River Plate Fame), in the rank of Captain. He was the first Indian officer to command the cruiser, in which he took part in a number of combined exercise and paid good-will visits to several countries in the Far East and the Mediterranean.

From November 1950 to January 1953, Admiral Chatterji was the Indian Naval Adviser to the High Commissioner for India in London, being responsible for, among other things the training of several hundred cadets and junior officers attached to the Royal Navy. On his return to India, he was appointed the Commander-in-Charge, Bombay. In this appointment, he was in administrative and operational control of several ships attached to the Bombay Command and of establishments in Bombay, Lonavla, and Jamnager. He held this appointment for two years. Admiral Chatterji there after completed a course in the Imperial Defence College, England. On his return to India, he took over as the Deputy Chief of the Naval Staff in Feb 1958, and was promoted to Rear Admiral in the same appointment in March 1959.

In May 1962, Admiral Chatterji took over as Flag officer Commanding, Indian Fleet, Flying his flag in I.N.S. MYSORE he paid a good-will visit to amongst other countries, Thailand the first visit of an Indian Cruiser to that country.

In January 1964, in the rank of Vice Admiral, he assumed the appointment of the Commandant, National Defence College in the New Delhi. This institution is responsible for Imparting higher knowledge to senior officer of the Army, Navy, and Air force as well as of the civil services. He was promoted to the rank of Admiral on 1 March 1968. Equally proficient in both the operational and administrative fields, Admiral Chatterji at one time had the reputation of being one of the finest ship-handlers amongst the navies of the entire Common-wealth countries.

Admiral Adhar Kumar Chatterji assumed charge of the Indian Navy, as the 5th Chief of Naval Staff, on 03 March 1966. Born in 1914, he entered the Royal Indian Navy in 1933 as one of the first cadet-entry officers. He qualified as an anti-submarine specialist in the United Kingdom in 1940, and subsequently saw active service afloat in the Second World War in the Atlantic and Indian Ocean areas in various ships of the Royal and Royal Indian Navies.

In August 1947, Admiral Chatterji completed his staff course in the United Kingdom and on his return to India, was appointed Director of Naval Plans in Naval HQ. In June 1950, he assumed command of the flagship of the Indian fleet, INS *Delhi* (the erstwhile HMS *Achilles* of the Battle of River Plate Fame), in the rank of Captain. He was the first Indian officer to command the cruiser, in which he took part in a number of combined exercises and paid good-will visits to several countries in the Far East and the Mediterranean.

From November 1950 to January 1953, Admiral Chatterji was the Indian Naval Adviser to the High Commissioner for India in London, being responsible for, among other things the training of several hundred cadets and junior officers attached to the Royal Navy. On his return to India, he was appointed the Commander-in-Charge, Bombay. In this appointment, he was in administrative and operational control of several ships attached to the Bombay Command and of establishments in Bombay, Lonavla and Jamnagar. He held this appointment for two years.

Admiral Chatterji thereafter completed a course in the Imperial Defence College in England. On his return to India, he took over as the Deputy Chief of the Naval Staff (DCNS) in February 1958 and was promoted to Rear Admiral in the same appointment in March 1959. In May 1962, Admiral Chatterji took over as Flag Officer Commanding of the Indian Fleet. Flying his flag in INS *Mysore*, he paid a goodwill visit to Thailand, among other countries, which was the first visit of an Indian Naval vessel to that country.

In January 1964, in the rank of Vice Admiral, he assumed the appointment of Commandant of the National Defence College in New Delhi. This institution is responsible for imparting higher knowledge to senior officer of the Army, Navy, and Air Force as well as of the civil services. He assumed command of the Indian Navy with the rank of Vice Admiral and was promoted to the rank of Admiral on 01 March 1968. Equally proficient in both the operational and administrative fields, Admiral Chatterji at one time had the reputation of being one of the finest ship-handlers amongst the navies of the entire Commonwealth countries.

S. M. NANDA

S. M. Nanda (October 10, 1915 – May 11, 2009) was the Chief of Naval Staff of the Indian Navy from February 28, 1970 until February 28, 1973. He was Born on October 10, 1915 in Punjab and was raised in Menora. He was awarded Padma Vibhushan award in 1972. He became famous as The man who bombed Karachi because of his role in the 1971 Indo-Pak War..

Subsequently, he became an arms dealer with Crown Corporation, headed by his son Suresh Nanda, specializing in the international weapons trade.

His family has been involved in several high profile criminal cases, two of which involve bribes paid to individuals at the highest levels of government for facilitating arms sales, and a third one a hit-and-run case involving his grandson, where three policemen and three others were killed at a police checkpoint by a speeding car.

- Operation West End which exposed corruption between India's defence ministry and Crown Corporation, where Suresh Nanda is alleged to have paid bribes to the defence minister George Fernandes and other Samata Party officials for
- selecting the Barak Missile system by Israel Aircraft Industries over the objections of the Indian defence research organization head APJ Abdul Kalam.
- helping select Slovakian Armoured Recovery Vehicles by disallowing a lower-priced Czech quotation.
- The BMW case, where his grandson Sanjeev Nanda (son of Suresh Nanda), drove over 6 people including 3 policemen around 3 AM on 1999-01-10 possibly in a drunken state, in a BMW car at high speed. The car did not stop, but the trail it left in its wake could be followed in the morning to where it was being cleaned of blood and other human remains. This case is continuing at a higher court after Sanjeev Nanda was acquitted in a lower court believed to be a result of bribing the sole surviving witness, who said that he was not sure what hit them, it could have been a truck.

Since Independence in 1947, Admiral Nanda held a number of important appointments both ashore and afloat that gave him varied experience.

In 1948, he joined the Navy's first cruiser INS *Delhi* in the United Kingdom as her First Lieutenant. On his return to India, he served as the Director of Personnel Services at Naval HQ from 1949-51. He later commanded the destroyer, INS *Ranjit*, as well as a Frigate Squadron. Posted back to Naval HQ, he became the Chief of Personnel and was promoted to the rank of Commodore.

In 1957, Admiral Nanda commissioned the cruiser INS *Mysore* in the United Kingdom. Subsequently, he was appointed Director General, Naval Dockyard Expansion Scheme, at Bombay. He was awarded the Ati Vishisht Seva Medal (AVSM) in 1961. There after, he underwent a course at the Imperial Defence College in London, returning to Naval HQ to assume the appointment of Chief of Material.

Admiral Nanda became the Deputy Chief of the Naval Staff (DCNS) in May 1962 in the rank of Rear Admiral. He was appointed Managing Director of Mazagon Dock Ltd. Bombay, in December 1964 and served there for 18 months. During this period, the re-organisation scheme of the Mazagon Dock and Leander Class frigates project were simultaneously taken up and he was responsible for giving both a good start.

Admiral Nanda was awarded the Param Vishisht Seva Medal (PVSM) for the distinguished service of a very high order in 1966. He commanded the Indian Navy during the 1971 Indo-Pak War and steered it to a resounding victory. The Pakistan Navy was humbled and the Indian Navy had complete control over the Bay of Bengal and the Arabian Sea. He retired in 1973 after completing over 31 years of exceptional service.

Nanda died in New Delhi on 11 May 2009 at the age of 93.

S N KOHLI

Padma Bhushan, PVSM

CNS, 28 Feb 1973-29 Feb 1976

Admiral Sourendra Nath Kohli assumed charge of the Indian Navy, as the 7th Chief of Naval Staff, on 28 February 1973. Prior to this appointment, he was the Flag Officer Commanding-in-Chief of the Western Naval Command, the largest command in the Indian Navy.

Born on 21 June 1916, Admiral Kohli was educated at St. Stephen's College, Delhi. He then joined the Royal Indian Navy as a cadet in May 1936 and proceeded to the United Kingdom for training. Two years later he was commissioned as a Sub Lieutenant into the Royal Indian Navy on 25 June 1938. He qualified as a Communication Specialist in the United Kingdom in 1943. During the Second World War, Admiral Kohli saw action in the Persian Gulf and also in the Far Eastern theatre.

After Independence, Admiral Kohli was one of those specially chosen to head the expanding Indian fleet. He was deputed to the United Kingdom in December 1948 in connection with acquisition of destroyers and was appointed as the Commanding Officer of INS *Rana*, an Admiralty Class destroyer, when the ship was taken over from Royal Navy. Among the important appointments held by him since then are the senior officer of INS *Godavari*, a Hunt Class escort frigate and later the Commanding Officer of INS *Mysore*, a Crown Colony/Fiji Class cruiser.

On his appointment as the superintendent of the Naval Dockyard at Bombay he was promoted to the rank of Commodore. Admiral Kohli has served in a number of staff appointments in addition to seagoing commands and has the distinction of having been twice Director of Naval Plans. He has been the Naval Adviser in the UK and has served as Principal Staff Officer in Naval HQ, first as the Chief of Material and then as the Vice Chief of the Naval Staff (VCNS). He rose to Flag rank in August 1965 and as Rear Admiral; he commanded the Indian Fleet from 1967 to 1969, spearheaded by the aircraft carrier INS *Vikrant*. He was awarded the Param Vishisht Seva Medal (PVSM) for exceptional and distinguished service in January 1968.

Prior to taking over as the FOC-in-C of the Western Naval Command in Bombay, on 12 February 1971, Admiral Kohli was, for two years, the Commandant of the National Defence College, which is the highest seat of learning in the politico-military field of our country. During the 1971 Indo-Pak War, Admiral Kohli was responsible not only for all naval operations in the North Arabian Sea but also entrusted with the defence of our coastline from the borders with Pakistan to Goa.

In addition, he was the controlling authority for the safe routing of the entire Indian mercantile fleet. The Western Fleet under his intrepid and imaginative leadership was instrumental in delivering crippling blows on the Pakistan Navy. The daring raids on Karachi have passed into the annals of naval warfare as a master stroke of offensive policy. After the war, he was awarded the Padma Bhushan for "*Demonstrating exceptional ability, sagacity and fortitude in putting into effect the several plans for the defence of our harbours and coastline.*"

JAL CURSETJI

CNS, 29 Feb 1976-28 Feb 1979

Admiral Jal Cursetji assumed charge of the Indian Navy, as the 8th Chief of Naval Staff, on 28 February 1976. Born on 20 May 1919, he joined the Royal Indian Navy as a cadet in January 1938 and was commissioned in September 1940. He served on board various naval ships during the war and was in command of INS *Bombay* in 1944.

Specialising in hydrography, Admiral Cursetji commanded naval survey ships for a number of years. He was the Surveyor-in-Charge, Marine Survey of India from 1950-54 and in 1955, he became the first Indian Chief Hydrographer to the Government, an appointment he held for more than two years.

Admiral Cursetji's other important appointments were Naval Attaché in Washington and commanding aircraft carrier, INS *Vikrant*. Promoted to the rank of Rear Admiral, in December 1967, he took over as the Chief of Personnel at Naval HQ. In February 1970 he was appointed as the Vice Chief of the Naval Staff (VCNS) in the rank of Vice Admiral.

Admiral Cursetji was awarded the Param Vishist Seva Medal on 26 January 1971 for distinguished service of the most exceptional order. Prior to his taking over as Chief of the Naval Staff, on 29 February 1976, he was the FOC-in-C of the Western Naval Command, a post he held since 27 February 1973.

R L PEREIRA

CNS, 28 Feb 1979-28 Feb 1982

Admiral Ronald Lynsdale Pereira assumed charge of the Indian Navy, as the 9th Chief of Naval Staff, on 28 February 1979. Born on 25 May 1923, he was commissioned into the

Indian Navy on 25 May 1943. During World War II, he saw active service aboard gunboats in Burma and Malaysia between 1943-45 and thereafter, continued at sea with an amphibious task group based in Iraq, till 1946.

After Independence in 1947, Admiral Pereira served for several years as a Gunnery Specialist, both afloat and ashore, before taking over as Officer-in-Charge of the Gunnery School, Cochin in 1956. A graduate of the Defence Services Staff College, he has served as Deputy Commandant of the National Defence Academy in Pune and as the Director of Combat Policy & Tactics at Naval HQ. He commanded the Indian Navy's Flag Ship, INS *Delhi* and commanded an anti-submarine warfare frigate, INS *Khutar*. He is considered as one the architects of the modern Indian Navy.

Admiral Pereira held the appointments of Flag Officer Commanding Eastern Fleet (FOCEF), Flag Officer Commanding of the Southern Naval Command and the Flag Officer Commanding-in-Chief of the Western Naval Command. In 1971 he was awarded the Ati Vishisht Seva Medal (AVSM) and in 1977 was awarded the Param Vishisht Seva Medal (PVSM). He is a keen sportsman having represented the Indian Navy in Hockey in 1946 and in Golf in the 1960s.

O. S. DAWSON

O. S. Dawson (Oscar Stanley Dawson) was an Admiral and former Chief of Naval Staff of India.

He was born in Burma and received early education there. He served as the Chief of Naval Staff from 28 February 1982 to 30 November 1984. He was one of the architects of Project Seabird.

PVSM, AVSM, ADC

CNS, 28 Feb 1982-30 Nov 1984

Admiral Oscar Stanley Dawson assumed charge of the Indian Navy, as the 10th Chief of Naval Staff, on 28 February 1982. Born in Burma, he also had his high school education there. When the Japanese occupied Burma in March 1942, he shifted to India where he continued his studies. Commissioned in the Royal Indian Naval Volunteer Reserve (RINVR) on 07 January 1943, Admiral Dawson was subsequently thereafter absorbed in the regular cadre of the Royal Indian Navy (RIN). Even as a junior officer his career was marked with distinction and the sea has always been his first love. He participated in World War II in the Arakan Operations (Burma), on convoy escort duty in the Bay of Bengal and the Arabian Sea and in mine-sweeping operations soon after the war.

Trained as a specialist in Navigation & Direction in the United Kingdom, Admiral Dawson has held various afloat and ashore appointments. He served as the Naval ADC to President Dr. Rajendra Prasad, from 1953-54 and since 02 March 1981 is the Honorary Naval ADC to the President.

Subsequent to his graduation from the Defence Services Staff College in 1957, Admiral Dawson served as the navigating officer of the aircraft carrier, INS *Vikrant* and also as the Fleet Navigating Officer. Later, he held appointments of Officer-in-Charge, Navigation & Direction School and that of the Director, Tactical School and Chief Staff Officer at Cochin.

Graduating from the National Defence College, in New Delhi in 1973, Admiral Dawson has to his credit 19 years of sea service which included important sea commands of the INS *Talwar* and INS *Nilgiri*. He served as the Flag Officer Commanding, Eastern Fleet, from February 1978 to March 1979. His important shore appointments include INS *Circars*-the Commanding Officer of the Boys' Training Establishment and the Director of Naval Operations (DNO) at Naval HQ during the 1971 Indo-Pakistan Conflict, for which he was awarded the Ati Vishisht Seva Medal (AVSM).

As the General Manager, Goa Shipyard Limited, Admiral Dawson introduced a Corporate Development Plan for the Shipyard and also brought about progressive management practices which improved the relationship between the workers and management. He was awarded the Param Vishisht Seva Medal (PVSM) for distinguished service of exceptional order on Republic Day 1981. He served as Flag Officer Commanding-in-Chief of the Southern Naval Command before assuming the office of Chief of Naval Staff (CNS).

During the latter half of his tenure as CNS, Admiral Dawson was also Chairman of the Chiefs of Staff Committee (COSC). He retired from the Navy on 30 November 1984, after 41+ years of glorious naval service. He was appointed as the High Commissioner of India to New Zealand in August 1985 and returned to Bangalore in September 1987, on completion of his tenure there.

LAXMINARAYAN RAMDAS

Admiral (retired) Laxminarayan Ramdas served as Chief of Naval Staff of the Indian navy taking the reins on November 30, 1990. He was commissioned in the Indian navy on September 1, 1953.

Career

Ramdas was trained as a communication specialist in the Royal Naval Staff College in the United Kingdom. He then went on to head in the Naval Academy in Kochi, Kerala. One of his major accomplishments was the reconnaissance and interdiction of enemy vessels and bombing of East Pakistan during the 1971 Indo-Pakistan war. Among the awards he won during his time in the Indian were: Vir Chakra, Param Vishisht Seva Medal, Ati Vishisht Seva Medal and the Vishisht Seva Medal.

He is also a keen sports person, enjoying cricket, golf and quite naturally yachting. In 2004 he was awarded the Ramon Magsaysay Awards for peace for his efforts in trying to demilitarise and denuclearize South Asia.

Admiral Laxminarayan Ramdas assumed charge of the Indian Navy, as the 13th Chief of Naval Staff (CNS), on 30 November 1990. Born on 05 September 1933, he was commissioned into the Indian Navy on 01 September 1953 after training at the Royal Naval College in Dartmouth, England.

A Communication Specialist, Admiral Ramdas underwent Royal Naval Staff College at England and as a Commander he established and commanded the Naval Academy at Cochin where he distinguished himself for which he was awarded Vishisht Seva Medal (VSM). During the 1971 Indo-Pak Operations, whilst in command of INS *Beas*, Admiral Ramdas took part in the most effective naval blockade of East Pakistan (Bangladesh) which frustrated Pakistan's attempt to evacuate 91,000 of their troops who eventually surrendered to the Indian Forces.

INS *Beas* also captured a large number of ships carrying contraband to East Pakistan, bombarded Cox Bazar and took part in the landing and other operations in an area infested with mines and submarines. For his resolute, bold, gallant and imaginative action in the face of great danger, he was decorated with the Vir Chakra. He later commanded a Patrol Vessel Squadron in the Indian Navy.

Admiral Ramdas served as Naval Attaché in Germany for three years. He held the appointments of Director of Personnel, Director of Naval Signals and Director of Naval Operations at the Naval HQ. Other notable appointments he held were Assistant Chief of Naval Staff (Operations), Flag Officer Commanding Eastern Fleet, Controller of Warship Production & Acquisition, Deputy Chief of Naval Staff (DNCS) and Flag Officer Commanding-in-Chief of the Southern Naval Command.

Prior to taking over as Chief of the Naval Staff, Admiral Ramdas was the Flag Officer Commanding-in-Chief of the Eastern Naval Command which he held since February 1989. A distinguished sportsman, an enthusiast of sailing and adventure activities, he promoted sports and adventure activities in the Navy to a great extent. He is a recipient of Param Vishist Seva Medal (PVSM) and the Ati Vishist Seva Medal (AVSM) in addition to the Vir Chakra (VrC) and the Vishist Seva Medal (VSM). Married to Lalita Ramdas since 19 October 1961, he has three daughters and three grandchildren. His interests include history, golf, cricket and yachting.

VISHNU BHAGWAT

Vishnu Bhagwat is a former Chief of the Naval Staff of India. He is the first and only chief of naval staff who was sacked while still serving. It was for the first time in the history of independent India that a service headquarter had refused to implement the order of an incumbent government.

Career

He went to School at The Lawrence School Sanawar on a prestigious Govt. of India scholarship for talented children. He is extremely proud of his school. Vishnu Bhagwat was commissioned into the Indian Navy on 1 January 1960. A graduate of the National Defence Academy, he was awarded the Telescope for the Best All-Round Cadet on the training ship, INS Tir and the Sword of Honour for the Best All-Round Midshipman of the Fleet.

In his 36 years of service he had a vast and varied experience in combat operations, warship production, acquisition and acceptance, personnel management and command. He was actively associated with the 1961 Goa Liberation Operations. During the 1971 Indo–Pak war his ship was in the escort groups for missile boats responsible for humbling the adversary. A Specialist in Communication and Electronic Warfare, he was Flag Lt. to Chief of the Naval Staff in 1968–70 and Naval Assistant to Chief of the Naval Staff in 1986-87.

Vishnu Bhagwat completed his first major command in INS Amini with the Western Fleet before being assigned as the Fleet Operations Officer of the same Fleet (1978–79). He commissioned the third Rajput class guided missile destroyer (DDG), INS Ranjit in September 1983 and was in command for 2½ years during which the ship set new fleet standards/records in weapons, sensors and operations.

On promotion to the Flag rank in 1988 he served as additional DG Defence Planning Staff, Chief of Staff of Western Naval Command and commanded the Eastern Fleet. He was Deputy Chief of the Naval Staff for two years at the Naval Headquarters. Prior to taking over as the Chief of the Naval staff on 1 October 1996, he was Flag Officer Commanding-in-Chief Western Naval Command.

A Graduate of National Defence College, Bhagwat is a recipient of Ati Vishisht Seva Medal (AVSM) in 1986 and was conferred the Param Vishisht Seva Medal (PVSM) on 26 January

1996. Admiral Bhagwat completed his first major command in INS *Amini* with the Western Fleet, before being assigned as the Fleet Operations Officer of the same fleet, from 1978-79.

He commissioned INS *Ranjit* in November 1983 and was in command of the vessel for 2½ years during which the ship set new fleet standards/records in weapons, sensors and operations. On promotion to the Flag rank in 1988, he served as the Additional Director General Defence Planning Staff, Chief of Staff of Western Naval Command and as the Flag Officer Commanding Eastern Fleet.

Admiral Bhagwat was Deputy Chief of Naval Staff (DCNS) for two years at Naval Headquarters. Prior to taking over as the CNS on 01 October 1996, he was the Flag Officer Commanding-in-Chief of the Western Naval Command. A Graduate of National Defence College (NDC), the Admiral is a recipient of the Ati Vishisht Seva Medal (AVSM) in 1986 and was conferred the Param Vishisht Seva Medal (PVSM) on 26 January 1996. His primary extra-professional interests are International Economics and History.

Sacking

Vishnu Bhagwat was appointed to chief of naval staff from 30 September 1996 and was sacked on 30 December 1998 under Article 310 of the Constitution of India. The unprecedented and much publicised row between the government and the admiral began after the Cabinet appointments committee appointed Vice-Admiral Harinder Singh as deputy chief of the naval staff.

Refusing to accept the Cabinet order, Admiral Bhagwat went public with his opposition to the government's decision. The government said that a series of actions from Admiral Bhagwat "were in deliberate defiance of the government."

The Supreme Court of India later dismissed a petition by the sacked Navy chief challenging the Government's decision to dismiss him from service and the punitive measure to strip him of the title of admiral.

Other controversies

In 2003, Bhagwat reportedly questioned installation of Veer Sarvarkar's portrait in the Central Hall of Parliament of India. This invited the ire of the Shiv Sena, a political party of India.

SUSHIL KUMAR

Admiral Sushil Kumar, a Nagercoilite Christian from Tamil Nadu, was a Chief of Naval Staff in the Indian Navy. His Christian surname is Isaacs which he dropped as not to confuse his initial with his brother who is also in the Service. He is often said to instruct his men with a quote from the Holy Gita "Do thy duty, reward is not thy concern"'. He was one of the highest ranking Indian christians in the Indian armed services, and the Indian Government.

Background

Admiral Sushil Kumar assumed charge of the Indian Navy, as the 16th Chief of Naval Staff, on 30 December 1998. A specialist in hydrography and amphibious warfare, he is also a qualified air warfare instructor. He has participated in the 1961 Goa Liberation and in both the Indo-Pakistan Wars of 1965 and 1971. As Director of Naval Operations, he was decorated with an Uttam Yudh Seva Medal for his exceptional conduct in Operation Pawan and in Operation Cactus (Liberation of Maldives). He was awarded the Naosena Medal (NM) for gallantry whilst in command of INS Ghorpad. He is an alumnus of the National Defence College and was an instructor at the Defence Services Staff College, Wellington. His training abroad includes a deputation to the Royal Navy onboard HMS Dampier in 1963 and a course in amphibious warfare with the US Navy at Coronado, San Diego, in 1976.

Admiral Kumar has held operational commands and important posts such as the Vice Chief of Naval Staff, the Flag Officer Maharashtra Area, Commander of the Flotilla in Mumbai and Fortress Commander Andaman & Nicobar Islands. He was the Flag Officer Commanding-in-Chief of the Southern Naval Command in Kochi, before being appointed as the Chief of Naval Staff. During his tenure as CNS, Admiral Kumar was the highest-decorated 'serving' officer in the Indian Navy and upon his retirement on 29 December 2001, he completed 40+ years of distinguished service. He is a keen yachtsman and has the rare distinction as a Naval Officer to have played polo on the international circuit with an international rating of 4+ goals.

MADHVENDRA SINGH

PVSM, AVSM, ADC

CNS, 29 Dec 2001-31 July 2004

Admiral Madhvendra Singh is former chief of Indian Navy. He was the 17th Chief of Naval Staff.

Admiral Madhvendra Singh assumed charge of the Indian Navy, as the 17th Chief of Naval Staff, on 29 December 2001. His father, the late Major General K. Bhagwati Singh (retd.), was the first batch of Indian Cadets to pass out of the Indian Military Academy-along with Field Marshal SHFJ Manekshaw. The late Major General K.B. Singh (retd.) has the distinction of having Indian Commission Number One.

After completing his schooling at the St. Xavier High School in Jaipur (Rajasthan), Madhvendra joined the National Defence Academy (NDA) at Khadakvasla in July 1958 and was commissioned into the Indian Navy on 01 January 1963. As a Cadet on board INS *Krishna*, he was awarded the Binocular for standing first in the overall Order of Merit and the Telescope for being the Best All Round Cadet. Later he was also awarded the coveted Sword of Honour on being adjudged the best all round Midshipman of the Fleet.

Admiral Singh specialised in Gunnery and has also undergone the Advanced Gunnery Course at the Royal Military College of Science at Shrivenham, United Kingdom. He is a Graduate of the Defence Services Staff College (DSSC), Wellington and a post-graduate of the Naval War College at Newport, USA and the National Defence College in New Delhi. He has commanded the aircraft carrier INS *Viraat;* the guided-missile destroyer INS *Ranvir*; the guided-missile frigate INS *Talwar* and the Naval Academy at Kochi.

Admiral Singh has also held important staff and training appointments, both afloat and ashore. As a Flag Officer, he has served as Chief of Staff of the Western Naval Command, the Chief Instructor (Navy) at the Defence Services Staff College (DSSC), Wellington and as the Flag Officer Commanding, Western Fleet, prior to taking over as the Assistant Chief of Naval Staff (Policy & Plans) at Naval HQ in June 1994.

On promotion to Vice Admiral on 02 January 1995, he took over as the Controller of Warship Production & Acquisition (CWP&A) at Naval Headquarters and later took over as the Deputy Chief of Naval Staff (DCNS). He was appointed as the Flag Officer Commanding Southern Fleet on 23 October 1996 and took over as the Flag Officer Commanding-in-Chief, Western Naval Command on 31 March 1998. He was later appointed as the Vice Chief of Naval Staff (VCNS) in New Delhi on 03 April 2001.

The highlight of Admiral Singh's tenure at Mumbai was the successful conduct of the International Fleet Review (IFR) in February 2001 in which 70 Indian Navy and 30 foreign naval ships were reviewed by the then incumbent President of India K.R. Narayanan in Mumbai harbour.

The prestigious event was attended by the then serving CNS, Admiral Sushil Kumar and senior naval officers from 30 other countries. He has twice been commended by the CNS and is a recipient of the Param Vishist Seva Medal (PVSM) and the Ati Vishist Seva Medal (AVSM) for distinguished service of a very high order. He took part in the liberation of Goa in December 1961 and in maritime operations in 1965 and 1971, as also in Operation Pawan in Sri Lanka in 1987. During the Kargil War in 1999, he was commanding the Western Maritime Theatre.

Admiral Singh is very fond of the outdoors and enjoys golf, yachting, riding and skeet shooting. An enthusiastic environmentalist, he is keen on preserving our maritime heritage and history. The Admiral is married to Mrs. Kaumudi Kumari and they have a son, a daughter and a grandson. Mrs. Kumari is a special educator and has worked in schools run by the Spastic Society of India. Upon his retirement on 31 July 2004, he completed more than 41 years of distinguished service to the nation and to the Indian Navy.

ARUN PRAKASH

PVSM, AVSM, VrC, VSM, ADC

CNS, 31 July 2004-31 Oct 2006

Admiral Arun Prakash PVSM, AVSM, VrC, VSM, Indian Navy, (born in Anantnag, in the Jammu and Ladakh districts in October 1944) served as Chief of Naval Staff of the Indian Navy and Chairman, Chiefs of Staff Committee from 31 July 2004 to 31 October 2006.

Admiral Arun Prakash assumed charge of the Indian Navy, as the 18th Chief of Naval Staff, on 31 July 2004. He was born in Anantnag, in the Kashmir valley, in October 1944. His father served in the Kashmir Civil Service, retiring as the District Commissioner of Leh, and young Arun's early childhood was spent in various towns of the Valley as well as Jammu and Ladakh districts. Although his two elder brothers served in the Indian Army, he was struck by *sea fever* from an early age and joined the National Defence Academy (NDA) as a Naval Cadet in 1961. He was formally commissioned into the Executive Branch of the Indian Navy on 01 January 1966.

Early life and education

Raised in the Kashmir Valley, where his father rose to be a District Commissioner of Leh

Early Naval Career

Specializing in naval aviation, he qualified as a pilot in the Seahawk jet fighter, flying from the deck of the aircraft carrier INS Vikrant in 1968. His assignments in naval aviation, included flying Islander aircraft with Indian Navy Air Squadron 550, Vampire and Kiran aircraft with Indian Navy Air Squadron 551, and Seahawk and Sea Harrier aircraft with Indian Navy Air Squadron 300. In the 1971 Indo-Pakistan War, Lieutenant Prakash flew Hawker Hunter aircraft for the 20th Squardon

Lightinings, & in his first mission against Chakala base, he blasted the Twin engine Beechcraft of Chuck Yeager which was parked on the tarmac. It was this action, which forced Chuck Yeager to call up Washington & requested them to send the US Seventh Fleet to Bay of Bengal. For his gallantry in air action over West Pakistan and Jammu and Kashmir, he received the Vir Chakra.

In 1976, he flew the Super Constellation for maritime air reconnaissance with Indian Navy Air Squadron 312. In 1983, while in command of Indian Navy Air Squadron 300, he supervised the training of Indian Navy crew members in the United Kingdom for the Sea Harrier and ferried the newly acquired aircrtaft back to India. He commanded two Air Squadrons and the naval air station INS Hansa. In his aviation assignments, he logged more than 2,500 hours in the air in single and multi-engined, shore-based and carrier-based aircraft.

As a junior officer, he served afloat in the aircraft carrier INS Vikrant, INS Kirpan, and INS Delhi. He commanded the missile boat INS Chatak, the training frigate INS Beas, the antisubmarine warfare frigate INS Vindhyagiri, and the aircraft carrier INS Vikrant.

Arun Prakash graduated from the Indian Air Force Test Pilots School in 1976, the Defence Services Staff College in 1979, and the U.S. Naval War College in 1990.

Admiral Prakash specialized in aviation, and qualified as an aircraft carrier pilot on the Sea Hawk jet fighter from the deck of INS *Vikrant* in 1968. His aviation tenures include service in a number of Indian Naval Air Squadrons, namely INAS 550 *Flying Fish*, INAS 551 *Phantoms* and INAS 300 *White Tigers*. In 1976, when the maritime reconnaissance role came to the Indian Navy, he converted to, and briefly flew the four-engined Super Constellation with the INAS 312 *Albatross* unit. He has commanded two Air Squadrons, and the Naval Air Station INS *Hansa*. While in command of INAS 300, he supervised the conversion and operational training of the crew on the Sea Harrier VSTOL fighter in 1983, and ferried the aircraft back to India from the United Kingdom. He has flown

2500 hours on a variety of single and multi-engined aircraft from the aircraft carrier and ashore.

As a young officer, Admiral Prakash served afloat on the aircraft carrier INS *Vikrant*, the ASW frigate INS *Kirpan* and the light cruiser INS *Delhi*. In subsequent years, he was privileged to command a variety of seagoing units which included the missile boat INS *Chatak*, the training frigate INS *Beas* and the ASW frigate INS *Vindhyagiri*, and the aircraft carrier INS *Viraat*. He commanded the Eastern Fleet from 1995 to 1997. On promotion to Rear Admiral in 1993, he served as ACNS (Air) and as the Assistant Chief of Personnel.

In the rank of Vice Admiral, he has been the Commandant of the National Defence Academy (from 1997 to 1999) and Chief of Personnel at Naval HQ (from 1999 to 2001). In October 2001, he was appointed the first Commander-in-Chief of the newly created Andaman & Nicobar Command and served in that capacity till taking over as Flag Officer Commanding-in-Chief of the prestigious Western Naval Command-the sword arm of the Indian Navy-on 31 December 2002. He took over as the Vice Chief of Naval Staff at Naval HQ on 17 October 2003 and held that post till he became the Chief on Naval Staff on 31 July 2004. He was appointed as the Chairman Chiefs of Staff Committee (COSC) on 28 January 2005.

Admiral Prakash graduated from the IAF's Test Pilots School in 1976, from the Defence Services Staff College (DSSC) in 1979 and from the US Naval War College in 1990. As a young Lieutenant, during the 1971 war, he served with an IAF fighter-bomber unit (No.20 *Lightnings* Squadron) flying Hawker Hunters, and was awarded the Vir Chakra for gallantry in air action over West Pakistan and Jammu & Kashmir. He is the recipient of the Vishisht Seva Medal (1985), the Ati Vishisht Seva Medal (1991) and the Param Vishisht Seva Medal (2002) for distinguished services rendered. The Admiral comes from a family with a strong military tradition; his two elder brothers, having both retired after distinguished careers in the Indian Army, and many nephews and nieces either serving in the armed forces or married to service officers. The Admiral and Mrs. Kumkum Prakash have one daughter who is married to a retired IAF pilot. Upon his retirement on 31 October 2006, he completed more than 40 years of distinguished service to the nation and to the Indian Navy.

Career as a Flag Officer

Promoted to Rear Admiral in 1993, he served as Assistant Chief of Naval Staff (Air) and Assistant Chief of Personnel. As a Vice Admiral, he was Commandant of the National Defence Academy in 1997-1999, and Chief of Naval Personnel at Naval Headquarters in 1999-2001. In October 2001, he became the first commander-in-chief of the newly established United Andaman and Nicobar Command. Then, on 31 December 2002, he became Flag Officer Commanding-in-Chief of the Western Naval Command. Following this assignment, he became Vice Chief of Naval Staff for a brief period before being promoted to Admiral and becoming the 20th Chief of Naval Staff, Indian Navy, on 31 July 2004.

Arun Prakash retired as Chief of Naval Staff on 1 November 2006. While serving as Chief of Naval Staff, Prakash played an important role in renewing the Indian Navy's relationships with the United States Navy and in developing a vision of India's maritime strategy.

NIRMAL KUMAR VERMA

Admiral Nirmal Kumar Verma is the current Chief of the Indian Navy, having taken office on August 31, 2009.

Early life

Born on November 14, 1950, he joined the Indian Navy at the age of 19. He studied at the Royal Naval Staff College in the UK, and the Naval War College in the US.

Military career

Verma took charge of the Naval Academy in Goa, and subsequently became commander of a series of Indian Navy ships, including INS Viraat, India's only aircraft carrier. He rose to the rank of Flag Officer Commanding-in-Chief (FOC-in-C) of the Eastern Naval Command, and was appointed Chief of the Indian Navy upon the retirement of Sureesh Mehta on

August 31, 2009. During his career he has been awarded several decorations, including the Param Vishisht Seva Medal and the Ati Vishisht Seva Medal.

SUREESH MEHTA

Chief of the Naval Staff & Chairman, Chiefs of Staff Committee

Admiral Sureesh Mehta assumed charge of the Indian Navy, as the 19th Chief of Naval Staff, on 31 October 2006. Born on 18 August 1947, he is the first service chief from the armed forces to be born post Indian Independence. He is an alumnus of the National Defence Academy (NDA) and was commissioned into the Executive Branch of the Indian Navy in July 1967. Shortly thereafter, he joined the Indian Naval Air Arm and extensively flew the Hawker Sea Hawk from the aircraft carrier Vikrant. He is a graduate of the prestigious Defence Services Staff College (DSSC) at Wellington and has also carried out instructional duties as a directing staff in that institute. He also attended the National Defence College (NDC) at New Delhi in 1994. His most distinguishing ship appointments include the command of INS *Beas*-a Leopard Class frigate and the first indigenously-built, guided-missile frigate of the Indian Navy-INS *Godavari*.

On promotion to Rear Admiral in 1995, Admiral Mehta was appointed as the Flag Officer Naval Aviation (FONA), where he was responsible for marshalling the resources of the entire aviation fleet of the Indian Navy. In October 1998, he was appointed as Flag Officer Commanding Western Fleet, a post he held with distinction till April 2000. It was during his tenure as FOC Western Fleet, that the incident of piracy aboard the MV Alondra Rainbow occurred in November 1999. This Japanese tanker was stopped by naval units under his command and the pirates were brought to book by his flagship, INS *Delhi*. He has also had the distinction of commanding INS *Garuda*, the Indian Navy's premier naval air station in Kochi, Kerala.

During Admiral Mehta's tenure as Assistant Controller of Warship Production & Acquisition and Assistant Controller Carrier Projects at Naval Headquarters, he initiated wide ranging initiatives to revitalize the naval fleet and was responsible for commencement of a host of important and critical ship & aircraft acquisition programs, in preparation for blue water operations of the Indian Navy in the 21st century. In his further appointments as the Assistant Chief of Personnel (Human Resources Development), Controller Personnel Services and Chief of Personnel at Naval HQ, he was responsible for the entire Personnel Management Policy of the Indian Navy.

Admiral Mehta was appointed as Director General (DG) Coast Guard on 13 January 2003 and he guided the force with the vision of establishing a strong, vibrant and visible Indian Coast Guard. He established linkages with India's maritime neighbours-both near and afar-and created common operating doctrines for tackling incidents at sea. He pursued a vigorous growth for the Coast Guard fleet and organisation, aided by active modernization programs. On the issue of piracy at sea, he has tailored Coast Guard operations towards adopting a pro-active approach in combating piracy in Indian and neighbouring waters.

Prior to taking charge as CNS, Admiral Mehta served as the Flag Officer Commanding-in-Chief (FOC-in-C) of the Eastern Naval Command from 30 September 2005. It was during his tenure at the ENC, that the first-ever Presidential naval fleet review was held on the country's east coast, which saw participation by over 66 warships and 50 aircraft of the Indian Navy. He also held the office of Deputy Chief of Naval Staff (DCNS) from 2004 to 2005. He was awarded the Ati Vishist Seva Medal (AVSM) in 1995 and the Param Vishist Seva Medal (PVSM) in 2005 for exceptional meritorious services. Admiral Mehta and Mrs Maria Teresa Mehta have two children. He was appointed as the Chairman Chiefs of Staff Committee (COSC) on 28 September 2007.

Military career

After graduating, Admiral Mehta joined the Fleet Air Arm of the Indian Navy, where he flew the Hawker Sea Hawk off the aircraft carrier, INS Vikrant. He served as the Flag Officer Commanding-in-Chief (FOC-in-C) of the Eastern Naval

Command (ENC) from 30 September 2005 till his appointment as the Naval Chief. He was appointed as the Chairman of the Chiefs of Staff Committee (COSC) on 28 September 2007.

Awards and Distinctions

In 1995, Admrial Mehta was awarded the Ati Vishist Seva Medal. In 2005, he received the Param Vishist Seva Medal.

High Commissioner to New Zealand

After retirement the Indian government appointed him as India's High Commissioner to New Zealand

V S SHEKHAWAT

PVSM, AVSM, VrC, ADC

CNS, 30 Sep 1993-30 Sep 1996

Admiral Vijai Singh Shekhawat assumed charge of the Indian Navy, as the 14th Chief of Naval Staff, on 30 September 1993. Having grown up in a military environment, he spent his childhood years in various cantonments including Peshawar (Pakistan) and Dhaka (Bangladesh) in the then undivided India. His father, a paratrooper, was amongst the first officers to be commissioned from the Indian Military Academy (IMA). Passing through several schools as the family moved on transfers, his main education was in Colonel Brown's School and St. Joseph's Academy in Dehradun, Bishop Cotton Boys' School in Bangalore and St Joseph's College in North Point, Darjeeling.

His interest in the sea developed early from reading stories of sailing ships, pirates and far off islands, and joining the navy was almost a foregone conclusion. He was selected for the 7th Course of the Joint Services Wing, National Defence Academy, then at Clement Town, Dehradun in January 1952. He was first in overall order of merit and awarded the President's Gold Medal for the best all-round cadet on passing out in December 1953. During his Academy days, he was an outstanding sportsman and was awarded Blues in Athletics, Boxing, Football, Swimming and Riding. His early riding experience with the Mysore and the Gwalior Lancers stood him in good stead and he won the first prize in Cadet's Show Jumping at the first post-war Army Horse Show held in New Delhi in 1954. He was a member of the academy debating teams participation in inter-university debates, notably against Oxford University, and also a prominent member of the Dramatics.

Admiral Shekhawat has been a keen mountaineer having done the basic and advanced mountaineering courses from the Himalayan Mountaineering Institute in Darjeeling. He was a member of the successful Annapurna III (24,858 feet) mountaineering expedition to Nepal in 1961 and has done extensive rock climbing in Wales, U.K. His present active sporting interest is tennis.

After early sea training in frigates and cruisers as cadet and midshipman, he was commissioned on 01 July 1956 and held various assignments in fleet ships before being sent to U.K. in 1959 as 2nd Gunnery Officer for INS *Talwar*, and later, Navigating Officer on her return passage through the Mediterranean Sea and the Suez Canal.

A pioneer of the submarine arm, Admiral Shekhawat did his basic submarine training in the U.K. in 1963-64 and then in the USSR in 1966-67. He has been the Executive and Commanding Officer of several submarines, commanded the submarine base and the 8th Submarine Squadron at Vizag and was Director of the Submarine Arm in 1975-77. He commissioned INS *Kalvari* (1967) and INS *Karanj* (1969)-two Foxtrot Class submarines-in the Baltic Sea and sailed them through the Atlantic Ocean and round the Cape of Good Hope to India, the Suez Canal being closed after the Arab-Israel War of 1967.

Admiral Shekhawat attended the US Naval War College in Newport, USA in 1977-78 and subsequently commanded INS *Himgiri* from 1981-82. He was awarded the Vir Chakra for gallantry whilst in the command of INS *Karanj* during the 1971 Indo-Pak War, the Ati Vishisht Seva Medal for distinguished service in 1984 and the Param Vishisht Seva Medal in 1991 for exceptional services. He has had close association with the training of junior officers and was an instructor on board the Cadet and Midshipmen training vessels from 1957-59 and also at the National Defence Academy, Pune from 1961-63. He again served at the National Defence Academy from 1979-81 as Chief Instructor and Deputy Commandant. On promotion to Flag Rank in June 1984, Admiral Shekhawat served as the Assistant Chief of Naval Staff (Operations) at Naval HQ. He commanded the prestigious Western Fleet, the strike force of the Indian Navy during 1986-87, coinciding with the period of Operation Brasstacks, and was Flag Officer Commanding Maharashtra Area (FOMA) during 1987-88.

Promoted to Vice Admiral in August 1988, he was the Director General of the tri-service Defence Planning Staff until August 1990. From December 1990 to October 1992, he was the FOC-in-C of the Eastern Naval Command, with maritime defence responsibilities for the entire eastern seaboard and the Andaman & Nicobar Islands. From November 1992 to September 1993, he was the Vice Chief of the Naval Staff (VCNS) and assumed the appointment of the Chief of the Naval Staff (CNS) on 30 September 1993. His long years at sea have taken him to most countries of the Indian Ocean littoral and he is deeply interested in the economic and maritime developments in the region. Extensive reading and travel in South East Asia, East and West Africa, the Far East, the Arab countries, the erstwhile Soviet Union, Europe and the USA have given him a keen insight in to global geo-strategic issues. The Admiral and Mrs. Binu Shekhawat have two sons, the younger of whom is a pilot in the Indian Navy.

JAYANT GANPAT NADKARNI

PVSM, AVSM, NM, VSM, ADC

CNS, 30 Nov 1987-30 Nov 1990

Admiral Jayant Ganpat Nadkarni assumed charge of the Indian Navy, as the 12th Chief of Naval Staff, on 30 November 1987. Born in Bombay on 05 December 1931, he did his early schooling in the city and joined the Indian Mercantile Marine Training Ship DUFFERIN in 1946.

On completion of three years' of training on board the DUFFERIN, Admiral Nadkarni graduated with distinction in

December 1948. He then joined the Royal Indian Navy (RIN) in March 1949 and proceeded to the United Kingdom for his initial training. He received training there, from 1949-53, during which he served on aircraft carriers and destroyers.

Admiral Nadkarni subsequently returned to India as the commissioning crew of the Hunt Class destroyer, INS *Ganga*. Subsequently, he specialised in Navigation and Direction and was the Navigating Officer of the cruiser, INS *Delhi* for over four years. He has also held command of INS *Talwar* and INS *Delhi*. In the latter appointment, he was also the Senior Officer, First Training Squadron.

His important shore appointments include Chief Instructor at Defence Services Staff College, Chief of Staff of the Western Naval Command and the Senior Directing Staff at National Defence College, New Delhi.

Promoted to the rank of Rear Admiral in December 1980, he commanded the Western Fleet from May 1981 to August 1982. Promoted to the rank of Vice Admiral in August 1982, he held the post of Chief of Personnel at Naval HQ until April 1984. He was then appointed as the Flag Officer Commanding-in-Chief of the Eastern Naval Command and became the Vice Chief of Naval Staff at Naval HQ in February 1986.

Admiral Nadkarni was awarded the Vishisht Seva Medal for distinguished service in 1969, the Naosena Medal in 1977, the Ati Vishisht Seva Medal in 1983 and the Param Vishisht Seva Medal (PVSM) in 1985. He is a graduate of the Defence Services Staff College (and the Naval War College, New Port, Rhode Island. He retired from the Indian Navy after 41 years service on 30 November 1990.

Admiral Nadkarni is married to Mrs. Vimal Nadkarni and they have two sons, one of whom is a Commander in the Indian Navy. Since retirement he has settled in Pune.

He was one of the founding members of the Centre for Advanced Strategic Studies, a think tank in Pune and served as its first Director for three years. He writes on defence subjects frequently in newspapers and internet magazines.

RADHAKRISHNA HARIRAM TAHILIANI

PVSM, AVSM

CNS, 30 Nov 1984-30 Nov 1987

Admiral Radhakrishna Hariram Tahiliani assumed charge of the Indian Navy, as the 11th Chief of Naval Staff, on 30 November 1984. Born on 12 May 1930, he was commissioned into the Indian Navy's naval aviation branch on 01 September 1950. A qualified test pilot, his major commands at sea include INS *Trishul* and aircraft carrier, INS *Vikrant*.

On elevation to the rank of Rear Admiral in December 1977, Admiral Tahiliani assumed charge of Flag Officer Goa Area and later as Flag Officer Commanding Western Fleet (FOCWF). Subsequently, he served in Naval HQ as Assistant Chief of Naval Staff (ACNS) and Deputy Chief of Naval Staff (DCNS) and was the first incumbent when the latter post was elevated to that of a Vice Admiral.

In February 1982, Admiral Tahiliani was appointed as the Flag Officer Commanding-in-Chief of Southern Naval Command. In March 1983, he was appointed as the Flag Officer Commanding-in-Chief of Western Naval Command and served in this capacity for a year, till he was appointed as the Vice Chief of Naval Staff (VCNS) in May 1984.

Admiral Tahiliani has the rare distinction of having been the Flag Officer Commanding-in-Chief of two Naval Commands. He is a graduate of the Naval War College, USA and the National Defence College, New Delhi. He is a recipient of the Param Vashisht Seva Medal (PVSM) and Ati Vishisht Seva Medal (AVSM) for his distinguished service. He retired on 30 November 1987, after completing nearly 37 years of service.

B S SOMAN

CNS, 04 Jun 1962-03 Mar 1966

Vice Admiral Bhaskar Sadashiv Soman assumed charge of the Indian Navy, as the 4th Chief of Naval Staff, on 04 June 1962. Born in March 1913, at Gwalior, he was selected for the Royal Indian Marine in 1931. After his initial training in the

United Kingdom, he returned to India as a Sub Lieutenant in August 1934. During World War II, he served as First Lieutenant and for a time, as the Commanding Officer of HMIS *Cornwallis* in the Red Sea and the Persian Gulf in 1939 and 1940 respectively. He took part in capturing the Italian Submarine Gallilio off Aden, Yemen.

Later he commissioned HMIS *Khyber*, a fleet mine-sweeper of the Royal Indian Navy. He was the Senior Instructor in combined operations training establishments at Mandapam, Tamil Nadu and Hamla near Bombay. He was one of the first Indian Officers to be promoted to the rank of Acting Captain in June 1947. During the months following Partition in 1947, he was the first Indian to be appointed to the key post of Chief of Personnel at Naval HQ. In October 1949, he went to sea in command of INS *Jumna*. He carried a number of goodwill visits to some of our neighbouring countries in the Persian Gulf, Malaya and East Africa.

In 1952, he took over from a Royal Navy Officer as the Naval Officer-in-Charge, Vizag where the Boys' Training Establishment, INS *Circars* is situated. In January 1954, he went to Cochin, the largest training center of the Indian Navy. Towards the end of 1956, he was appointed as the Commodore-in-Charge, Bombay and with the subsequent upgrading and re-designation of this appointment in 1958 he was promoted to the rank of Rear Admiral and re-appointed as the Flag Officer, Bombay.

In April 1960, Vice Admiral Soman took over as Flag Officer Commanding the Indian Fleet. During the 1961 Goa Operations, he was in command of the naval operations. He was the Chief of Naval Staff during the 1965 Indo-Pak War, but the Indian fleet remained bottled in harbour due to political reasons and did not face any action. The Vice Admiral retired in 1966, after more than three decades of service.

2

Historical Background of Indian Navy

The Indian Navy is the naval branch of the armed forces of India. It currently has approximately 55,000 personnel on active duty, including 5,000 members of the naval aviation branch, 1,200 marine commandos and 1,000 Sagar Prahari Bal soldiers, making it the world's fifth largest navy in terms of personnel. The Indian Navy currently operates around 170 vessels, including the aircraft carrier INS *Viraat*, along with operational jet fighters. Though the primary objective of the navy is to secure national maritime borders, India also uses its navy to enhance its international relations through joint exercises, port visits and humanitarian missions, including disaster relief. In recent years, the Indian Navy has undergone extensive modernisation and expansion with an intention to increase its capabilities as a recognised blue-water navy.

Role

The Indian Navy sees several principal roles for itself:

- In conjunction with other armed forces of the union, act to deter or defeat any threats or aggression against the territory, people or maritime interests of India, both in war and peace;
- Project influence in India's maritime area of interest, to further the nation's political, economic and security objectives;

- In cooperation with the Indian Coast Guard, ensure good order and stability in India's maritime zones of responsibility.
- Provide maritime assistance (including disaster relief) in India's maritime neighbourhood.
- To play a key role as part of 'a pluralistic security order' for a better world.

History

India has a maritime history dating back to 7,600 years. The first tidal dock is believed to have been built at Lothal around 2300 BCE during the Indus Valley Civilization, near the present day Mangrol harbour on the Gujarat coast. The Rig Veda written around 1500 BCE, credits Varuna with knowledge of the ocean routes and describes naval expeditions. There is reference to the side wings of a vessel called Plava, which give stability to the ship under storm conditions. A compass, Matsya yantra, was used for navigation in the fourth and fifth century AD. The earliest known reference to an organisation devoted to ships in ancient India is to the Mauryan Empire from the 4th century BCE. Emperor Chandragupta Maurya's Prime Minister Kautilya's Arthashastra devotes a full chapter on the state department of waterways under *navadhyaksha* (Sanskrit for Superintendent of ships). The term, *nava dvipantaragamanam* (Sanskrit for sailing to other lands by ships, i.e. Exploration) appears in this book in addition to appearing in the Buddhist text, *Baudhayana Dharmasastra* as the interpretation of the term, *Samudrasamyanam*.

Sea lanes between India and neighbouring lands were the usual form of trade for many centuries, and are responsible for the widespread influence of Indian Culture on other societies. Powerful navies included those of the Maurya, Satavahana, Chola, Vijayanagara, Kalinga, Maratha and Mughal empires. The Cholas excelled in foreign trade and maritime activity, extending their influence overseas to China and Southeast Asia.

During the 17th and 18th centuries, the Maratha and Kerala fleets were expanded, and became the most powerful Naval

Forces in the subcontinent, defeating European Navies at various times. The fleet review of the Maratha navy took place at the Ratnagiri fort in which the ships Pal and Qalbat participated. The 'Pal' was a three masted fighter with guns peeping on the broadsides. Kanhoji Angre and Kunjali Marakkar, the Naval chief of Saamoothiri, were two notable naval chiefs of the period.

Colonial Era

The British Indian Navy was established by the British while India was a colony in 1830 as *Her Majesty's Indian Navy* (earlier by the East India Company in 1612 as *Honourable East India Company's Marine*.

The first Indian to be granted a commission was Sub Lieutenant D.N Mukherji who joined the Royal Indian Marine as an engineer officer in 1928. Indian sailors started a rebellion also known as The Royal Indian Navy mutiny, in 1946 on board ships and shore establishments which spread all over India. A total of 78 ships, 20 shore establishments and 20,000 sailors were involved in the rebellion. When India became a republic on 26 January 1950, it became known as the Indian Navy, and its vessels as Indian Naval Ships (INS). On 22 April 1958 Vice Admiral R. D. Katari assumed office as the first Indian Chief of the Naval Staff.

Invasion of Goa

The first engagement of the Navy in any conflict was *Operation Vijay* in the 1961 invasion of Goa. The operation followed years of escalating tension between Portugal's anti-decolonialist stance and India. On 21 November 1961, Portuguese troops fired on the passenger ship *Sabarmati* near Anjadip Island, killing one and injuring another. Shortly after, the Indian government decided to militarily intervene and end Portuguese rule in Goa. Indian ships provided fire support to navy and army landing troops. During the operation, the *INS Delhi* sank one Portuguese patrol boat. Indian frigates *INS Betwa* and *INS Beas* sunk the Portuguese frigate NRP Afonso de Albuquerque after a brief fight.

Indo-Pakistan Wars

The Navy has been involved in two wars between India and Pakistan. Its activity in the Indo-Pakistani War of 1965 largely involved patrolling of the coast. The Pakistani Navy attacked the Indian coastal city of Dwarka and returned to their home port, although they did not achieve any strategic objective. However, the Navy did play a significant role in *Operation Trident*: the bombing of Karachi harbour in the 1971 war, on 4 December 1971. The attack was a success, and 4 December has been celebrated as Navy Day ever since. The attack was followed by *Operation Python* before the center of conflict shifted to the eastern India-Pakistan border and the Bay of Bengal. To show solidarity with its ally Pakistan, the United States sent Task Force 74 led by the *USS Enterprise* into the Bay of Bengal. A task force led by *INS Vikrant* was stationed to counter the *Enterprise* task force; Soviet Navy submarines also trailed the U.S. task force. A confrontation was averted when the U.S. task force moved towards South East Asia, away from the Indian Ocean.

The sinking of the Pakistani Navy's lone long-range submarine *PNS Ghazi* after an attack by the destroyer INS Rajput., enabled an easy Indian blockade of East Pakistan. The missile boats *INS Nirghat* and *INS Nipat* each sank a destroyer; the *INS Veer* destroyed a minesweeper. The naval aircraft, Sea Hawks and Alizés, operating from the *Vikrant* were also instrumental in sinking many gunboats and merchant navy vessels. There was one major casualty, the frigate *Khukri* (sunk by the *PNS Hangor*), while the *Kirpan* was damaged in the western sector of conflict. Ultimately, the naval blockade of Karachi Port and the complete blockade of East Pakistan's ports were successful in cutting Pakistani troops off from reinforcements, supplies, and evacuation routes. These actions proved decisive in India's victory in the war.

Operation Cactus

In 1988, the Indian Navy joined the Indian Air Force in successfully thwarting a coup attempt by PLOTE in the Maldives. A naval maritime reconnaissance aircraft detected a vessel hijacked by PLOTE rebels. One of the hostages on-board included a senior Maldivian minister and *Operation Cactus* was launched to secure the vessel. After military intervention by INS *Godavari* and Indian marine commandos, the rebels surrendered.

1999-2001 Operations

During the 1999 Kargil conflict between India and Pakistan, the Western and Eastern fleets were deployed in the Northern Arabian Sea, as a part of *Operation Talwar*. The intent was to safeguard India's maritime assets from a potential Pakistani naval attack, as also to deter Pakistan from escalating to a full-scale war by blocking India's sea-trade routes. Indian Navy's aviators and commandos also fought along side Indian Army personnel during the Kargil War.

The Indian Navy was a part of the joint forces exercises, Operation Parakram, during the 2001–2002 India–Pakistan standoff. More than a dozen warships were deployed.

Later in 2001, the Indian Navy provided escort to United States warships travelling through the Strait of Malacca to take part in Operation Enduring Freedom.

Disaster relief

2004 Indian Ocean earthquake

During the 2004 Indian Ocean earthquake crisis, the Indian Navy deployed 27 ships, 19 helicopters, 6 naval aircraft and over 5000 Naval personnel in disaster relief operations. These deployments were a part of various area-specific relief operations including *Operation Madath* in the Indian states of Andhra Pradesh and Tamil Nadu, *Operation Sea Waves* in the Andaman and Nicobar Islands, *Operation Castor* in Maldives, *Operation Rainbow* in Sri Lanka and *Operation Gambhir* in Indonesia. This was one of the largest relief mobilisations that the Indian Navy had undertaken. Indian Naval groups were able to start large scale rescue operations in neighbouring countries within 12 hours from the time of the tsunami, and was the first foreign navy to reach the affected areas.

The quick deployment of forces during relief operations was a testing ground for the Navy's amphibious, as well as force projection capabilities. Deficiencies in the response led to modernisation of the naval forces after the tsunami, including the acquisition of Landing Platform Docks (LPD) like the INS *Jalashwa* (formerly the USS *Trenton*), as well as smaller amphibious vessels. Part of the Eastern Fleet, the *Jalashwa* is the second-largest ship currently in-service with the Indian Navy.

Operation Sukoon

During the 2006 Israel-Lebanon conflict, the Indian Navy evacuated 2,286 Indian nationals and expatriates, including 436 Sri Lankan and 69 Nepali citizens, from war-torn Lebanon. This operation was named *Operation Sukoon*, meaning "Peace and tranquility". In the year 2006, ten naval doctors from India served for 102 days on USNS *Mercy* and conducted about 10 medical camps in Philippines, Bangladesh, Indonesia and East Timor. Indian Navy has also provided relief materials to survivors of cyclones in Bangladesh and Myanmar. Two ships from the Indian Navy carried the first international aid material for the victims of Cyclone Nargis in Myanmar.

Anti-piracy operations

In October 1999, a coordinated effort by the Indian Navy and the Indian Coast Guard led to the release of a hijacked Japanese cargo ship, MV *Alondra Rainbow*, from pirates.

Piracy off the coast of Somalia has caused significant concerns in India as most of its sea-trade routes pass through the region. The Indian Navy responded to these concerns by deploying the frigate INS *Tabar* in the Gulf of Aden in October 2008. Within a month of its deployment, the *Tabar* had prevented attempts by pirates to board two cargo ships and also destroyed a pirate "mother ship". As of 11 November 2008, the frigate had escorted 35 ships safely through the pirate-infested region. The pirates had hijacked a fishing trawler from Thailand and made it their mothership. There were also reports of India deploying destroyer INS *Mysore* to augment the frigate INS *Tabar* in anti-piracy operations. On 21 November 2008

India was granted permission to enter Somalian territorial waters to intercept suspected pirate vessels. 23 pirates were arrested by Indian Navy while attempting to hijack a merchant ship near the Gulf of Aden. Anti-piracy patrols were carried out after a request was made by the Seychelles government, resulting in the arrest of nine pirates. Further ships has been send to give a boost to anti-piracy operations. While preventing a pirate attack on a Liberian vessel MV Maud, two pirates were killed and the remaining six were apprehended. On 7 December 2009, the Indian Navy successfully repulsed a pirate attack on a US-owned tanker in the Gulf of Aden off Somalia coast. The Indian Navy was awarded by the U.N for anti-piracy operations in the Gulf of Aden. By June 2010, Indian Navy had escorted about thousand ships of fifty nations in the Gulf of Eden.

Personnel

Commissioned Officers

The Commander of the Navy is the Chief of Naval Staff (CNS). Admiral Nirmal Kumar Verma, who was formerly the Eastern Naval Commander at Visakhapatnam, has assumed responsibility as the head of Navy from incumbent Admiral Sureesh Mehta, who retires from service.

While the provision for the rank of Admiral of the Fleet exists, it is primarily intended for major wartime use and honour. No officer of the Indian Navy has yet been conferred this rank. (Both the Army and Air Force have had officers who have been conferred with the equivalent rank-Field Marshals Sam Manekshaw and Cariappa of the Army and Marshal of the Indian Air Force (MIAF) Arjan Singh.)

Enlisted Personnel

Organisation

The Indian Navy is divided into the following broad categories:

- Administration
- Logistics and Material
- Training

- Fleets
- Naval Aviation
- Submarines

Commands

The Indian Navy operates four Commands. Each Command is headed by a Flag Officer Commanding-in-Chief in the rank of Vice Admiral.

Commands	HQ Location	Current FOC-in-C
Western Naval Command	Mumbai	Vice Admiral Vinod Bhasin
Eastern Naval Command	Visakhapatnam	Vice Admiral Anup Singh
Southern Naval Command	Kochi	Vice Admiral K N Sushil
Far Eastern Naval Command	Port Blair	Vice Admiral Vijay Shankar

The Far Eastern command, a joint Navy, Army and Air force command was set up in the Andaman and Nicobar Islands in 2001 as a strategic area of defence.

It was created to safeguard India's strategic interests in Southeast Asia and the Strait of Malacca. The Indian Navy plays a major role in patrolling the area with the Indonesian Navy, Royal Malaysian Navy and Royal Thai Navy. India and Australia signed an agreement to provide maritime security in the Asia Pacific region.

Bases

In 2005, the Indian Navy commissioned *INS Kadamba* at Karwar, 100 km from Goa. This is the third operational naval base after Mumbai and Vishakapatnam and the first to be controlled exclusively by the Navy. (The other bases share port facilities with civilian shipping, but this one is for purely naval use.) Built under Phase I of the multi-billion dollar 'Project Seabird', it is the largest naval base in the region. Asia's largest Naval academy INS Zamorin, was inaugurated at Ezhimala, in January 2009 by the Prime Minister of India. Another naval base is being planned for the eastern shores, near Vishakapatnam at a cost of USD 350 million.

The base, which will be located fifty km south of Vishakapatnam in Rambilli Mandal, will have comprehensive anti-aircraft, anti-submarine and amphibious capability. The Indian Navy is setting up a Naval Station in Madagascar, to monitor and patrol the coast of Mozambique as well as the Southern Indian Ocean. The Indian Navy also has berthing rights in Oman.

Marine Commando Force

The Marine Commando Force (MCF), also known as *MARCOS*, is a special forces unit that was raised by the Indian Navy in 1987 for direct action, special reconnaissance, amphibious warfare and counter-terrorism. In 1988, the MARCOS successfully rescued several hostages, including Maldives' then-Minister of Education, aboard a ship hijacked by PLOTE mercenaries during Operation Cactus. The MARCOS are also deployed to prevent infiltration through the Jhelum and Wular Lake and are involved in covert counter-terrorism operations in and around lakes and rivers in Jammu and Kashmir. The MARCOS were also involved in the rescue mission of hostages captured by the terrorists in Taj Mahal Palace & Tower luxury hotel in Mumbai as part of a large terrorist attack in Mumbai metropolis in November 2008.

Ships

The names of all commissioned ships (and Naval Bases) of the Indian Navy are prefixed with the letters INS, designating *Indian Naval Ship* or *Indian Navy Station*. The fleet of the Indian Navy is a mix of domestic built and foreign vessels and is expanding with new inductions. India often build destroyers, frigates and corvettes.

Destroyers

The Indian Navy currently operates the *Delhi* and *Rajput* class guided-missile destroyers. The next-generation, *Kolkata* class vessels are expected to be commissioned starting in 2012.

Frigates

The guided-missile frigates currently in service are the *Talwar* class, *Brahmaputra* class and *Godavari* class. The *Nilgiri class* (variants of the British Leander class) vessels have all been decommissioned. The 3 *Advanced Talwar* class frigates (Krivak IV) are also scheduled for delivery by 2012. The next-generation *Shivalik* class vessels, which will have a lot of stealth features incorporated into them are planned for commissioning in 2010.

Corvettes

The Indian Navy currently operates the *Kora*, *Khukri*, *Veer* and *Abhay* class corvettes. The next-generation Project 28 and Project 28A class of corvettes are expected to be commissioned starting in 2012.

Amphibious Warfare Vessels

The Indian Navy has an Amphibious transport dock of the Austin class, re-christened as INS Jalashwa in service.

Aircraft Carriers

The Indian Navy presently has one aircraft carrier in active service — INS *Viraat*. The carrier is planned for decommissioning after the induction of the first domestically built *Vikrant* class aircraft carrier. The Indian Navy will also induct the Russian-built INS *Vikramaditya* in 2014.

SUBMARINES

Diesel Submarines

The Indian Navy currently maintains a fleet of diesel-electric submarines, primarily of the Sindhughosh and Shishumar classes. India signed a deal for six Scorpène class submarines with MESMA air-independent propulsion and construction has begun.

These submarines will join the Indian Navy from 2012 onwards. The Indian Navy may arm its *Kilo* class submarine fleet with the BrahMos cruise missiles after successfully completing test launches from the submarine. India will issue request for proposals for another six submarines in financial year 2008-09.

Unmanned Submarines

The National Institute of Oceanography has developed the Autonomous Underwater Vehicle (AUV) that has applications in the field of Oceanographic research. Also an Autonomous Surface Vehicle (ASV) has been developed.

Nuclear Powered Submarines

In January 1988, India leased for three years an ex-Soviet Charlie class nuclear powered guided missile submarine with eight Ametist (SS-N-7 Starbright) anti-shipping missile launchers. In the Indian Navy, the vessel was christened INS *Chakra*, and the submarine was manned by an Indian crew. Upon expiration of the ship leasing term in 1991, the submarine was returned to Russia and joined the Pacific Fleet of the Russian Navy. India's indigenously designed and built nuclear-powered ballistic missile submarines of the Arihant class are expected to be commissioned starting in 2011. The lead vessel of the class, INS Arihant, was launched for sea-trials on July 26, 2009 in Visakhapatnam.

Planned Acquisitions

The Navy is purchasing from Russia the Kiev class aircraft carrier *Admiral Gorshkov* (INS *Vikramaditya*), which will be delivered to India by 2012. The Indian Navy is also negotiating with Russia for the acquisition of further *Advanced Talwar* class frigates, and six conventional submarines. India started a program in 1985 to develop indigenous technologies for building a nuclear-powered submarine, known as the Advanced Technology Vessel (ATV) project. The first Advanced Technology Vessel is called INS Arihant, was launched on July 26, 2009. The hull for the vessel has been built by Larsen & Toubro at its A naval version of a nuclear reactor has been developed at the Indira Gandhi Centre For Atomic Research, Kalpakkam and will be deployed on the submarine's hull after miniaturization. The Prototype Testing Centre (PTC) will be used to test the submarine's turbines and propellers. A similar facility is operational at Vishakapatnam to test the main turbines and gear box.

Once the vessel is completed, it may be equipped with K-15 as well as Sagarika/Agni-III ballistic missiles and advanced Indian made sonar systems. According to defence sources, the ATV is expected to be commissioned in 2010. Each unit will cost one billion U.S. dollars. Government has given approval for constructing the follow on SSBN's which will be larger than the Arihant class submarines. Approval has also been given for the construction of SSN's which will escort the SSBN's.

India is reportedly paying two billion dollars for the completion of two Akula-II class submarines which were 40-60% completed. Three hundred Indian Navy personnel are being trained in Russia for the operation of these submarines. India has finalized a deal with Russia, in which at the end of the lease of these submarines, it has an option to buy them. According to report, the first submarine will be commissioned into the Indian Navy in September, 2009. The first submarine will be named INS Chakra, it is currently undergoing trials in the Pacific ocean.

Aircraft

The naval air-arm is an important component of the Indian Navy. The Indian Navy air arm consists of Sea Harrier jets that operate from the aircraft carrier INS *Viraat* and also from INS *Jalashwa*. Recently, the Harriers were modernized for Beyond Visual Range missile capability. The Kamov-31 provide the Airborne Early Warning cover for the fleet. In the anti-submarine role the Sea King, Ka-28 and the domestic built HAL Dhruv are used. The MARCOS use Sea King and HAL Dhruv helicopters while conducting operations. Reconnaissance operations are carried out by Tupolev 142, Ilyushin 38, Dornier Do 228 aircraft, as well as HAL Chetak helicopters. The Aircraft used for carrying out roles of a strategic bomber and as a maritime strike are carried out by 4(3 more on order) Tupolev Tu-22M, which is also capable of performing reconnaissance missions. The UAV arm consists of around 30 UAVs like Heron and Searcher-IIs that are operated from ships and shore for better surveillance. The Indian Navy also maintains a four aircraft aerobatic display team, the *Sagar Pawan*. The Sagar Pawan team will be replacing their present Kiran HJT-16 aircraft with the newly developed HJT-36 aircraft. The Indian Navy has also placed an order for 8 P-8I Poseidon long-range maritime reconnaissance (LRMR) aircraft.

In January 2004, the Indian Navy signed a contract for the delivery of 12 MiG-29K and 4 MiG-29KUB which will be operated from INS *Vikramaditya*. The first MiG-29KUB manufactured for the Navy took to the skies in May 2008. The first four aircraft were delivered to India in February 2009. There were also reports that the Indian Navy would purchase an additional 30 MiG-29Ks and-KUBs for the Indigenous Aircraft Carrier. The Indian Air Force also has a maritime strike role, providing support to the Indian Navy. It operates SEPECAT Jaguar and Sukhoi Su-30MKIf. Aircraft in this role. The Jaguars are armed with the Sea Eagle missile, which will be replaced with the Harpoon missile. Su-30MKI and the Il-38 will be armed with the air-launched version of the Brahmos cruise missile.

Weapon Systems

The Indian Navy uses modern technology and weapon systems, most of which are imported from foreign countries. Others, like the BrahMos supersonic cruise missiles, are jointly developed with Russia-a major stride in defence research. There are reports on the joint development by India and Israel of the Barak-II missile system, an improved, longer range version of the Barak-I air defence missile which is operational on Indian Navy ships. The Barak-I is used on most of the main ships of the Indian Navy. The Indian Navy's nuclear deterrence capability is based on *Sukanya* class ships armed with the *Dhanush* ballistic missiles that has a range of 350 km.

India has a number of foreign made cruise missile systems, including the Klub SS-N-27. It also has its own Nirbhay cruise missile systems under development. The Sagarika (Oceanic) submarine launched ballistic missile (SLBM), which has a range of at least 700 km (some sources claim 1000 km) forms part of

India's nuclear triad. Another successful program has been the adaptation of the Yakhont anti-ship missile system into the BrahMos by the NPO and the DRDO. The BrahMos has been tailored to Indian needs and uses a large proportion of Indian-designed components and technology, including its fire control systems, transporter erector launchers, and its onboard navigational attack systems. The successful test of Brahmos from INS Rajput (D51) provides Indian Navy with precision land attack capability.

Electronic Warfare and Systems Management

Sangraha is a joint electronic warfare program of the Defence Research and Development Organisation (DRDO) and the Indian Navy. The system comprises a family of electronic warfare suites, such as Ajanta and Ellora, for use on different naval platforms capable of intercepting, detecting, and classifying pulsed, carrier wave, pulse repetition frequency agile, frequency agile and chirp radars.

The systems employ a modular approach facilitating deployment on various platforms like helicopters, vehicles, and small ships. Certain platforms, apart from ESM (electronic support measures), have ECM (electronic countermeasure) capabilities. Advanced technologies like multiple-beam phased array jammers are employed in the system for simultaneous handling of multiple threats.

The Indian Navy also relies on information technology to face the challenges of the 21st century. The Indian Navy is implementing a new strategy to move from a platform centric force to a network-centric force by linking all shore-based installations and ships via high-speed data networks and satellites. This will help in increased operational awareness. The network is referred to as the Navy Enterprise Wide Network (NEWN). The Indian Navy has also provided training to all its personnel in Information Technology (IT) at the Naval Institute of Computer Applications (NICA) located in Mumbai. Information technology is also used to provide better training, like the usage of simulators and for better management of the force.

Fleet Reviews

The President of India is entitled to inspect his fleet, as he is the supreme commander of the Indian Armed Forces. The first President's fleet review by India was hosted by Dr. Rajendra Prasad on October 10, 1953. President's reviews usually take place once in the President's term. In all, nine fleet reviews have taken place, the most recent being in February 2006, when President Dr. APJ Abdul Kalam took the review. The Indian Navy also conducted an International fleet review named *Bridges of Friendship* in February 2001 in Mumbai. Many ships of friendly Navies from all around the world participated, including two from the U.S. Navy. Once in two years navies from the Indian Ocean region meet at the Andaman and Nicobar Islands and the event is named as *MILAN* (Sanskrit: Get together).

NAVAL EXERCISES AND COOPERATION

India often conducts naval exercises with other friendly countries designed to increase naval interoperability and also to strengthen cooperative security relationship. Some such exercises take place annually like the *Varuna* with the French Navy, *Konkan* with the Royal Navy (UK), *Indra* with Russian Navy, *Malabar* with the U.S. Navy and *Simbex* with the Republic of Singapore Navy. The Indian Navy also conducted exercise with the People's Liberation Army Navy in 2003 and will send ships to the South China Sea to participate in the fleet review.

In 2007, the *TROPEX* (Theatre-level Readiness Operational Exercises) was held during which Indian Navy experimented the doctrine of influencing a land and air battle to support the Indian Army and the Indian Air Force. Apart from the Indian Ocean, India has steadily gained influence in the Pacific Ocean. In 2007, Indian Navy conducted naval exercise with Japan Maritime Self-Defence Force and U.S Navy in the Pacific and also signed an agreement with Japan in October 2008 for joint naval patrolling in the Asia-Pacific region.

Naval aircraft from Indian and US Navy flying in formation over Indian Navy aircraft carrier *INS Viraat* during Malabar 2007.

India has also held naval exercise with Vietnam, Philippines and New Zealand.

In 2007, India and South Korea decided to conduct annual naval exercise and India participated in the South Korean international fleet review. In addition, Indian Navy will also be increasing naval cooperation with other allies, particularly with Germany and Arab states of the Persian Gulf including Kuwait, Oman, Bahrain and Saudi Arabia. India held the first Indian Ocean Naval Symposium (IONS) with an objective to provide a forum for all the littoral nations of the Indian Ocean to cooperate on mutually agreed areas for better security in the region. The Indian Navy is increasingly used in international diplomacy. Since 2000, the Indian naval ships have made port calls in Israel, Turkey, Egypt, Libya, Greece, Oman, Thailand, Indonesia, Australia, New Zealand, Tonga, South Africa.

Kenya, Qatar, Oman, United Arab Emirates, Bahrain, Kuwait and other countries in 2005-2007.

The first Atlantic Ocean deployment of the Indian Navy happened in 2009. During this deployment, the Indian Naval fleet will conduct exercise with the French, German, Russian and British Navies.

Exploration

The Indian Navy regularly conducts adventure expeditions. The sailing ship and training vessel INS *Tarangini* began circumnavigating the world on 23 January 2003, intending to foster good relations with various other nations; she returned to India in May of the following year after visiting 36 ports in 18 nations. INS Tarangini returned to port, after a ten month long overseas voyage named Lokayan 07. Lt. Cdr. M.S. Kohli led the Indian Navy's first successful expedition to Mount Everest in 1965; the Navy's ensign was again flown atop Everest on 19 May 2004 by a similar expedition. Another Navy team also successfully scaled Everest from the north face, the technically more challenging route. The expedition was led by Cdr Satyabrata Dam, belonging to the elite submarine arm. Cdr. Dam is a mountaineer of international repute and has climbed many mountains including the Patagonias, the Alps among others. This team's record is unmatched by any other navy. The Navy was also the first to send a submariner to summit Everest.

An Indian Navy team comprising 11 members successfully completed an expedition to the Arctic pole. To prepare, they first travelled to Iceland, where they attempted to summit a peak. The team next flew to eastern Greenland; in the Kulusuk and Angmassalik areas, they used Inuit boats to navigate the region's ice-choked fjords. They crossed northward across the Arctic Circle, reaching seventy degrees North on skis. The team scaled an unnamed peak of height 11,000 feet and named it "Indian Peak".

The Indian Naval ensign first flew in Antarctica in 1981. The Indian Navy succeeded in Mission Dakshin Dhruv 2006 by traversing to the South Pole on skis. With this historic expedition, they have set the record for being the first military team to have successfully completed a ski traverse to the Geographic South Pole. Also, three of the ten member team-the expedition leader-Cdr. Satyabrata Dam, leading medical assistants Rakesh Kumar and Vikas Kumar are now amongst the few people in the world to have visited the two poles and summited Mt. Everest. Indian Navy became the first organization to reach the poles and Mt.Everest. A solo circumnavigation voyage named 'Sagar Parikrama' is underway by Cdr. Dilip Donde.

Ongoing expansion

In 2004, India bought the Russian aircraft carrier, *Admiral Gorshkov* for the equivalent of US$1.5 billion. It will cost an additional US$1.5 billion to refit, and is expected to join the Indian Navy in 2012 as INS *Vikramaditya*. A further US$700 million will be spent to purchase 12 single-seat MiG-29K and four dual-seat MiG-29KUB fighters, six Kamov-31 attack and reconnaissance anti-submarine helicopters; also included are training facilities for pilots and technical staff, delivery of simulators and spare parts, and establishment and maintenance of Indian Navy facilities. Upgrades include removing missiles from the carrier foredeck to make way for a 14.3-degree ski-jump. The Mig-29's will be delivered to the Indian Navy in 2009.

In April 2007, India began construction of a 40,000 tonne *Vikrant* class aircraft carrier at a cost of $800 million and scheduled to operate 30 aircraft, including Naval LCA, MiG-29K, and Sea Harrier combat aircraft, as well as HAL Dhruv, Ka-31, and Sea King Mk.42 helicopters. Four turbine engines will power the ship. The carrier is being constructed by state-run Cochin Shipyard Limited and will be commissioned by 2012-13. The Indian Minister of State for Defence, Pallam Raju, went on record in September 2006 stating that the aircraft carrier is likely to be commissioned by 2011. There are plans to build more aircraft carriers domestically.

The Indian Navy is currently undergoing rapid expansion and modernisation. Yantar, a plant in Kaliningrad, Russia, was awarded a US$1.56 billion contract to build three additional 1135.6 frigates. The increased price is due to more sophisticated armaments such as BrahMos cruise missiles. The Navy has government approval for an additional eight warships.

The Indian Navy has signed a deal with Boeing to supply eight P-8 Poseidon Anti Submarine Warfare/Maritime Surveillance Aircraft. The first aircraft will be delivered 4 years after the signing of the contract, that is 2012. Also there are plans to induct four AEW&C aircraft's that will be based on super carriers.

Future Prospects

India is expected to spend about US$40 billion on military modernisation from 2008 to 2013. A major chunk of those purchases were made for the Indian Navy. Work on the third aircraft carrier is to start in 2010 and will be inducted into the Navy by 2017. Order has been placed for seven Project 17A class frigates. India is currently focusing on expanding its submarine fleet. Also newer technology like the Unmanned Underwater Vehicle (UUV) is being developed for the Indian Navy.

After ordering six Scorpene submarines as part of Project 75, Indian Navy is now on the look out for six next-generation submarines in a project worth over Rs 30,000 crore. These six diesel-electric submarines built in India under Project-75I, will be equipped with air-independent propulsion boosting their operational capabilities and will have high degree of stealth, land-attack capability and ability to incorporate futuristic technologies. RFI has been issued to Rosoboronexport, French (Armaris), HDW and other firms, two rounds of discussions have already taken place.

The RFP (request for proposal) for six MRMR aircraft with anti-submarine warfare (ASW) capabilities was issued on 11 July 2008 to Italian Alenia Aeronautica's ATR-72-500MP aircraft, Brazilian Embraer P-99, French Dassault's Falcon 900DX and Russian Antonov-72P. The contract is expected to be signed by June 2009 and deliveries to begin by 2012. The contract is estimated to cost Rs. 1,600 crore. The Navy is also planning to induct more UAVs. The India-Israel joint venture to convert the Chetak helicopters into unmanned UAV's that can operate from ships is progressing steadily. All these will be linked with space-based reconnaissance systems. On 13 January 2009, India has issued a request for proposals (RFPs) for six Medium Range Maritime Reconnaissance (MRMR) aircraft. The new aircraft, which will replace the ageing fleet of 10 Islander aircraft in service, are to be equipped with an Airborne Early Warning system. The Indian Coast Guard has an additional requirement for six MRMRs without an Airborne Early Warning system. The MRMR is required to have a range of 500 nautical miles and an endurance of 6 hours. Aircraft competing for the order include a variant of Boeing's P-8I, and possibly the turboprop ATR-72MP, EADS C-295, Dassault's Falcon 900MPA and Embraer P-99A platforms. For the Coast Guard RFP, contenders could be the ATR-42MP, C-295 or CN-235MP.

In August 2009, the U.S. Navy and Northrop Grumman briefed the Indian Navy on the E-2D Advanced Hawkeye. This covered potential use of this platform to satisfy its current shore-based and future carrier-based Airborne Early Warning and Control (AEW&C) requirements. The Indian Navy reportedly expressed interest in acquiring up to six Hawkeyes.

Indian Navy has issued a tender for procurement of 16 advanced, multi-role naval helicopters to AgustaWestland, EADS and Sikorsky. The order is likely to be expanded to 60 helicopters. The helicopters will be equipped with anti-ship and anti-submarine warfare equipment including cruise missiles and torpedoes, and also be capable of being refuelled in flight. The type will operate from both naval vessels and land bases.

Global bids has been floated to acquire eight mine countermeasure vessels (MCMVs), to replace the twelve Pondicherry class ocean minesweepers in service.

France's DCN International, Fincantieri of Italy, Izar of Spain, Kangnam Shipbuilding Co. of South Korea and Northrop Grumman of the U.S have been invited to participate in the bidding process. Six of the craft will be produced at Goa shipyard under transfer of technology.

With the recent and ongoing upgrades and inductions, independent analysts expect that the Indian Navy may soon become a blue-water navy. India's navy is already the most powerful in the region, and with further upgrades in the future, aims to control the Indian Ocean Region, from the coast of East Africa to Australia. India is also the only Asian navy to regularly operate aircraft carriers. The aim is to have a total of three Aircraft carriers resulting in two fully operational Carrier battle groups and an additional Aircraft carrier eventually in refit making India an operating Blue-water navy.

The ambitious long term plan that was recently revealed shows a road-map to blue water navy with six aircraft carriers.

HISTORY OF THE INDIAN NAVY

India has a rich maritime history dating back 5,000 years. The world's first tidal dock is believed to have been built at Lothal around 2300 BCE during the Indus Valley Civilization, near the present day Mangrol harbour on the Gujarat coast.

The Rig Vedas written around 1400 BCE, credits Varuna with knowledge of the ocean routes and describes naval expeditions. There is reference to the side wings of a vessel called Plava, which give stability to the ship under storm conditions. A compass, Matsya yantra, was used for navigation in the fourth and fifth century AD.

The earliest known reference of an organization devoted to ships and sailing in ancient India is from the Mauryan Empire of the 4th century BCE. Emperor Chandragupta Maurya's Prime Minister Kautilya's Arthashastra devotes a full chapter on the state department of waterways under *navadhyaksha* (Sanskrit for Superintendent of ships). The term, *nava dvipantaragamanam* (Sanskrit for sailing to other lands by ships, i.e. Exploration) appears in this book in addition to appearing in the Buddhist text, *Baudhayana Dharmasastra* using the term, *Samudrasamyanam* (Sanskrit for sea voyage).

Sea lanes between India and neighboring lands were the usual form of trade for many centuries, and are responsible for the widespread influence of Indian Culture on other societies, particularly in the Indian Ocean region. Powerful navies included those of the Maurya, Satavahana, Chola, Vijayanagara, Kalinga, Maratha and Mughal empires. The Cholas excelled in foreign trade and maritime activity, extending their influence overseas to China and Southeast Asia.

Chola expeditions

The Imperial Cholas initiated their grand naval conquests during the reign of two of its most illustrious monarchs, Raja Chola (ruled 985-1014) and his son Rajendra Chola (ruled 1012-1044). Under Rajendra Chola, the Cholas expanded their empire with the use of their strong navy and subdued many kingdoms of South-East Asia and occupied the region which included Myanmar, Malaya, Sumatra etc., and sent ambassadors to countries as far off as China.

INDIAN NAVIES OF THE POST-CLASSICAL AGE

Kozhikode

Manavikraman, Samoothiri Raja of Kozhikode began the naval build-up in 1503 in response to Portuguese attempts at extracting trading privileges. He commanded and appoited Mohammed Kunjali as Marakkar (admiral) of his fleet. Over the course of the next century, the Samoothiri Rajas successfully repelled various attempts by the Portuguese to overthrow their rule, with each side enlisting various allies over time. 4 generations of Kunjali Marakkars served the Samoothiri Rajas.

However, over time differences between Mohammed Ali, Marakkar IV, and his masters increased, culminating with his self-declaration as the "Lord of the Indian seas". The Samoothiris then collaborated with the Portuguese to defeat Mohammed Ali in 1600. Later, they allied with the Dutch East India Company to defeat the Portuguese.

Maratha Navy

The Maratha Empire was established by Chhatrapati Shivaji in 1674. From its inception, the Marathas established a Naval force, consisting of cannons mounted on ships.

The dominance of the Maratha Navy started with the ascent of Kanhoji Angre as the *Darya-Saranga* by the Maratha chief of Satara. Under that authority, he was master of the Western coast of India from Mumbai to Vingoria (now Vengurla) in present day state of Maharashtra, except for Janjira which was affiliated with the Mughal Empire. Until his death in 1729, he repeatedly attacked the colonial powers of Britain and Portugal, capturing numerous vessels of the British East India Company and extracting ransom for their return.

On 29 November 1721 a joint attempt by the Portuguese (Viceroy Francisco José de Sampaio e Castro) and the British (General Robert Cowan) to humble Kanhoji also failed miserably. Their combined fleet consisting of 6,000 soldiers in no less than four Man-of-war ships led by Captain Thomas Mathews failed miserably. Aided by Maratha naval commanders Mendhaji Bhatkar and Mainak Bhandari, Kanhoji continued to harass and plunder the European ships until his death in 1729.

The 'Pal' was a three masted Maratha man-of-war with guns peeping on the broadsides.

COLONIAL INDIAN NAVY

Establishment of the Bombay Marine

The English East India Company was established in 1612.

In 1612, Captain Thomas Best encountered and defeated the Portuguese at the Battle of Swally. This encounter, as well as piracy, led the English East India Company to build a port and establish a small navy based at the village of Suvali, near Surat, Gujarat to protect commerce. The Company named the force the *Honourable East India Company's Marine*, and the first fighting ships arrived on 5 September 1612.

This force protected merchant shipping off the Gulf of Cambay and the rivers Tapti and Narmada. The ships also helped map the coastlines of India, Persia and Arabia.

In 1686, with most of English commerce moving to Bombay, the force was renamed the *Bombay Marine*. The Bombay Marine was involved in combat against the Marathas and the Sidis and participated in the Anglo-Burmese Wars. The Bombay Marine recruited many Indians but commissioned no Indian officers until 1928.

Expansion of Her Majesty's Indian Navy

In 1830, the Bombay Marine became *Her Majesty's Indian Navy*. The British capture of Aden increased the commitments of Her Majesty's Indian Navy, leading to the creation of the *Indus Flotilla*. The Navy then fought in the China War of 1840.

Her Majesty's Indian Navy resumed the name *Bombay Marine* from 1863 to 1877, when it became *Her Majesty's Indian Marine*. The Marine then had two divisions; the Eastern Division at Calcutta and the Western Division at Bombay.

In recognition of the services rendered during various campaigns, *Her Majesty's Indian Marine* received the title the *Royal Indian Marine* in 1892. By this time it consisted of over 50 vessels.

The Royal Indian Marine in World War I

When mines were detected off the coasts of Bombay and Aden, the Royal Indian Marine went into action with a fleet of minesweepers, patrol vessels and troop carriers. Besides patrolling, the Marine ferried troops and carried war stores from India to Iraq, Egypt and East Africa.

The first Indian to be granted a commission was Sub Lieutenant D.N Mukherji who joined the Royal Indian Marine as an engineer officer in 1928.

The Royal Indian Navy in World War II

In 1934 the Royal Indian Marine became the Royal Indian Navy (RIN). Ships of the RIN received the prefix HMIS for His Majesty's Indian Ships. At the start of the Second World War, the Royal Indian Navy was very small and had eight warships. The onset of the war led to an expansion.

The sloops 'HMIS Sutlej' and 'HMIS Jumna' played a key role in Operation Husky – the invasion of Sicily.

Indian sailors started a rebellion also known as The Royal Indian Navy mutiny, in 1946 on board ships and shore establishments, which spread all over India. A total of 78 ships, 20 shore establishments and 20,000 sailors were involved in the rebellion.

Independence of India

India gained independence from the United Kingdom in 1947, but senior British officers continued to serve with the navy of India. When India became a republic on 26 January 1950, the name was changed to the Indian Navy, and the vessels were redesignated as Indian Naval Ships (INS).

Vice Admiral R.D. Katari was the first Indian Chief of Naval Staff, appointed on April 22, 1958.

Partition of India

Upon the Partition of India, the Indian Navy was split between India and Pakistan, and the vessels were divided between the two nations.

INDIAN NAVY OPERATIONS

Portuguese-Indian War

The first involvement of the Navy in any conflict came during the Liberation of Goa in 1961 with the success of Operation Vijay against the Portuguese Navy. Four Portuguese frigates-the NRP Afonso de Albuquerque, the NRP Bartolomeu

Dias, the NRP João de Lisboa and the NRP Gonçalves Zarco- were deployed to patrol the waters off Goa, Daman and Diu, along with several patrol boats (Lancha de Fiscalização).

Eventually only the NRP Afonso de Albuquerque saw action against Indian Navy ships, the other ships having fled before commencement of hostilities. The *NRP Afonso* was destroyed by Indian frigates *INS Betwa* and *INS Beas*. Parts of the Afonso are on display at the Naval Museum in Mumbai, while the remainder was sold as scrap.

Indo-Pakistani war of 1965

There were no significant naval encounters during the Indo-Pakistani War of 1965.

On September 7, 1965 a flotilla of the Pakistani Navy carried out a small-scale bombardment of the Indian coastal town and radar station of Dwarka, 200 miles (300 km) south of the Pakistani port of Karachi. Codenamed Operation Dwarka, it did not fulfill its primary objective of disabling the radar station. There was no significant Indian retaliation, since 75% of the Indian naval vessels were undergoing maintenance or refitting in the harbor. Some of the Indian fleet sailed from Bombay to Dwarka to patrol the area and deter further bombardment. Operation Dwarka has been described as an "insignificant bombardment" of the town was a "limited engagement, with no strategic value." The Pakistani largely involved patrolling of the coast.

Indo-Pakistani war of 1971

The Indian Navy played a significant role in the bombing of Karachi harbour in the 1971 war. On December 4, it launched Operation Trident during which missile boats *INS Nirghat* and *INS Nipat* sunk the minesweeper *PNS Muhafiz* and destroyer *PNS Khyber*. The destroyer *PNS Shahjahan* was irreparably damaged. Owing to its success, December 4 has been celebrated as Navy Day ever since.

The operation was so successful that the Pakistani Navy raised a false alarm about sighting an Indian missile boat on December 6. Pakistan Air Force (PAF) planes attacked the supposed Indian ship and damaged the vessel before it was identified as being another Pakistani Navy ship, *PNS Zulfiqar* which suffered numerous casualties and damage as a result of this friendly fire.

During Operation Python on December 8, the frigate *PNS Dacca* was severely damaged by *INS Veer* and the oil storage depot of Karachi was set ablaze. On the western front in the Arabian Sea, operations ceased after the Karachi port became unusable due to the sinking of Panamian vessel *Gulf Star*. An Indian frigate, *INS Khukri* was sunk by submarine *PNS Hangor*.

On the eastern front, the submarine *PNS Ghazi* was sunk outside Vishakhapatnam harbor. Indian naval aircraft, Sea Hawks and Alizés, from the aircraft carrier INS Vikrant were instrumental in sinking many gunboats and merchant navy vessels in the Bay of Bengal. The successful blockade of East Pakistan by the Indian Navy proved to be a vital factor in the Pakistani surrender.

Operations after 1971

The Indian Armed Forces initiated Operation Cactus to prevent a coup attempt by a group of Maldivians led by Abdullah Luthufi and assisted by about 200 Sri Lankan Tamil mercenaries from the People's Liberation Organisation of Tamil Eelam (PLOTE) in Maldives in 1988. After Indian paratroopers landed at Hulhule and secured the airfield and restored the democratically-elected government at Malé, the Sri Lankan mercenaries hijacked the freighter *MV Progress Light* and took a number of hostages, including the Maldivian Transport minister and his wife. The Indian Navy frigates INS Godavari and INS Betwa captured the freighter, rescued the hostages and arrested the mercenaries near the Sri Lankan coast.

During the 2006 Lebanon War, the Indian Navy launched Operation Sukoon to successfully evacuate 2280 persons from Lebanon, including Indian, 436 Sri Lankan and 69 Nepali and 7 Lebanese citizens.

Since November 2, 2008 an Indian Navy frigate INS Tabar accompanied by the destroyer INS Mysore has been on an anti-piracy mission off the Gulf of Aden.

INDIAN COAST GUARD

The Indian Coast Guard (ICG) is one of four branches of the Indian Armed Forces, tasked with the mission to guard the Republic of India's maritime interests. The Indian Coast Guard's organization is similar to that of other Para Military Forces of India. It was created on 18 August 1978 as an independent entity as per the Coast Guard Act. It operates under the effective control of the Ministry of Defence.

The ICG mission is to protect India's maritime interests, including its coastline, exclusive economic zone and shipping. It is also tasked with Indian maritime law enforcement relating to ocean resources, shipping, customs and revenue, maritime environment, protected species as well as narcotics. The coast guard works in close cooperation with the Indian Navy, Indian department of Fisheries, Department of Revenue (Customs) and the Central and State Police forces. The ICG is generally headed by a naval officer of the rank of Vice-Admiral.

History

The establishment of the Indian Coast Guard was first proposed by the Indian Navy to provide non-military maritime services to the nation. And it is considered as one of the best coast gaurds in the world In the 1960's, sea-borne smuggling of goods was threatening India's domestic economy. The Indian Customs Department frequently called upon the Indian Navy for assistance with patrol and interception in the anti-smuggling effort.

The Nag Chaudhri Committee was constituted with participation from the Indian Navy and the Indian Air Force to study the problem. In August 1971, the committee identified the need to patrol India's vast coastline, register fishing vessels in order to identify illegal activity and the need for a capable and well-equipped force to intercept illegal vessels. The committee also looked at the number and nature of the equipment, infrastructure and personnel required to provide these services.

By 1973, India had started a program to acquire the equipment and started deputing personnel from the Indian

Navy for these anti-smuggling and law enforcement tasks, under the provisions of the Maintenance of Internal Security Act. The Indian Navy sensed that the nature of these duties diverged from its core mission as a military service. Based on the inputs from the Chief of Naval Staff, on August 31, 1974, the then Defence Secretary submitted a note the Cabinet Secretary outlining the need for the Coast Guard.

In September 1974, the Rustamji Committee was setup with participation from the Indian Navy and the Department of Revenue to examine the gaps in security and law enforcement between the roles of the Indian Navy and the central and state police forces. The discovery of oil off Bombay High further emphasized the need for a maritime law enforcement and protection service. The committee submitted its recommendation for the establishment of the Indian Coast Guard under the Ministry of Defence on July 31, 1975.

Bureaucratic wrangling followed, with the Cabinet Secretary making a recommendation to place the service under the Ministry of Home Affairs. Fortunately, Prime Minister Indira Gandhi overruled the Cabinet Secretary and decided to place the service under the Ministry of Defence.

An interim Indian Coast Guard came into being on February 1, 1977 equipped with two small frigates and five patrol boats deputed from the Indian Navy. The duties and functions of the service were formally defined in the Coast Guard Act, which was passed on 18 August 1978, and came into effect the next day. Vice Admiral V.A. Kamath of the Indian Navy was the founding Director General. Vice Admiral Kamath proposed a plan to develop the ICG into a potent force by 1984, but the full potential of this plan has not been realized due to a resource crunch.

The Indian Coast Guard conducts exercises with the other coast guards of the world. In 2006, the Indian Coast Guard conducted exercises with Japanese and Korean counterparts. In May 2005, the Indian Coast Guard agreed to set up liaison links with Pakistan Coast Guard which is formally known as the MSA Maritime Security Agency.

Major historic achievements of the service includes the first ever recapture of a pirated ship at high seas, the MV Alondra rainbow. After the 2008 Mumbai attacks, the Indian government has initiated a program to expand the ICG force, assets and infrastructure.

Rank Structure

Coast Guard Rank Structure	Equivalent Indian Navy Rank Structure
Director General	Vice Admiral
Inspector General	Rear Admiral
Deputy Inspector General+	Commodore
Deputy Inspector General	Captain
Commandant	Commander
Commandant (Junior Grade)	Commander
Deputy Commandant	Lieutenant Commander
Assistant Commandant	Lieutenant
Assistant Commandant†	Acting Lieutenant
Assistant CommandantÊ%	Midshipman

+ With three years seniority † Under training after completion of Phase III afloat training and during sub courses Ê% Under training after completion of Phase II afloat training

Organization

The Indian Coast Guard operations are split into 3 regions: Western Region headquartered in Mumbai, Eastern Region headquartered in Chennai and the Andaman & Nicobar Region headquartered in Port Blair. The force has a strength of 5440, including 633 officers.

The ICG is led by the Director General of Coast Guard, usually a commissioned officer of rank *Vice Admiral* from Indian Navy. The current ICG DG is Vice Admiral Anil Chopra, AVSM. Each region is headed by an Inspector General (IG) or a Deputy Inspector General (DIG). The IG and DIG are commissioned Coast Guard Officers, often graduates of the Indian defence service colleges.

Each of the regions is further divided into multiple districts, typically covering a coastal state or a union territory.

Bases

The Indian Coast Guard operates:

- 29 Coast Guard Stations
- 2 air bases, in Daman and Chennai
- Air enclaves at Goa, Kolkata and Port Blair.

3

Different Types of Ships in Indian Navy

This is a list of all Indian Navy Ships and submarines presently in service or being built. Speculative or planned procurements are NOT included here. Note: uc = Under Construction (Applies only to ships classes where some are in service while others are being built)

CENTAUR CLASS AIRCRAFT CARRIER

The *Centaur* class of aircraft carriers of the British Royal Navy was the last of the light fleet carrier designs started during the closing years of World War II.

History

Originally conceived as a class of eight vessels, with the end of hostilities, work on all the ships was suspended and four units *Monmouth*, *Polyphemus*, *Arrogant* and *Hermes* were cancelled outright. The four remaining vessels remained uncompleted for the best part of a decade. The earlier light fleet carriers of the *Colossus* and *Majestic* classes were completed before work resumed on the larger ships. With the extended completion periods of the units, and the rapid advances in aircraft carrier design at the time of their building, it was almost inevitable that large differences should be seen between the various members of the class.

HMS *Centaur*, the first to be completed, was commissioned in 1954. The ship had an axial flight deck and was thus unsuitable for operating the jets then rapidly supplanting piston engine aircraft in the Fleet Air Arm. *Centaur* was commissioned in Belfast and after completing her sea trials, she then steamed into Portsmouth Dockyard and for the next six months in 1954 the ship underwent a substantial reconstruction to provide for an angled flight deck, However, service in this new configuration did not last long and the ship was decommissioned in 1964. Conversion to a "commando carrier" configuration was cancelled in 1965.

HMS *Albion* and HMS *Bulwark*, the next two members of the class completed spent their lives inextricably linked. They both took part in Operation Musketeer, during the Suez Crisis, and they were both later converted into commando carriers. In this role, instead of carrying fast jets, they carried helicopters and marines.

They were worked hard in the 1960s, with each taking turns deploying 'east of Suez' to the Far East Fleet. The link was broken when *Albion* was decommissioned in 1973. *Bulwark* lingered on a few years longer until 1976. However, in 1979, *Bulwark* was recommissioned in the anti-submarine role. It was only a short change though as an engine room fire in 1980 finally saw the old ship withdrawn from service.

The final ship of the class, started as *Elephant* but now HMS *Hermes* had a longer service life than any of the others in British hands. Not being completed until 1959, some 15 years after being started, *Hermes* incorporated a full angled flight deck and other changes compared to *Centaur*, *Albion* and *Bulwark*.

After fulfilling the role of a light attack carrier for a number of years, *Hermes* was converted to a commando carrier to replace *Albion* in the early 1970s. However, a return to operating fixed wing aircraft beckoned at the end of the decade. *Hermes* was fitted with a ski-jump to enable the ship to operate the new Sea Harrier aircraft then coming into service. In this role, the ship saw considerable action in the Falklands War, acting as the flagship of the aircraft carrier task force. *Hermes* finally left Royal Navy service in 1984, and was sold to India. As INS *Viraat*, the ship continues in active service as of 2010.

Design

The *Centaur* class were intermediate in size between the *Colossus* and *Majestic* class light carriers and the *Audacious* class fleet carriers. At first this did not prove to be a hindrance. However, as the 1960s progressed, and jets continued to get larger and heavier, the point was eventually reached where the *Centaurs* could not sustain a balanced air wing of conventional aircraft. *Hermes* survived the longest as a conventional carrier, even operating the Blackburn Buccaneer. However, *Hermes* was not large enough to operate the Phantom FG.1.

In roles they were not originally designed for, the class also proved successful. The loss of *Albion* and *Bulwark's* helicopter capability was keenly felt in the Royal Navy for many years, until an effective replacement, in the form of HMS *Ocean* was commissioned in 1998. *Hermes* also performed sterling service as a platform for the Sea Harrier and made a vital contribution to the winning of the Falklands War, the largest naval conflict since 1945.

RUSSIAN SUBMARINE K-152 NERPA

The K-152 *Nerpa* is a 8,140-tonne (8,010-long-ton) Project 971 Shchuka-B (NATO: Akula II) type nuclear-powered attack submarine. Construction was started in 1993, but suspended due to lack of funding. *K-152 Nerpa* was launched in October 2008 and entered service with the Russian Navy in late 2009. The submarine will eventually be leased to the Indian Navy in 2010 and recommissioned as the INS *Chakra*.

While *K-152 Nerpa* was undergoing sea trials in the Sea of Japan on 8 November 2008, an accident caused the deaths of some twenty sailors and injury to twenty-one others. A fire suppression system discharged gas in the bow of the sub, suffocating civilian specialists and navy crew members.

Construction

The *Nerpa* was laid down at the Komsomolsk-on-Amur shipyard in 1993, but its completion was delayed for nearly a decade due to a lack of funds caused by the economic crisis of the early 1990s. The partly-constructed vessel was mothballed until 2004, when Rosprom (the Federal Agency for Industry) signed an agreement with the Indian government to complete the submarine and lease it to the Indian Navy. The vessel was intended to be completed by 2007, but underwent further delays. In 2007, it was transferred to the Vostok shipyard in the closed city of Bolshoy Kamen, Primorsky Krai, for fitting-out. It was launched in October 2008 for sea trials, following which it was due to be handed over to the Russian Defence Ministry. Reports in the Indian media suggest that the resumption of construction was underwritten with Indian funding.

The standards of the vessel's construction were criticised by several commentators. Alexander Golts, defense editor of the *Yezhednevny Zhurnal* newspaper, said that in the 1980s, the Amur shipyard turned out submarines "one after another, like pancakes," but from 1993 to 2008 had produced just one. "The old specialists had left, and the new ones lacked professionalism." An unnamed worker at the Amur shipyard told *Komsomolskaya Pravda* that there were "questions about the quality of the metal that was used in building the nuclear submarine", some of which had been bought from China, and alleged that "when the first trials of the submarine were carried out water was leaking in between the seams! So it is not surprising that the work dragged on."

During May 2009, the repairs were reported to be almost complete and new sea trials were planned for June 15–20. However, by October 2009, the work had still not been completed due to the shipyard's electrical supply having been disconnected. Nikolai Povzyk, the head of the shipyard, complained they had not been paid the 1.9 billion rubles (63.8 million dollars) owed for the work carried out on the Nerpa.

Pending lease to India

As of 2008, Russia had an agreement pending with India worth US$2 billion for the lease of *Nerpa* and another Project 971 Shchuka-B class submarine. Of this, *K-152 Nerpa* will be leased for 10 years to India at an estimated cost of US$650 million. After being handed over to the Indian Navy, it would be commissioned as *INS Chakra*. *Nerpa* is the Russian word for the Baikal seal, and *Chakra* is a weapon. Indian naval crews earlier trained to operate the submarine near St. Petersburg and another group of sailors was expected to arrive in Vladivostok in late 2008 for joining sea trials. The training of the crew was viewed as crucial to India's own nuclear submarine program, known as the Advanced Technology Vessel (ATV).

After the 2008 accident, there were conflicting reports over the status of the lease. A Russian defense industry official denied that talks had been held with India on the delivery of the nuclear submarine. "Russia did not launch talks on a contract to supply India with the Nerpa nuclear-powered submarine." General of the Army Nikolai Marakov stated that Russia would commission the *Nerpa* and that it would join seven other Akula class submarines in Russia's Pacific Fleet. "The sum of $650-780 million, which Rosoboronexport and the Amur Shipbuilding Plant had negotiated over a long period of time with the Indian Ministry of Defense, will now be found in Russia," he said.

However, in May 2009, both Russian and Indian defense officials confirmed that the *Nerpa* would be joining the Indian Navy by the end of 2009, after Russian President Vladimir Putin visited the yard & announced an immediate release of 1.2 billion roubles, for the submarine construction.

On December 28, 2009, Nerpa was commissioned and joined the Russian Navy. The submarine underwent further adjustments in February 2010. As of August 2010 Russia was training a crew from the Indian Navy to sail the ship to India in fulfillment of the lease agreement.

2008 accident

An accident aboard *K-152 Nerpa* occurred at 8:30 PM local time on 8 November 2008, during an underwater test run in the Pacific Ocean. A total of 208 people-81 military personnel and 127 civilians-were on board at the time of the accident. At least 20 people were killed by asphyxiation and at least 21 more were injured, marking the worst Russian submarine disaster since the *Kursk* sank in 2000. Three of the dead were military personnel and the rest were civilians from the Vostok,

Zvezda, Era and Amur shipbuilding yards who were members of the acceptance team.

The incident involved the accidental triggering of a fire extinguishing system which sealed two forward compartments and released freon R-114B2 (Dibromotetrafluoroethane) gas into them. According to survivors, those affected by the gas release were caught off guard and may not have been alerted in time due to warning sirens sounding only after the gas had already begun pouring in. Some of the victims were reported to have been unable to don breathing kits before they suffocated.

On 10 November, a Russian Navy statement blamed the disaster on an "unsanctioned operation" of the fire suppression system aboard the *Nerpa*. Preliminary investigations concluded that the system had triggered automatically without human intervention. On 13 November, naval investigators announced that a crewman had turned on the system "without permission or any particular grounds".

SINDHUGHOSH CLASS SUBMARINE

Sindhughosh class submarines are Indian variants of the Kilo class diesel-electric submarines in active service with the Indian Navy.

The *Sindhughosh* submarines, designated 877EKM, were designed as part of *Project 877*, and built under a contract between Rosvooruzhenie and the Ministry of Defence (India).

The submarines have a displacement of 3,000 tonnes, a maximum diving depth of 300 meters, top speed of 18 knots, and are able to operate solo for 45 days with a crew of 53. The final unit was the first to be equipped with the 3M-54 Klub (SS-N-27) antiship cruise missiles with a range of 220 km.

Incidents

January 10, 2008-The INS *Sindhughosh* collided with cargo ship MV *Leeds Castle*. The submarine is reported to have sustained superficial damage to its conning tower. As a result, the submarine was out of service for a month. The cargo ship was in restricted shallow waters.

February 26, 2010. A fire on board INS *Sindhurakshak* killed one sailor and injured two others. The fire was due to a defective battery.

INS *Sindhuvijay* has been upgraded with the hydro acoustical USHUS complex and the CCS-MK radio communications system.

SHISHUMAR CLASS SUBMARINE

The Shishumar class vessels are diesel-electric submarines, currently in active service with the Indian Navy.

These submarines are an Indian variant of the German HDW Type 209 submarine. They were commissioned between 1986 and 1994. The first two vessels were built at HDW, while the remainder were built at Mazagon Dock Limited (MDL), Mumbai under a technology transfer agreement.

These submarines have a displacement of 1660 tons when surfaced, a speed of 22 knots (41 km/h), and a complement of 40 including eight officers.

History

India signed the agreement for these submarines with HDW in 1981. The initial agreement called for delivery of four submarines which were delivered to the Indian Navy between 1986 and 1994. A subsequent agreement for the construction of 2 more submarines to be constructed at MDL was cancelled after the Pokhran-II nuclear tests in 1998.

VELA CLASS SUBMARINE

Vela class submarines of the Indian Navy were variants of the Soviet Foxtrot class submarines.

The last Vela Class will decommission in 2011.

DELHI CLASS DESTROYER

The *Delhi* class destroyers are guided-missile destroyers of the Indian Navy. Three ships of this class are in active service.

The *Delhi* class vessels are the largest warships to be fully designed and built in India, although they will soon be superseded by the Kolkata class destroyers and the Vikrant class aircraft carriers. They were built at Mazagon Dock Limited in Mumbai.

Development

The development of the ship began as Project 15 in 1977. The ships were designed indigenously and built by Mazagon Docks Limited (MDL) at a cost of Rs 7 Billion each.

The *Delhi* class has both Soviet and Western design influences, incorporating elements of the *Sovremenny* class destroyer, the *Rajput* class (*Kashin-II*) destroyer, and the *Godavari* class frigate.

These vessels are fully fitted with flag facilities. The *Delhi* class is also capable of operating in a NBC environment. Radar cross-section reduction is presumed to be minimal, to the extent that some sharp angles have been flattened.

In the main air defence role, a pair of 2 3S-90 launchers-one installed forward of the bridge and the other atop the dual helicopter hangar-are fitted with the Shtil SAM system. The Shtil system consists of the Russian Shtil missile and 24 such missiles are carried in a below-decks magazine. The launchers elevate up to 70° but have a limited firing arc of 30° within the centreline. The launcher groups require a crew of 20 men and weigh about 50 tons.

The *Delhi* class is being upgraded with the Rafael Barak point air defence missile system, which overcomes the limited firing arc of the Shtil system. It has an eight-cell vertical launch system and the missile command-to-line-of-sight (CLOS) radar guidance with a range from 500m to 10 km. The missile's maximum range is 32 km. The ship has a surveillance capacity of over 350 km and can sterilise an area of 250 km.

The ships also have a quadruple 533mm torpedo launcher, which can also be used to launch SS-N-15 'Starfish' or possibly SS-N-16 'Stallion' ASW missiles, so is capable of hitting targets ranging from 50 km to 120 km. It is also equipped with two RBU-6000 anti-submarine rocket launchers with 12 tubes. Their range is 6 km and the maximum engagement depth is 500m.

Each ship can support two helicopters, the Sea King or the HAL Dhruv. The Sea King helicopters are equipped with a Super Searcher radar and primarily used in air surveillance and anti-submarine roles. The helicopters are capable of flying four and half hours non-stop. The HAL Dhruv helicopters are primarily for utility roles. The INS *Delhi* has a crew of approximately 30 officers and 350 sailors.

The ships are equipped with four chaff launch systems and the BEL Ajanta radar interceptor. The TQN-2 jamming system is supplied by the Italian company, Elettronica. The ship's hull mounted active search sonar capability is based on the TSM2633 by Thales Underwater Systems or the APSOH by Bharat. The *Delhi* Class also has a variable depth sonar, Model 15-750 developed and manufactured in India by Indal and Garden Reach.

RAJPUT CLASS DESTROYER

The *Rajput* class guided-missile destroyers built for the Indian Navy are modified versions of Soviet Kashin class destroyers. They are also known as Kashin-II class. The ships were built in Russia after considerable Indian design modifications to the *Kashin* design. The helicopter pad in the original design was replaced with a flight elevator.

Rajput class destroyers were the first ships in the Indian Navy to deploy the BrahMos supersonic cruise missile systems. The systems were deployed during a mid-life refit of the ships. The missile system has 8 missiles with bow mounted launchers.

INS Ranvijay was deployed with updated vertical launchers for the BrahMos missile. The *Kashin* class ship was designed to fulfill a variety of roles including anti-aircraft and anti-submarine warfare to defend carrier task forces from submarines, low-flying aircraft, and cruise missiles. Five units of a variant of the modified *Kashin* class design were built in the former USSR for export to India in the 1980s.

GODAVARI CLASS FRIGATE

The *Godavari class* frigates (formerly, Type 16 or Project 16 frigates) are guided-missile frigates of the Indian Navy. The

Godavari class was the first significant indigenous warship design and development initiative of the Indian Navy. Its design is a modification of the Nilgiri class frigate with a focus on indigenous content of 72%, a larger hull and updated armaments.

The class and the lead ship, INS Godavari are named after the Godavari River. Three ships of this class currently serve in the Indian Navy. Subsequent ships in the class, INS Ganga and INS Gomati also take their names from Indian rivers.

INS *Gomati* was the first Indian Navy vessel to have digital electronics in her combat data system. The ships combine Indian, Russian and Western weapons systems.

History

The concept for the Godavari class originated from the lessons learnt in the Indo-Pakistan War of 1971. There was a need for a ship unique to Indian requirements, for deploying a hybrid of indigenously-designed, as well as Russian and European weapons systems.

One of the requirements was to deploy two Sea King helicopters from the ship. The Nilgiri class vessels were too small for this. So the final design incorporated a larger hull.

Design

Although the Directorate of Marine Engineering suggested replacing steam propulsion with gas turbines, it was decided not to do so, since Bharat Heavy Electricals Limited and Hindustan Aeronautics Limited had made heavy investments in facilities and tooling for design of steam turbines and auxiliary systems. For armaments, the missile and gun package of the Soviet Nanuchka class corvette was to be installed on the frigate. The keel of the lead ship INS Godavari was laid in 1977 at Mazagon Dock Limited in Bombay. She was commissioned in December 1983.

NILGIRI CLASS FRIGATE

The *Nilgiri* class frigates are updated versions of the Leander class, designed and built for the Indian Navy by

Mazagon Dock Limited in Mumbai. Six ships were built between 1972-81. Vessels of the class formed the 14th Frigate Squadron.

The class and its lead ship, INS *Nilgiri* are named for the Nilgiri Hills. Subsequent ships in the class are also named for hill ranges of India.

The *Nilgiri* class is being decommissioned by the Navy. At least four ships have been decommissioned, with the remainder being used primarily for training and testing roles. These are due to be decommissioned by 2009-10, once the Shivalik class vessels enter service.

History

The *Nilgiri* Class frigates served as the mainstay & workhorse of the Indian Navy during the 1980s and early 1990s and they formed the 14th Frigate Squadron. The last two vessels (F41, F42) have more powerful engines than the remainder.

INS Taragiri (F41) had a serious fire in July 1994, but was repaired and was back in active service in 1995.

Westinghouse supplied the Indian Navy with ASW sonar systems, two hull mounted arrays and three variable depth sonar arrays which are installed inside towed bodies built by Fathom Ocean Ltd. Transducer elements in both cases are identical. INS Udaygiri (F35) underwent a refit at Naval Dockyard, Mumbai. The remaining vessels in the series were expected to have their armaments brought into line with later ships.

INS Himgiri (F34) was used as a trial ship for the indigenous APSOH (Advanced Panoramic Sonar Hull) sonar.

KHUKRI CLASS CORVETTE

The Khukri class corvettes were intended to replace the ageing Petya II Class corvettes of the Indian Navy.

The first two were ordered in December 1984 and the remaining in 1985. The diesel engines are assembled in India, under license by Kirloskar Group. Around 65% of the ship contains indigenous content.

SHARDUL CLASS LANDING SHIP

Shardul class landing ships are large amphibious warfare vessels built at Garden Reach Shipbuilders and Engineers for the Indian Navy.

The class has an indigenous content of over 90% with state-of-the-art equipment.

History

INS *Shardul* was the first vessel commissioned at Karwar Naval base INS Kadamba. The second ship INS Kesari was commissioned at the Vishakapatanam Naval base, and later moved to Port Blair. The third ship INS *Airavata* was handed over to the Indian Navy of sea trials in 2008 and was expected to enter active service in August 2008 with Eastern command of the Indian Navy. The ship was commissioned into service on 19 May 2009.

MAGAR CLASS LANDING SHIP

The Magar class landing ships are amphibious warfare vessels of the Indian Navy, currently in active service. Only two ships of the class were designed and built by Hindustan Shipyard Limited, with fitting completed at Garden Reach Shipbuilders and Engineers.

The ships are stationed at the naval base in Vishakapatnam on India's east coast.

It can operate two medium-lift helicopters, which are primarily meant for "inserting" a small team of Special Forces (marine commandos). To discharge its cargo and most of the troops, it needs to be "beached" through its 'bow-door' (in the front).

INS Magar fire

On the 22nd of February 2006, at around 5 pm local time, an accidental fire broke out on the ship. It was caused while the ship was engaged in dumping expired ammunition, and one of the boxes of ammunition caught fire. At the time of the accident the Magar was in the Bay of Bengal, around 40 nautical miles (70 km) from Vishakapatnam. Casualties included three deaths and a further six sailors sustaining injuries. The injured were rushed to a naval hospital in Vishakapatnam by the Sea King helicopter on board.

LANDING CRAFT

Landing craft are boats and seagoing vehicles used to convey a landing force (infantry and vehicles) from the sea to the shore during an amphibious assault. Most renowned are those used to storm the beaches of Normandy, the Mediterranean, and many Pacific islands during WWII. This was the high point of the landing craft, with a significant number of different designs produced in large quantities by the United Kingdom and United States.

Because of the need to run up onto a suitable beach, WWII landing craft were flat-bottomed, and many designs had a flat front, often with a lowerable ramp, rather than a normal bow. This made them difficult to control and very uncomfortable in rough seas. The control point (bridge was far too fancy a description for the facilities of the LCA and similar craft) was normally situated at the extreme rear of the vessel as were the engines. In all cases they tended to be known by an abbreviation derived from the official name rather than by the full title.

Origin

In the days of sail, the ship's boats were used as landing craft. These rowing boats were sufficient, if inefficient, in an era when marines were effectively light infantry, participating mostly in small-scale campaigns in far-flung colonies against less well-equipped indigenous opponents.

However during World War I, mass mobilization of troops equipped with rapid-fire weapons quickly rendered such boats obsolete; after the disastrous landing phase of the Battle of Gallipoli in 1915, military powers around the world tended to avoid large-scale amphibious warfare altogether.

The British produced a landing craft in 1920 that could put their then-current medium tank directly onto a beach. From 1924 it was used with landing boats in annual exercises in amphibious landings. It would later be given the name "Landing

Craft, Mechanized" (abbreviated to LCM). In the 1930s the British Army carried out divisional-sized amphibious landing exercises. A boat for landing infantry, the Landing Craft Assault, was drawn up after research by the Inter-Service Training and Development Centre in 1938.

The United States revived and experimented in their modern approach to amphibious warfare between 1913 to mid-1930s, when the United States Navy and Marine Corps became interested in setting up advanced bases in opposing countries during wartime; the prototype advanced base force officially evolved into the Fleet Marine Force (FMF) in 1933. In 1939, during the annual Fleet Landing Exercises, the FMF became interested in the military potential of Andrew Higgins's design of a powered, shallow-draught boat. These LCVPs, dubbed the 'Higgins Boats', were reviewed and passed by the U.S. Naval Bureau of Construction and Repair. Soon, the Higgins boats were developed to a final design with a ramp, and were produced in large numbers.

WW2 Types

Nine-ton Landing Craft Navigation (LCN) were used by British "Combined Operations Assault Pilotage Parties" (Royal Marine and Special Boat Service crew) for surveying landing sites.

The "Landing Craft Control" (LCC) were 56-foot (17 m) U.S. Navy vessels, carrying only the crew (Scouts and Raiders) and newly-developed radar. Their main job was to find and follow the safe routes in to the beach, lanes which had been cleared of obstacles and mines. There were 8 in the entire Normandy invasion (two per beach). After leading in the first wave, they were to head back out and bring in the second wave. After that, they were used as all-purpose command and control assets during the invasion.

The smallest landing craft were amphibians such as the U.S.-designed Landing Vehicle Tracked, an amphibious (and sometimes armored) personnel carrier. These were operated by Army personnel, not naval crews. They had a capacity of about three tons. The British introduced their own amphibian the

Terrapin. Of the landing craft proper the smallest were the U.S. Landing Craft Personnel, Large (10 tons) and the British Landing Craft Assault (LCA) (13 tons). These were small craft intended to be transported around by larger vessels then lowered into the water off the target beach. Typically they could carry 36 fully armed soldiers. The LCPL sometimes came with an enclosed cockpit and was often used as a command boat. It lacked a loading ramp which the LCA did have.

The U.S. Landing Craft Vehicle/Personnel (LCVP), also known as a Higgins Boat, was a more flexible variant of the LCPL with a wide ramp — it could carry 36 troops or a small vehicle such as a Jeep, or a corresponding amount of cargo.

Landing Craft, Mechanized were larger (36 tons), capable of carrying one small tank or 100 troops.

None of the above was capable of making a voyage longer than about 6–12 hours, mainly through fuel limitations.

The Landing Craft Utility (LCU) is used to transport equipment and troops to the shore. They are capable of transporting tracked or wheeled vehicles and troops from amphibious assault ships to beachheads or piers.

Then came the Landing Craft Infantry (Large) or LCI(L), capable of making serious voyages under its own power (some were sailed directly from the United Kingdom to take part in the Operation Torch landings, and U.S. Navy LCIs island hopped across the Pacific). LCI(L)s were about 158 feet long and 23 feet wide and carried around 200 troops. There were several sub-types of the craft, with the LCI(L) infantry carrier dominating; but LCIs also served as rocket (LCI(R)) and mortar (M), and gunboat (G) platforms, as well as a flotilla flagship (FF). While still intended to run up on the beach, these tended to have a normal type bow with stepped ramps on each side for the troops to disembark. The LCI was re-classified Landing Ship Infantry (LSI) by the U.S. in 1949.

Of a similar size was the Landing Craft Tank, which could carry up to 4 Tanks or other vehicles. These had a ramp at the front which was dropped for the vehicles to get ashore. Behind the ramp was an open space known as the *Tank Deck*. There were several different designs and sizes varied. The next step was the Landing Ship Tank. This carried more vehicles than the LCT (20 in the US-built versions) and had normal looking bows, although the bows were actually formed by doors which were opened for the unloading ramp to drop. Fully loaded, these displaced more than 3,000 tons, rather more than any Royal Navy destroyers of the period.

Finally there was the Landing Ship Dock, which had a large open compartment at the back. Opening a stern door and flooding special compartments allowed this area to be open to the sea and LCI-sized vessels could enter or leave.

Initial British nomenclature used different type names leading to alternate names such as Assault Landing Craft, Infantry Landing Craft and Tank Landing Craft.

Due to their rather small size the majority were not given names and were simply given serial numbers, e.g., *LCT 304*. The LSTs were an exception to this being much the same size as a small cruiser. Three British-built LSTs were named as well, HMS *Boxer*, *Bruiser* and *Thruster* which were somewhat larger than the U.S. design; they also had proper funnels.

Armament

DUKWs, LCAs and LCMs had no fixed armament, but there were ways for troops on board to use their own weapons.

LCIs and LCTs carried weapons such as the Oerlikon 20 mm cannon each side of the bridge structure. LSTs had a somewhat heavier armament.

Imperial Japanese Navy landing craft

The Imperial Japanese Navy operated the following types of landing craft during World War II

- *Chuhatsu*
- *Daihatsu*
- *Mokusei Daihatsu*
- *Shohatsu*
- *Toku Daihatsu*

Current Landing Craft

landing craft were made famous by their use during World War Two, and the descendants of these early landing craft are used by many armies and navies today.

Amphibious mechanized utility and landing craft

The mechanized utility and landing craft, more commonly known as an amphibious landing craft or boat. This was the kind used during the second world war, and while the mechanized landing crafts of today are similar in construction, a lot of improvements have been made. Normally using diesel engines, the best amphibious landing boats (such as the LCM-8 of the US Navy) are capable of a military lift of 183 metric tons at a speed of 22 km/h, carrying even heavy equipment like M1 Abrams tanks with little trouble. Amphibious landing craft normally mount several machine guns or similar weapons for the defense of troops and/or vehicle crews inside.

Air-cushioned landing craft

The air cushioned landing craft (Landing Craft Air Cushion, or LCAC in the US Navy) is based on small to mid sized multi-purpose hovercraft, Also known as "over the beach" ("OTB") craft, they allow troops and material to access more than 70 percent of the world's coastline, while only approximately 15 percent of that coastline is available to conventional landing craft. Like the mechanized landing craft, they are usually equipped with mounted machine guns, although they also support grenade launchers and heavy weapons. These vehicles are commonly used in the United States Navy, the Royal Navy, the Russian Navy, and the Hellenic Navy.

Special purpose craft

Some Landing craft were converted for special purposes either to give défence for the other landing craft in the attack or as support weapons during the landing.

Landing Craft Assault (Hedgehog)

The LCA(HR) was a conversion of the British LCA which carried 24 spigot mortars, the Royal Navy's Hedgehog anti-submarine weapon instead of personnel. The mortars were fired as a barrage onto the beach to clear mines and other obstructions. Having discharged its mortars and its duty the LCA(HR) would then leave the beach area. They were towed to the beach by larger craft such as the LCT which would carry the assault teams of the Royal Engineers with their specialist vehicles and equipment to complete the beach clearance.

There were 3 flotillas (of 18, 18 and 9 craft) used at Juno, Gold and Sword beaches.

Landing Craft Gun

The Landing Craft Gun (LCG) was similar and was intended to give supporting fire to the landing. Apart from the Oerlikons as per a normal LCT they had two 4.7 inch destroyer guns. Crewing was similar to the LCF. LCGs played a very important part in the Walcheren operation in October 1944.

There were a variants on the LCG: LCG(L)3 and LCG(L)4 both having 2 4.7 inch guns and LCG(M) which carried British Army 25 pounder gun-howitzers.

Landing Craft Flak

The Landing Craft Flak (LCF) was a conversion of the LCT intended to give anti-aircraft support to the landing. They were first used in the Dieppe Raid early in 1942. The ramp was welded shut, and a deck built on top of the Tank deck. They were equipped with several light anti-aircraft guns—a typical fitting was eight 20 mm Oerlikons and four QF 2 pdr "pom-poms" and had a crew of 60. Royal Navy examples had mixed crews, with the operation of the craft being the responsibility of RN crew and the manning of the guns being done by Royal Marines. They carried two naval officers and two marine officers.

Landing Craft Rocket

Finally there was the Landing Craft Rocket, known as the Landing Craft Tank (Rocket) (LCT(R)) to denote that it was a modified LCT.

This had a large set of launchers for the British RP-3 60 lb (27 kg), 3 in (76 mm) rockets mounted on the covered-over tank deck. The full set of launchers was "in excess of" 1,000 and reloads totaling 5,000 rockets were kept below. The firepower was claimed to be equivalent to 80 light cruisers or 200 destroyers.

The method of operation was to anchor off the target beach, pointing towards the shore. The distance to the shore was then measured by radar and the elevation of the launchers set accordingly. The crew then vanished below (apart from the commanding officer who retreated to a special cubby hole to control things) and the launch was then set off electrically. The launch could comprise the entire set or individual ranks of rockets.

A full reload was a very labor-intensive operation and at least one LCT(R) went alongside a cruiser and got a working party from the larger ship to assist in the process.

Landing Craft Support

The Landing craft Support were used to give some firepower close in.

The Landing Craft Support (Medium), LCS(M), Mark 2 and Mark 3 were used at Normandy. The crew was Royal Navy with Royal Marines to operate the weapons: two 0.5 inch Vickers machine guns and a 4-inch mortar to fire smoke shells.

The Landing Craft Support (Large) was a converted Landing Craft, Infantry (Small). Armour was added to its wooden hull and a turret with an anti-tank gun fitted. The LCS(L) Mark 1, had a 2–pdr (40 mm) gun in a Daimler armoured car turret. The Mark 2s had a 6–pdr (57 mm) anti–tank gun.

Inflatable landing craft

Inflatable boats were often used to transport amphibious troops from high speed transports and submarines. The United States used a 7 man Landing Craft, Rubber (Small) (LCR-S) and a 10 man Landing Craft, Rubber (Large) (LCR-L).

Landing barges

Landing barges were adaptations of British Thames barges and lighters as landing craft. In size they came between the landing craft and landing ships. They were used at all beaches during the landings at Normandy manned by British crews.

Some were fitted with engines while others were towed to the beach. They were used for defence, transportation, supply (food, water and oil) and repair (fitted out with workshops).

Those fitted for vehicle carrying had a ramp fitted in place at the rear and they had to back onto beaches. They would work from ships and coasters to the shore and back.

Two flotillas were made up of "flak barges" to provide defence of the beaches. Like landing craft, flak barges carried A/A guns: two 40 mm Bofors and two 20 mm Oerlikon, with army gunners and naval crew.

The "Landing Barge Kitchen" (LBK) was fitted with a large superstructure containing the galley. With a crew of 20 plus they could carry food for 800 for a week and provide 1,600 hot and 800 cold meals a day, including freshly baked bread.

CAR NICOBAR CLASS FAST ATTACK CRAFT

The *Car Nicobar* class of fast attack crafts are being built at Garden Reach Shipbuilders and Engineers for the Indian Navy. The ships will be cost-effective platforms for patrol and rescue operations at sea. The vessels are the first water-jet propelled ships of the Indian Navy.

INS *Car Nicobar* and INS *Chetlat* are based in Chennai under India's Eastern Naval Command.

The class and the lead vessel, INS *Car Nicobar*, are named for the *Car Nicobar* island. Subsequent vessels of the class are also named for Indian islands.

Design

The vessels have improved habitability with fully air-conditioned modular type accommodation. They have sensors/ radars, an efficient gun turret of indigenous design and sewage treatment plant to comply with the conditions laid down by the International Maritime Organisation.

Weapons

One 30mm CRN-91 gun fitted on the forepeak. The CRN-91, which is a naval version of the 2A42 30mm Medak gun, is controlled by an electronic fire control system developed & jointly produced by the Ordnance Factory Board (OFB) and Bharat Electronics Limited (BEL). It also mounts two 12.7mm Heavy Machine Guns.

BANGARAM CLASS PATROL VESSEL

The *Bangaram class* patrol vessels of the Indian Navy are designed for interdiction against fast moving surface vessels and for search-and-rescue operations in coastal areas and in the exclusive economic zone.

The vessels are designed and built by Garden Reach Shipbuilders and Engineers. The diesel generators on board are supplied by Cummins India. The electronic equipment on board is from Bharat Electronics Limited, ECIL and Hindustan Aeronautics Limited.

TRINKAT CLASS PATROL VESSEL

The Indian Navy commissioned the design and construction of the *Trinkat class* patrol vessels for fisheries protection, anti-poaching, counter-insurgency and search-and-rescue operations in coastal areas and in the exclusive economic zone.

The vessels were designed and built by Garden Reach Shipbuilders and Engineers. The vessels of the class are named after islands from the Andaman and Nicobar Islands or the Lakshadweep Islands.

ADITYA CLASS TANKER

The *Aditya class* tankers of the Indian Navy are fleet replinishment ships. They are enhancement of the Deepak class tankers.

4

Indian-Subcontinent Database

Almost always limited by the lack of proper decision making and allocation of priorities on the Indian Government's part and the uncertainty of the same about it's role, the Indian Navy has nevertheless, always striven to maintain a credible, professional and independent Air arm to provide for increasing strategic and tactical demands of the subcontinent.

The origins may be traced back to as early as 1948, when a newly set up Directorate of Naval Aviation under the command of Capt.H.C Ranalds of the Royal Navy, put forth ambitious and highly optimistic expansion plans envisaged an inventory of 300 aircraft, 54 of them being elemental to a two-carrier strike group and the Hawker Sea Fury FB.11 as the primary shore based strike fighter. After realistic abatement in 1950, expansion plans were revised to initiate the acquisition of a small carrier and shore based ASW and strike force.

Following the approval for the creation of a Fleet Air Arm by the Defence Minister's committee, on 24 October 1950, a Royal Navy (RN) team was deputed to New Delhi, to help create the necessary infrastructure. The Navy had already deputed up to 13 volunteers to the UK in March 1949 and following flight training at Donibristle, three of them moving on to ASW conversion at Losseimouth with two others proceeding to operational conversion on fighters. The very first aircraft to be acquired by the Indian Navy was the Shorts

Sealand Mk.1L amphibian, ten examples of the type to equip a Fleet Requirement Unit (FRU) at INS Garuda, in Cochin. The Navy then proceeded to execute it's plans through the purchase of an aircraft carrier, INS 'Vikrant' (ex-HMS Hercules), followed by a total of 74 Hawker Seahawk Mk.6/Mk.100/Mk.101 fighters, 12 Breguet Alize' ASW aircraft and numerous other types.

After the liberation of Goa in 1961, the Navy took over the ex-Portuguese airfield at Dabolim and rechristened it as the the new INS Hansa (formerly a lodger unit of an IAF airbase at Sulur in the state of Tamil Nadu), on 2 September 1964. The magnificent base soon became the hub of all naval aviation and hosts six squadrons which include disembarked carrier aircraft. Goa is also home to the headquarters of Indian Naval Aviation, established in 1986 and headed by a Flag Officer Naval Aviation (FONA). The Aircrew Categorization and Standardization board (AIRCATS) which also conducts annual Flight Safety Inspection of all naval air squadrons, was also established at Goa in 1983.

Combat proven in the 1971 Indo-Pak war and boasting of invaluable contributions ever since, the Naval Air Arm has since forced the Indian government to reevaluate it's stance and hence accrued additional roles, resources and funds to satisfy it's growing importance.

In comparison to the IAF, the range of aircraft types operated by the Indian Navy seem to have similar degree of diversity even if they cannot compare in terms of absolute strength in numbers. Each aircraft type, despite being built to more limited specifications, is operated in numerous roles including combat, most having been accoutered with state of the art equipment for the purpose. For the heavy logistics and transport role however, the Indian Navy has no aircraft of it's own and depends on the IAF. The second aircraft carrier, INS Viraat (ex-HMS Hermes) was purchased in 1986, while the INS Vikrant was retired in 1997. The current Indian Naval Air Arm consists of 5000-10000 personnel and more than 170 aircraft equipping over 13 squadrons at six major Naval Air Stations (NAS) and a single aircraft carrier. With the inking of the deal with Russia that provides for the refit and acquisition of the carrier Gorshkov and MiG-29K, the initiated construction of the indigenous 37,500 ton aircraft carrier and joint development of the Naval LCA, the Indian Navy is all set for it's next major expansion.

INAS 312 "Albatross/The Mighty Props"

Since independence, long range Maritime Patrol (MP) had been the sole responsibility of the Indian Air Force (IAF) which followed a British model and manual of joint operations. In 1961, the IAF effected the transfer of 7 Lockheed L1049G Super Constellation aircraft from the national carrier Air-India which had replaced the type with the Boeing-707, and proceeded to convert at least five units of the type to MPA configuration equipped with the ASV-21 radar.

In 1966, the Indian Navy (IN) put forth a proposal to transfer the command and control of all MP aircraft and the associated responsibilities from the Air Force to the Navy, quoting inadequate coverage of the maritime zones and underutilization of the assets during the 1965 War with Pakistan, cost effectiveness and superior coordination and cooperation through the use of naval personnel who were already familiar with the regions of expected operation.

The Air Force was quick to reject the proposal, citing the importance of already existent maintenance facilities (although major maintenance was carried out by Air India, at Bombay), airfield arrangements and experience, despite the fact that they had generated an overall MP effort of just 10 hours per day during May and September 1965, against the Navy's requirement of 80 hours per day in the Arabian Sea alone, even when working in conjunction with other naval aircraft operating from Santa Cruz.

After some discussions, the Government of India (GoI) decided to let the IAF continue with the Super Connies and reopen the debate if and when newer MP Aircraft (MPA) were acquired at a later stage. Thereafter, both the IAF and the IN began to search for a suitable dedicated MP/ASW aircraft for the purpose and the first option to be considered was the Breguet Atlantique-1. In October 1968, a French Aeronavale

Atlantique, flying in formation with IN Alizes, gave a demonstration at INS Hansa in Dabolim, Goa. This was followed by a thorough evaluation by a joint IAF-IN team plus ASW trials against the submarine Kalvari. Although the aircraft was found to conform to all requirements, the decision on who would operate these aircraft, had still not been made and no new aircraft were acquired at this point.

During the 1971 War with Pakistan, the lack of sufficient airborne ASW assets among other reasons, led the deployment of two obsolete Blackwood class Frigates against a modern Daphne class submarine of the Pakistani Navy, leading to the loss of the one of the former. Although the IAF did fly some useful maritime reconnaissance and Search And Rescue missions with the L1049G, the Navy was dissatisfied overall. The IN thus pressed forth their immediate requirement of a new MP/RASW aircraft and the need for it to perform constant coordinated action with other ASW and Patrol assets which could be made possible only though operation by the Navy itself. This finally led to Government approval for the acquisition of four new MPAs in May 1973 shortly after which the Ilyushin Il-38 'May' MRASW was selected.

In June 1975, the Government also reopened the debate on who, the Air Force or the Navy, should get to operate the latter. For the purpose, the Defense Ministry prepared an analytical statement of 20-25 pages which included all the points of view and it was finally concluded that it would be more prudent to let the Navy operate the Il-38s while the Air Force could possibly undertake their maintenance. With the Il-38 scheduled to arrive in mid-1977, the IAF concluded that it would now be best if the Navy took over the Super Connies and wrote the latter in 1976, offering to immediately hand over the aircraft albeit with a provision that the Il-38s should revert to the Air Force if it was found within the first six months that the Navy could not cope with both the flying and maintenance of the Super Connies, keeping in mind that the Navy had no experience in the flying, handling patterns and navigation of a giant 4-engined aircraft of similar type. Thereafter, four naval aviation pilots, four co-pilots, six to eight observers and some maintenance personnel were given a brief flying and technical course by the IAF's No.6 squadron, based at Pune. On completion, all naval crew plus some IAF flying instructors, navigation instructors and maintenance personnel were deputed to INS Hansa at Dabolim (Goa) to form an ad-hoc squadron. In all, the IAF transferred five L1049Gs while retaining two of the same which were freighter configured (with a large cargo door on the port side) for the transport role.

After six weeks of preparation, Lt Cdr Bhinde became the first naval pilot to undertake a solo flight, soon to be followed by four other pilots. Despite the lack of manpower at the base due to a large contingent of personnel being deputed to the USSR for training on the Il-38, dissimilar infrastructure and facilities were quickly set up for the L1049G type. On 18 November 1972, the squadron INAS 312 'Albatross' was formally commissioned at INS Hansa. The Super Constellation was finally phased out of naval service in 1983 but the IAF interestingly, kept it's two freighters operational for a little while longer. Air India terminated it's Super Constellation maintenance and overhaul facilities on 31 March 1984 due to a spares shortage and the IAF was soon to retire it's last Super Connie.

The requirement for additional and more capable aircraft became apparent when two squadrons of MPAs themselves were not enough to ensure adequate coverage, especially over the Bay of Bengal. In the mid-80s, the USSR offered the Tupolev Tu-142M-Mod4 (NATO: Bear-F) MRASW and the proposal was quickly followed up with an order after the initial attempts to sell a downgraded version of the aircraft were rejected. Between May and August 1987, four sets of 10 crewmembers each began ground training at Riga in the USSR after a mandatory prerequisite Russian language course. The first three Tu-142Ms of the Indian Navy were flown from Simferopol to Dabolim on 30 March 1988, after a 9.5 hr flight covering over 7000 km. Two more Tu-142Ms were flown in on 13 April and on 16 April 1988, INAS 312 was officially reraised and recommissioned with the new aircraft, under the command of Cdr.Pandey. The remaining three Tu-142Ms arrived between August and October of the same year. Reliable reports do indicate a total of 10 aircraft being acquired eventually, although this figure cannot be confirmed beyond doubt.

Efforts were already underway to convert the small abandoned IAF airfield on the eastern coast near the town of Arakonnam, around 90 km from the city of Chennai in the state of Tamil Nadu, into a fully fledged naval airfield/base, in order house the entire squadron of Tu-142s.

For the purpose, the Navy added another 1450 acres of land to the existing 750 acres and extended the runway from 1530 meters to 4500 meters. INS Rajali, the new naval airbase, was officially commissioned on 11 March 1992, under the command of Capt. Vasan, and was also home to the squadron INAS 561, which catered to the training of Chetak helicopter pilots of the SAR Chetak flight (INAS 321). The new base housed a dedicated ATC complex and a special maintenance hangar and base support facility for the Tu-142M among other features.

The roles of the Tu-142M include long range maritime patrol of typically 12/14/16 hours endurance, ASW, ASV, homing in of and coordination of strike packages. The aircraft are operated out of both INS Rajali (East) and INS Hansa (West) for routine long range patrols and are also serviced at both bases.

All MPA pilots need to receive basic training followed by multi-engine training at the IAF's Transport Training Wing (TTW) in Yelahanka before converting to their respective aircraft while Observers receive specialist training in ASW and communications. Each Tu-142M carries 10 crewmembers including the Pilot/Commander, Co-Pilot, Flight Engineer (Cheif petty officer), Flight Signaller, Flight Gunner for the tail turret and five Navigators/Observers. The Observers act as the Weapon System and Sensor officers while a senior navigator coordinates the entire ASW phase of the mission.

Major upgrade plans for the Tu-142M were announced in the late 90s with mentions of the Leninets Sea Dragon (*Morskoi Zmei*) sensor suite and the air launched Klub ASCM but developments, if any, soon faded into obscurity for the next few years. It seemed certain that the Sea Dragon upgrade had been chosen until it was revealed in 2003-04 that plans to upgrade the Tu-142M with the same, were scrapped primarily on cost grounds.

Apparently, Rosoboronexport had demanded a massive USD $888.9 million for the upgrade of the Tu-142M fleet, against a maximum of USD $555.5 million sanctioned by the IN and also refused to cooperate for a joint upgrade with Israeli participation. Although the original deal to equip the Il-38 with the Sea Dragon suite proceeded as planned, a wholly Israeli sensor suite on the lines of the upgrade package applied to the Dornier/HAL Do-228 of the INAS 310 squadron, was chosen instead for the Tu-142M.

By early 2004, the IN had completed refitting a single Tu-142M (IN-315) with the Elta EL/M-2022A-V3 radar which replaced the Leninets Korschun system plus a complete ELINT and COMINT package with nose and fuselage mounted V/UHF antennae and an underfuselage P-band antenna farm. The complete upgraded to be standardized on the type includes all the sensors installed on the upgraded Do-228 plus additional SATCOM, ELINT and EW equipment.

It is also expected that the upgraded aircraft would act as the primary command link between India's Nuclear Command Centre and the ATV SSN currently being built indigenously for the Indian Navy. Although the Russian upgrade offer was rejected, the Tu-142Ms will progressively receive the air launched version of the Novotar Klub cruise missile.

The aircraft is also one of the intended primary platforms for the Indo-Russian Brahmos-A air launched supersonic multi-mission cruise missile whose development has recently been initiated. Upto four Brahmos-A under each wing, are expected to be the standard payload. Other recent announcements included the intention to overhaul and modernise the Tu-142M's Kuznetsov NK-12MV engines at the Motorostroitel aircraft factory in Samara, Russia. The factory also undertakes the major overhaul of around 15 Indian NK-12MV engines, yearly.

In the future, the Tu-142M will receive the Brahmos-A supersonic cruise missile, with 4-6 rounds carried underwing and 2 carried on the fuselage.

INAS 315 "The Winged Stallions"

Following the French Atlantique, the second MPA to be evaluated by the Indian Navy was the BAe Nimrod. A Naval team visited the UK in September 1973 and the Nimrod was also found to be suitable. Acquisition and purchase in foreign exchange, of either the Atlantique or the Nimrod was however threatened and finally ruled out due to the financial situation caused by the oil crisis of October 1973.

Eventually, details of the potent Ilyushin Il-38 which entered service with the Soviet AV-MF some years earlier, had become available and the IN pressed for their acquisition, although the former was quite reluctant since each aircraft was essential for their own large scale maritime coverage worldwide. After some persuasion, the contract for the transfer of three ex-AV-MF Il-38s, was signed in February 1975, although the decision to reflect these in the Navy's budget and thus place them under the latter's command and control, came much later.

For training, a large contingent of naval aviators, mostly Alize' pilots, none of whom had experience on multi-engine types, left for Riga in September 1977 after completing the preliminary training and Russian language courses at INS Hansa itself. The formal commissioning of the new squadron 'INAS 315', under the command of Cdr. B.K Malik, took place on 1 October 1977, at INS Hansa. Two more Il-38s were eventually acquired and joined the squadron in 1983.

The Il-38 type in Indian service has proven to be popular and important, taking the roles of MR, ASW, ASV, SAR and Strike coordination. The aircraft is reputed to have a failure free service life for over 25 years and is a favorite among maintenance crew. The first major modification aiming to give the Il-38, missile capability, was commenced under 'Project *Yaduvansh*', from April 1990 onwards, with HAL Bangalore as the primary partner. The first successful drop trial of a dummy missile payload was carried out on 22 August 1991. Finally, on

15 May 1994, the first live firing of a Sea Eagle AshM was carried out under 'Operation Crocodile'

Since it's induction, INAS 315 has operated the aircraft from Dabolim, for 10-12 hour endurance sorties over the Arabian sea and by 10 June 1996, had over 25,000 hours of problem-free flying to it's name, 30,000 hours by 2002. INAS-315 was awarded the 'Best Naval Air Squadron' trophy on 16 August 1991 and the CNS trophy for 'Best Frontline Squadron' on 04 August 1992. Other notable achievements include SAR aid to the ship INS Sandhayak which was crippled by a cyclone in May 1990, SAR aid to INS Andaman, SAR aid to MV Najid II on 20 April 1991, for which Cdr Ranveer Singh received the Nausena Medal and SAR aid to a man overboard from a Japanese training squadron on 18 June 1995. In Jan 1993, an LTTE merchant ship MV Ahat, carrying arms and ammunition was successfully intercepted off the coast of Karikal. The first ever joint exercise with IAF MiG-27MLs was carried out on 01 August 1997 and on 23 July 1998, INAS-315 participated with a bilateral exercise between India and Male. On 12 Oct 1998, the squadron operated from Bhubhaneshwar airfield for the exercise 'SUMMEREX 98'. Despite consistent performance of the ageing Berkut system, the need to upgrade the aircraft was realized and the Indian Navy turned to Leninets for the Sea Dragon upgrade suite.

Tragedy struck on 1 October 2002, during the squadron's silver jubilee anniversary celebrations; At approximately 9:50 AM, IN-302 and IN-304, which were flying parallel to each other, clashed and suffered a Mid-Air Collision (MAC) above the airport. Both aircraft crashed, killing all 12 crewmembers as well as 3 people on the ground. The event left the country shattered and created a significant gap in maritime surveillance capabilities, thus forcing the Navy to accelerate it's attempts to acquire additional aircraft, a move initiated and announced much earlier.

The Indian Navy finally signed the contract for the upgrade of the five Il-38s, with Rosoboronexport in September 2002. The deal, valued at USD $205 million, will not only add the Leninets Sea Dragon radar with digital mission computer,

GOES-324 FLIR/CCD/Laser electro-optics system, a new ESM system, GPS/GLONASS and Magnetic Anomaly Detector (MAD) but will also implement a life extension refit that is expected to keep the aircraft active for 10 to 15 more years.

The Man-Machine Interface (MMI) will consist of two operator stations, each equipped with 13" AMLCD displays and a third console for the mission controller, equipped with a larger display. Structural changes include the addition of two hard points/pylons near the wing root.

The first Indian Il-38 (IN-305) flew to Russia for the upgrade in March 2002 and was delivered by early 2004. A short while after the loss of two Il-38s to the tragic MAC of October 2002, Russia generously offered two additional Il-38s from ex-AV-MF stocks as attrition replacements "free of charge" (this was actually, implicitly linked to the Gorshkov deal) and the original contract was modified accordingly. Russia herself is pursuing the upgrade for her own Il-38s to Il-38N (Novella) standard.

With the inevitable increase in MP demands, the Indian Navy began hunting for a third MPA type in the mid-90s. The Lockheed P-3C Orion, was brought to attention and deemed ideal, although sanctions and export restrictions would prevent their purchase, post 1998 nuclear tests at Pokhran. After the sanctions were lifted in September 2001, negotiations for the P-3C came back into the spotlight and the Navy officially listed out it's requirement for 8 to 10 new MPAs.

Lockheed Martin, hopeful of bagging a USD $1 billion deal, deputed a team to India in the June 2003, to discuss the details. On 27 May 2004, an American delegation, led by Ed Ross, director for South Asia for the Defense Security Cooperation Agency, held talks in New Delhi with Indian defense officials and mentioned the possibility of a deal by the end of the year. Despite the keenness of the involved parties and exports of American Arms worth $200 million to India in the recent years, the US Government has not cleared the sale of the aircraft to India. In addition, the Navy remains skeptical and suspicious of deals with American companies, after the outcomes of the post-1998 sanctions, including the grounding of the entire Sea king fleet due to export restrictions on US sourced spares. Irrespective of the possible purchase of newer aircraft, the Il-38SD will continue to serve with the Indian Navy until 2020.

INAS 550 "Flying Fish" and INAS 318 "Hawks"

INAS 550, Indian Navy's very first dedicated air squadron, was initially raised as a Fleet Requirement Unit (FRU) in 1951, to provide for training, communications, target towing and radar calibration. It started out with ten Shorts Sealand aircraft, based at Cochin in the south-western state of Kerala. The very first Sealand (IN 101), piloted by Lt.Cdr. Balbir D. Law, landed at Cochin on 4 February 1953. Prior to this, on 1 January 1953, the Indian Navy took over the civilian airfield (which was incidentally, a former RAF experimental airbase operating then Catalina flying boat) at Willingdon island, Cochin, and assumed responsibility for the operation of both civilian and military aircraft from the same, now designated INS Garuda, commissioned on 11 May 1953.

The FRU was formally commissioned on 11 March 1953 and recommissioned on 17 January 1959 as the Navy's very first air squadron. Between this period, ten Fairy Firefly aircraft fitted with winches to tow drogue/sleeve targets and three HAL HT-2 basic trainers were inducted in 1955-58 and 1952 respectively. Training and Maintenance establishments including the School for Naval Airmen (SFNA), Observer Training School, Naval Air Technical School (NATS), Naval Aircraft Repair Organisation (NARO) and Naval Aircraft Inspection Service (NAIS), were established between 1956 and 1961. INAS 550 retired it's Fireflies and HT-2s in 1964 and phased out the Sealand in the following year. To make up for this, two Dove (Devon) and two Breguet Alize were added to squadron and served until 1969 when they were replaced by two HAL HJT-16 Kiran Mk.1.

Urgent Fleet requirements for pilot and observer training, given the increasing numbers of the same, led to the proposal to acquire the Britten Norman BN-2A-21 Islander, in 1972. An initial order for six Islanders was placed and the first three aircraft arrived at Cochin, from the Isle of Wight, on 18 May

1976 while the remaining arrived at the end of the same year. Seventeen Islanders were acquired till date, including eleven BN-2A-21s (IN-126 to IN-136) and six BN-2Bs (IN-137 to IN-142). At least six of these were upgraded to BN-2T 'Turbine Islander' standard in 1996-97 and feature the Bendix-King RDR-1400 search radar. In Sept 1983, the Islanders got a local gun pod modification.

The acquisition of additional Islanders allowed for a few of the same to be stationed at the Andaman and Nicobar Islands and the first two Islanders from INAS 550 arrived at Port Blair in Feb 1981. This led the formation of the new squadron INAS 318 'Hawks' in 1984, which was gradually joined by Dornier/HAL Do-228-101 MPAs. The latest Naval Air Station, 'INS Utkrosh', was commissioned at Port Blair, on 11 May 1985. Although there was no hangarage at the time, a hangar was prefabricated on the mainland and erected within three weeks. Eventually, all the Islanders were withdrawn from Port Blair and INAS 318 operates the Do-228 alone. In May 2000, a flight of Islanders was positioned at INS Dega in Vizag. Out of the 17 Islanders acquired in total, 4 have been lost to attrition. This includes one Islander (IN-132) being ditched in the backwaters of Cochin in Decemeber 1981, another on 11 Jan 1983 and another (IN-134) on 17 May 1983. The latter two cases involved the loss of officers, Lt CP Omanakuttan, SLt HS Kavre and, Lt SG Pynamootil and Lt PB Jose respectively. Operation "Khoj" was commenced to locate the bodies of the former on 14 and 21 Jan respectively. IAF Helicopters located the wreckage of IN-134 and the bodies of SLt HS Kavre and Lt SG Pynamootil at N 09 14.8' E 77 07' on 27 May 1985.

In January 1986, IANS 550 acquired its first HAL HPT-32 "Deepak" trainer and between December 1986 and March 1987, acquired a total of eight HAL HPT-32 'Deepak' trainers, operating these for the basic flying training of pilots at the entry level. The first batch of 6 Naval pilots passed out in October 1987 after basic conversion training on these aircraft. Pilots may either train here or take up basic flying training with the IAF. INAS 550 participated in the IPKF operation in

Sri Lanka in December 1987. On 24 August 1988, Islanders IN-142 and IN-127 became the first fixed wing aircraft to land at the remote Lakshadweep Islands. One HPT-32 was lost on 30 November 1989, with its pilot, Lt Cdr Shyam Sunder.

The Indian Navy also took the delivery of six IAI Malat Searcher-II UAVs and a single Medium Altitude High Endurance (MALE) Heron UAV in 2002. The drones are in operation at INS Garuda and additional units have reportedly been purchased, with at least three Herons operational from INS Garuda. Some of these drones are also operated at INS Dega, in Vishakapatnam, on the south eastern coast, as well as from Porbander in Gujarat and Port Blair in the Andaman and Nicobar Islands. The total number of UAVs eventually acquired, are expected to equip as many as three squadrons.

INAS 330 "Harpoons" and INAS 336 "Flaming Arrows"

The requirement for additional and technologically modern assets to effectively counter the increasing threat of enemy underwater forces, lead to a proposal to acquire 12 Westland Sea King Mk.42 helicopters, in 1968. Following sanction for the acquisition of only six of these helicopters, in April 1969, an Indian team visited the UK and found the type to be suitable after thorough evaluation, leading to a formal order for the six helicopters plus a number of Mk.44 anti-submarine torpedoes, being placed in 1970.

Training of the first batch of pilots and observers, commenced on 27 September 1970 and the first two Sea King helicopters were handed over at Yeovil, on 3 November. These two helicopters proceeded to India and the Sea King squadron "INAS 330", was commissioned at INS Hansa in Dabolim, on 17 April 1971, with Cdr. MinnieWadhawan as the Commanding Officer. Despite the new dimension introduced, the squadron was replete with problems. One of the immediately evident problems was that the first batch of pilots were merely given conversion and familiarization training in the UK, leading to an urgent deployment of a second batch of pilots to the Royal Navy, in order to gain tactical flying experience. In addition, serviceability was very low and the Mk.44 Torpedoes had not yet been delivered. Operational evaluation of the Sea King's panoramic dunking sonar 195 (performance of which, was found to be extremely poor), commenced only by August and in the absence of torpedoes, flight trials with depth charges were started, followed by the first night flying sorties by August-end. Between May and the end of 1971, the squadron was tasked to carry out conversion flying, maintenance courses and evaluation of the potential ASW capabilities by the Tactical School.

However, the latter's Sea King dockets were given high security classification and based on the limited training and information given to the first batch of pilots, the helicopters were given limited deployment which eventually led to their ineffective and defensive utilization during the 1971 Indo-Pak war. Only after the loss of the single frigate INS Khukri, did the Sea Kings deploy to an abandoned airfield at Diu on the western coast, to stage a few ASW searches. With the delivery of all six Sea Kings, two of them were based at INS Garuda (Cochin) and four of them at INS Kunjali.

The latter had helipad facilities to accommodate helicopters from the ships stationed at the Bombay port and became a fully fledged helicopter base, only later on. Despite the arrival of the second batch by October, serviceability and utilization remained low and inefficient, due to the limited maintenance, no spares or workshop facilties and overpushing during the war.

The serviceability of the helicopter had gradually improved between November 1972 and July 1973, although equipment performance remained poor and flying hours, limited. A British team of specialists were summoned to investigate and isolate the causes for poor sonar performance and only after one years, could they address the problems.

After the situation was corrected, a second batch of six Sea King Mk.42s, were ordered and the first three arrived between August and November 1973. With the arrival of the new helicopters, serviceability greatly improved and evaluation of the Mk.44 Torpedo and intensive ASW exercises between the

Sea Kings and submarines, became possible. The remaining Sea Kings arrived by July 1974 and the second squadron, "INAS 336", was commissioned at INS Garuda, on 9 December 1974, under the command of Cdr. 'Cheify' Yadav. By now, serviceability and flying hours had become very high and coordinated ASW training between the helicopter and surface vessels as well as aircraft such as the Seahawk and Alize, became very frequent, with tactics considerably improved.

The Sea King Mk.42 type was embarked on the aircraft carrier INS Vikrant, from May 1975 onwards. On 19 July 1979, the Sea King Flight and Tactical Simulator (FATS), was commissioned at INS Garuda and INAS 336 became the Sea King training squadron. The capabilities of the helicopter, pushed for the order of additional units and standardization as the primary ship-borne ASW platform. Orders for three units of a new variant equipped with Recovery Assist Traverse (RAST), the Sea King Mk.42A, to operate from the last two Leader class frigates built in India, were placed in July 1977.

In the early 80s, the Indian Navy announced the arrival of a new generation, Type 16, "Godavari" class missile frigate, designed to accommodate not one but two Sea King helicopters. Keeping in mind, the need to supplement/replace the older generation Sea King variants as well, an international tender was floated in 1982, which required 20 new ASW/ASV helicopters (6 for INAS 330, 2 for INAS 336, 4 for a new squadron INAS 339, 2 each for the frigates *Godavari* and *Gomati* and 4 for MRSOW)

The two primary candidates chosen were the French Super Puma and an updated version of the British Seaking. Despite certain advantages such as composite rotor blades, the Super Puma was not selected because of the unavailability of a suitable AsHM. The British were not willing to integrate the Sea Eagle on the Super Puma and the French were not willing to sell the AM.39 Exocet due to a commitment made to Pakistan after supplying the same for the Pakistani Seakings. As a result, a conceptual upgrade to the Seaking was selected, also in consideration of existing operational experience, training, infrastructure and facilities. The Indian Navy was to select and evaluate the customized avionics and armament fit onboard the helicopter. So chosen was the Marconi Hermes ESM fit, Thomson-CSF HS-12 dunking sonar, LAPADS sonobuoys, Whitehead Motofides A244S torpedoes and BAe Sea Eagle AsHMs. Software for the integration was entirely developed by an Indian team which was deputed to Britain for inspection and modification.

The Sea King Mk.42B was essentially based on Westland's "Advanced Sea King" concept and featured RollS Royce Gnome H.1400-IT engines, composite main rotor blades, uprated transmission, strengthened airframe, Alcatel HS-12 Dunking Sonar, MEL MAREC-2 radar, GEC ASQ-902B tactical sonobuoy processor and were most importantly, armed with two BAe Sea Eagle sea-skimming Anti-ship missiles. The Sea King Mk.42C is a commando/troop transport and utility variant, with the nose mounted Telephonics RDR 1400C radar instead of the MEL Super Searcher and was intended to be deployed from landing ships.

Twelve Mk.42B and six Mk.42C variants were ordered in July 1983, followed by eight more Mk.42Bs at a later stage. The Mk.42A and Mk.42B variants continue to be operated by INAS 330 at Bombay and INAS 336 at Cochin and as an integral air element aboard the carrier INS Viraat, for ASW, ASV, training, SAR, communication, utility and other miscellaneous roles. The Mk.42C was inducted into a separate helicopter flight, initially known as the Indian Marine Security Force (IMSF) Flight, commissioned in January 1989, exclusively for use in Marine Commando operations and training. The flight, now renamed as "The Zappers", also caters to day/night SAR and general logistics. In a typical amphibious operation, the Sea King Mk.42C would be used to clear and secure the beach head, before the landing of troops. Four Mk.42s, one Mk.42A and three Mk.42Bs have been lost to attrition. The experience with the Seaking had the Navy draft a comprehensive and refined avionics and armament suite for the Naval Dhruv.

5

Synergising Indian Navy and the Coast Guard

Armed Forces all over the world are beginning to realise the importance of jointmanship, and accordingly enormous efforts have been made of late to promote jointmanship and bring about integration of the three armed forces in India. However, no attempt has been made to formally integrate the Coast Guard, which has also been termed as an armed force of the union, with the other forces, especially with the Indian Navy (IN).

Presently, the naval-coast guard relations are cordial and joint operations are conducted without any major hitch but in the absence of any formal mechanism, there is scope for problems in future. Although a beginning was made by incorporating a Coast Guard component into the tri-service command at Port Blair, the Coast Guard has been kept out of the ambit of Headquarters Integrated Defence Staff (HQIDS).

This reflects that the service is not likely to be placed under the Chief of Defence Staff (CDS) as and when it is created. For some inexplicable reasons, the Coast Guard (CG) has been treated like one of the Central Police Organisations (CPOs), even though the service is an armed force of the union and functions under the Ministry of Defence (MoD). The paucity of resources at sea requires that various agencies operating at sea must coordinate their efforts and pool their resources to obtain optimum results. As the two premium agencies operating in the seas around India, there is a need to institutionalise the relationship between the two services.

The two Indian maritime security forces, the IN and the CG are diverse services, but have a common role towards the nation's defence. "The CG ships and aircraft, and personnel manning them along with the shore infrastructure, have the inherent capability to switch over to a variety of specialised tasks in times of hostilities." They need to cooperate to optimise limited resources and to enhance their effectiveness in their areas of operation. This paper aims to analyse the problems likely to arise in future cooperation between the IN and the Indian CG and to suggest remedial measures. The irritants which have the potential to undermine mutual cooperation have been studied with the purpose of eliminating them. The study has been carried out with the aim that relationship between the IN and the CG does not suffer from inter-service rivalry and mutual bickering as has happened in the case of the Army and the Border Security Force (BSF).

It is intended to highlight the differences in service conditions of the two services with special reference to absence of common or equivalent rank structure, differences in recruitment and promotional norms and its likely impact on command and control while operating together. It is also intended to highlight the absence of clear cut guidelines for the jobs likely to be entrusted to the CG in times of war and in less than war situations to suggest remedial measures to overcome these shortcomings and to optimise IN and CG resources and their organisational structures to evolve a doctrine for the joint operations.

BACKGROUND

It has been three decades since the inception of the CG. The youngest unit of the Armed Forces, the Indian Coast Guard was formally inaugurated by the then Prime Minister Morarji Desai on 19 August 1978, making India one of the few countries to have established such a force to fulfil its obligations in the maritime zones under its jurisdiction. An interim CG organisation had been set up earlier within the Navy on 1

February 1977 with the aim of undertaking non-military maritime duties and enhancing ocean management. The requirement of the new organisation emerged from the preliminary discussions at the third United Nations Conference on the Laws of the Sea (UNCLOS).

The existing infrastructure and the organisation for the protection of life and property at sea had not kept pace with the substantial increase in the maritime activity taking place in the waters surrounding India. The Indian Navy (IN) was the only organisation capable of enforcing Indian jurisdiction in the maritime zones. It was therefore felt necessary to create an organisation for the safety of off-shore installations in peacetime, control of smuggling across the seas and for meeting various international obligations at sea like pollution control, search and rescue and preservation of various marine species. According to a former Director General (DG) of CG, "The Indian Coast Guard was created ... to maintain economic and environmental discipline ... in its waters, and protect national and other interests in its maritime zones."

It was probably felt that entrusting these additional responsibilities to the IN would not only dilute the primary function of a defence force but also expose the service to undesirable civilian influences. In addition, these peace-time law enforcement duties would have required large financial outlays and would have led to a substantial increase in the naval and consequently the defence budgets. This would have positively raised eyebrows in the littoral countries of the Indian Ocean in the Seventies and the Eighties and would have led to wider international ramifications. Based on some of these factors, it was decided to create an Indian CG organisation under the Ministry of Defence.

The CG Act was brought into force on Aug 19, 1978, constituting CG as the fourth Armed Force of the Union. The statutory duties of the CG as prescribed in the Act include protection of maritime and other national interests in the maritime zones of India, by such measures as the CG deems fit. These measures could provide for enforcing the provisions of the Maritime Zones of India (MZI) Act, assisting Customs and other authorities in anti-smuggling operations, providing protection and assistance to fishermen, ensuring safety and protection of artificial islands, off-shore terminals, installations and other structures and devices in the maritime zone, preserving and protecting the maritime environment and preventing marine pollution, safety of life and property at sea and assistance in collection of scientific data.

Although, the Rustomji committee, which recommended setting up of the CG, had recommended that in an emergency, the service be placed under the operational control of IN to supplement the naval fleet, there is no specific mention of this in the CG Act. Nevertheless, the CG has been assisting the IN and rendering yeoman service during peacetime operational commitments. For the first ten to twelve years of its operation the CG was basically manned by IN personnel and all the ships and establishments were commanded by IN officers or ex-IN officers who had joined the CG. Even today, the DG and some of the top hierarchy of the CG consist of naval and retired naval officers but at the lower levels the number of IN personnel manning the CG ships and establishments has come down drastically.

Today, most of the CG ships and establishments are commanded by CG officers. In the absence of common or equivalent rank structure and differences in promotional norms, difficulties have been experienced in command and control while operating together. Because of the lack of clear cut guidelines on the jobs likely to be entrusted to the CG in times of war and in less than war situation, there is a growing feeling in the lower echelons of the CG that they are doing most of the dirty jobs of the IN. On top of this, except a handful of officers, most of the CG officers have not served on IN units except during their initial training. They are, therefore, not totally aware of its operating procedures and this often creates problems in the smooth conduct of joint operations.

Growing Maritime Interests

Indian maritime interests are growing at a very fast pace in terms of sea trade, off-shore hydrocarbon explorations and other economic activities in the Exclusive Economic Zone (EEZ). Besides, a 7500 km border is open to sea and is easier to breach and the geopolitical scenario around us is not too encouraging as we continue to remain surrounded by hostile neighbours. Indian offshore oil assets are spread over an area of over 48,000 square kilometres and are expected to double by 2015. Overseas trade, 95 per cent of which transits through the sea, is expected to cross $ 400 billion by 2010 and $ 1 trillion by 2020, when over 8000 tankers are expected to be touching Indian ports. With growing trade, mostly by sea, there is a proportionate increase in Indian liabilities towards the protection of shipping, off-shore assets and protection of EEZ. Any laxity on the nation's part may cripple the economic lifeline of the nation. Thus, there is a need to consolidate Indian maritime defence in the best possible way. In a developing country like India, IN and the CG will never have adequate resources to meet all their requirements of platforms and equipment. Therefore, it would be logical to augment the resources of one service by making available the resources of the other in times of crisis. In view of the similarities of facilities required by the two services and the nationwide resource crunch, the cooperation between the two is inevitable.

COAST GUARD'S POTENTIAL FOR NATIONAL DEFENCE

Being a maritime service the CG possesses numerous resources and skills which could make enormous contribution to the nation's defence. In times of war, it could not only meet the naval requirement of additional ships and aircraft for various military tasks like patrolling and convoy escort, but also provide a vast pool of trained manpower which could be used to man the naval ships and aircraft. In times of hostilities it may be feasible to acquire additional weapon platforms from friendly countries, but it is virtually impossible to get trained manpower to man them at short notice. Today it takes five and a half years to train an officer through the National Defence Academy. Even if the Navy were to recruit graduates from outside, it would take two and a half years to train them to become effective watch-keeping officers. The two most demanding areas are training mariners and teaching command. It may be feasible to train and indoctrinate a large number of newly enlisted personnel into military life quickly and effectively but it takes time for them to acquire the ways of the sea by spending time at sea, whether on board an aircraft carrier or a CG boat. Similarly, command cannot actually be taught, because it is learnt through experience. The true lessons of command can only be acquired while commanding a ship.

The CG can provide the Navy with a cadre of experienced mariners who have gained the knowledge of the sea through extended and extensive sea-time on numerous ships, boats and small craft – experience that cannot be traded. With the basics of military training already provided, these mariners can take up any naval task, with very little additional training. The CG can also bring to the Navy a pool of officers with command experience. With numerous smaller ships and patrol vessels, these officers would be an invaluable asset for any sudden expansion of naval assets and responsibilities in times of a protracted war. It is therefore essential that CG should be able to "dissolve" into the Navy in case of any eventuality and the navy must be able to "fuse" CG in times of war by suitably equipping it and frequently exercising with it.

Challenge of Terrorism

A new phenomenon that has made naval CG cooperation even more crucial is the growing phenomena of terrorism. Hitherto confined to land, terrorism could spread its tentacles over Indian maritime assets also. Owing to the suitability of geographical environs, it is feared that terrorism may shift into maritime realm.

If so, terrorists could then exploit the vulnerabilities of global trade and shipping and disrupt the sea lines of communications passing through the neurological choke points. They could even carry out attacks on hub ports. Arms, weapons and explosives are readily available in the world market. A number of nations are ready to promote its proliferation – whatever be the pretext. Terrorism is here to stay and will remain an important element of the political process to intimidate governments and influence public opinion. The smuggling – limited to gold, silver and drugs till recently– has now proliferated to include weapons and explosives. Further, much of the military technology is freely available to the smugglers and terrorists. Their modus operandi is likely to become more sophisticated, due to easy accessibility of hi-tech equipment and connivance of the states themselves. Use of warships, aircraft or submarines to a limited extent cannot be ruled out.

To counter this threat, India needs to keep its coastline and the waters around under constant surveillance. Proactive and preventive capabilities are essential and the maritime forces have to play a lead role in such interfaces. With the resources currently available with the CG it is well nigh impossible for it to maintain continuous presence. The naval assets will have to be pressed into service to meet these terrorist threats which would continue to be supported by our enemies. It would be more of a low intensity conflict than an internal security problem. Even with the existing resources of the two services, the IN and the CG have just managed to bring the situation under control on the western and southern coasts.

PROBLEMS IN NAVAL COAST GUARD COOPERATION

Today, the CG and the IN are getting along fairly well. This, however, is due to the fact that, barring two short interregnums, CG has been headed by a naval officer. Despite this the bickering has started at the lower levels. The situation could worsen as time passes and the CG is manned totally by its own cadre of officers. This has happened in the case of the BSF and the Army, where the former was supposed to be a service with an army ethos and culture but as the army officers on deputation were phased out and BSF/Police officers took over, its orientation and attitude changed. Today, it has acquired police culture and resents being put under army command and control when the need arises. It is feasible that the CG could also evolve the same way in times to come, especially since the CG Act has no specific provision to place the CG under the operational control of the Indian Navy when the need arises.

The bureaucratic conflicts have the potential to cause considerable harm and may affect both the Navy and the CG. Some of the important problem areas that adversely affect the relationship between the IN and the CG have been analysed in the subsequent paragraphs. All of them have the potential to cause serious inter-service rivalry and bickering in future.

Service Conditions

Differences between the service conditions of the IN and the CG, especially the lack of common or equivalent rank structure and difference in promotional norms, has the maximum potential to cause problems in any future cooperation between the Navy and the CG. IN inducts officers through the National Defence Academy and the Naval Academy and as direct entrants in the technical branches. The CG officers are also inducted through the Naval Academy, but while the Naval officers join the Academy as cadets, the CG officers join as Assistant Commandants.

This anomaly can be basically attributed to the fact that the CG officers at the time of induction are usually older than their naval counterparts. As a result, by the time a naval officer finishes his Midshipman's time and gets commissioned, his course mate in the CG is already an Assistant Commandant of one and a half year seniority. Later, when a CG officer comes up for watch-keeping ticket, the naval officers who have already got the ticket are still junior to him. In the past CG officers have got their tickets under naval officers who were technically junior to them – purely by taking into account years of service. Further, if a CG officer got his promotion at the right time he could become a Commandant in eight years. By this time a much senior naval officer would not have been considered for promotion to the rank of Commander. In the absence of clear cut directives and common rank structure, the Commandant got equated to the Commander and led to serious problems.

One of the most glaring examples pertains to a CG ship based in the Andaman and Nicobar Islands in the early Nineties. The ship commanded by a naval Lieutenant-Commander, entered Campbell Bay during one of its patrols to the southern group of islands. When it had to sail, a problem arose as to who should make the sailing order. Commander CG District Ten (COMDIS 10) based at Campbell Bay was a Commandant who in service was much junior to the Commanding Officer (CO) of the ship who had not yet been considered for promotion to the rank of Commander. Both the CO and the shore authority felt that they ought to make the sailing order based on their own logic and thinking. The CO eventually made his sailing order and left harbour but was asked to return back by the Commander CG Region (COMCG) based at Port Blair. The CO of the ship at this juncture expressed his intention to hand over command to his Executive Officer (Second in Command). The CO was subsequently allowed to make the sailing orders and the matter was somehow hushed up and no clear cut directives were issued at that time on this contentious issue. This sort of an ambiguity can be catastrophic in times of war. Even today there are problems regarding the issuing of sailing orders in ANC, where the sailing orders for CG ships are being issued by COMCG rather than the Commander in Chief of ANC.

Another incident pertains to joint operations in Palk Bay. During an escort operation, which involved an IN and a CG ship jointly escorting a merchant ship repatriating Sri Lankan refugees, the CO of the IN ship, a Lieutenant Commander, was appointed the Officer in Tactical Command (OTC). However, the CO of the CG ship, who was a Deputy Commandant and whose total service was almost three and a half years less than the commissioned service of his naval counterpart, objected to it claiming that he was senior as he had become a Deputy Commandant before the naval officer had become a Lieutenant Commander. In order to avoid unpleasantness and to skirt the issue, an even more senior naval officer was appointed the OTC and the shore authority controlling the operations requested higher ups about the relative seniority of the COs by signal but failed to receive a definite reply.

The problem therefore definitely exists; unfortunately, no attempt has been made to address it. Rather than taking the problem head on, a deliberate attempt has been made to sweep the issue under the carpet. The remedy invented by the CG

Headquarters to remove these situations causing unpleasantness was to reduce the number of CG ships being commanded by naval officers.

The result was that Deputy Commandants of less than eight years service including time spent in Naval Academy, basic Sub-Lieutenant's courses and afloat training that is less than six years after the award of watch-keeping tickets were commanding ships like Inshore Patrol Vessels, Seaward Defence Boats and Fast Patrol Vessels, leading to a spurt in navigational accidents – numerous ships were damaged on account of grounding and mishandling during the mid-Nineties.

It is not intended to cast aspersions on the navigational skills of the CG officers, who are as good or as bad as any naval officer of equivalent seniority; but just to bring out the relative inexperience of some of these officers commanding ships.

Except for wartime risks and the risks inherent in operating and firing various hi-tech weapons, the CG officer is essentially doing the same job as the naval officer. When the day of reckoning comes, however, being an armed force of the Union, the CG too will have to go in harm's way and come under fire. Therefore, the CG officers justifiably feel that they should also get most if not all the facilities available to other defence personnel, like rations in kind for officers and sixty days annual leave.

In case of lower ranks, there exists a rank structure in the CG which is more or less equivalent to that of the Navy. Although in the formative years the promotions were much faster in the CG, and even today continue to be relatively fast, this has not really caused much problem. Due to the presence of a similar rank structure, there is generally a good understanding amongst the naval sailors and CG naviks about inter se seniority. Moreover, their direct interaction is also considerably less as compared to the officers. Initially, there were a few problems regarding the status of Pradhan Naviks (equivalents of Petty Officers in the Navy) who, according to the CG Rules, are not subordinate officers (equivalent of Senior Sailors in the Navy). There was also a problem of mess-men as the CG Naviks initially felt that it was not in their charter of duties to serve Senior Sailors or their equivalents in the CG. However, most of these problems have been resolved by now.

Common service conditions for the two services with a common or equivalent rank structure for the officers is considered a must for removing mutual irritants and enhancing cooperation between the two services. CG being the fourth Armed Force of the Union must be given privileges as applicable to the other defence forces. Qualifications and other requirements for entry in the CG should be made similar to those for the Navy. The promotion norms also need to be made similar. In order to retain the naval character of the force, it is felt that a significant number of the officers manning the CG should be naval deputationists. Similarly, as in the US, the CG officers should be deputed to naval ships and units. This will not only improve mutual understanding but also acquaint the officers with each other's operating procedures.

Sharing of Training Facilities

As of now, most of the training is common for the Navy and the CG. The CG is using the existing naval facilities for the basic and subsequent professional training of their officers and lower ranks. Some years back, a serious thought was being given to start a CG Academy near Hazira, but the idea seems to have been shelved now. It is essential that the CG should continue to use naval facilities for training. With the Naval Academy at Ezhimala becoming operational, the Navy should be in a position to meet the entire training requirement of the CG. The CG should also start inducting their officers after the "Plus Two" stage so that they could train together with the naval cadets in the Naval Academy just like the naval cadets train together with their Army and Air Force counterparts at the National Defence Academy. This will establish excellent lifelong rapport amongst the officers of the two services.

The subsequent professional training for the two services is generally carried out together. Almost all the CG officers and lower ranks complete their initial and subsequent professional training in the naval establishments. This system of training together needs to be continued if the two services are to operate together in times of war and in less than war situations. However, there is a growing feeling amongst the CG personnel, specially the officers, that they get a step-motherly treatment in the naval training establishments. In order to eliminate this feeling, it is necessary that all the major training establishments of the Navy training CG personnel should also have the CG personnel in their training teams.

This will enable the training package for the CG personnel to be continuously modified to suit the CG requirements. This will also eliminate the feeling of alienation that many CG officers suffer from when they are undergoing training in the naval establishments. It is also felt that all the naval personnel, especially the officers, should undergo a basic capsule on subjects like pollution control, anti-smuggling and anti-poaching operations. The CG should set up training facilities for training their personnel in these subjects and naval officers should also go there for short courses. At the same time, it is felt that the quantum of gunnery training being imparted to the CG officers needs to be enhanced so as to enable the CG to undertake its war-time responsibilities more effectively. It is also imperative that some Anti-Submarine Warfare (ASW) training should also be imparted to the CG personnel, especially officers. This along with the likely presence of sonar and ASW weapons in future CG ships will enable the CG ships to be used for anti-submarine patrols in times of war.

MAINTENANCE, LOGISTICS AND COMMUNICATION FACILITIES

The CG is presently utilising the logistics and communication facilities of the Navy and to some extent the maintenance facilities of the Navy. Of late, the CG has started setting up its own facilities. It is strongly felt that rather than duplicating the infrastructure, the CG should set up logistics, Communication and maintenance facilities where naval facilities do not exist, like Porbandar, Haldia and Campbell Bay. By this sort of an arrangement the two services can utilise each other's resources most optimally.

The CG should pay the Navy for the facilities used by it, including the training facilities and the manpower. As the finances for the CG are provided by the Department of Revenue (Customs), this could help in keeping the defence budget low.

Doctrines for Joint Operations

Today, the Navy and the CG are moving forward in their development without much regard to the other service's thinking and planning. They have a common role towards the nation's defence. The CG is expected to operate in support of the Navy in times of emergency. This requires a great deal of cooperation between the two services in peace-time so that the CG could change over to its war-time role more smoothly. The two services need to develop as forces complementary to each other so as to avoid wasting scarce national resources in duplicating infrastructure. This requires the two services to take a holistic view and plan their future developments with mutual consultation. If the CG is to function as an integral part of the Indian maritime force structure during hostilities, it should be provided with the wherewithal for playing such a role efficiently. In addition, the staff requirements of each new addition of either service need to be dovetailed keeping the integrated force requirements in mind. They need to ensure commonality of basic ship designs, common operation procedures, unambiguous command and control organisation for joint operations and cross deputations from one service to the other so that the personnel are not only familiar with one another but also with the problems and procedures of the other service. The Navy and the CG are two Armed forces of different characters and need a doctrine to govern their relationship, which must clearly highlight that the main roles of the CG are maritime law enforcement and marine safety missions. However, maritime defence should be one of the three missions of the CG and accorded equal importance. The following principles should govern this relationship:

(a) The CG should complement the Navy's capabilities rather than duplicate them, for optimum utilisation of scarce national resources.

(b) By incorporating combat capability in existing CG platforms, the CG could provide significant accretion to the maritime defence capabilities at a nominal cost and in LIC and other low threat scenarios, the CG should meet the Navy's platform requirements.

(c) In times of war or other emergencies the CG should carry out tasks such as Naval Control of Shipping, search and rescue, harbour defence and security and surveillance. As far as possible efforts should be made to allocate only such jobs as are similar to the tasks being performed by the CG in peace-time.

(d) The selection of ships and aircraft for the CG should be in consultation with the Navy to facilitate inter-operability and standardisation for logistics support. The CG should therefore avoid operations and procedures that would change in the event of the Navy's control, and develop its own combat system and command and control system.

As the CG grew out of the Navy, presently there are many areas of duplication as well as blurring of responsibilities. Efforts would have to be made to sort them out. The CG draws upon the expertise and the infrastructure of the Navy and will continue to do so for times to come. Within a short span of three decades, the CG has begun to acquire an independent identity of its own. While retaining its separate identity, the CG can provide significant support to the Navy, both in times of war and peace. The growing network of CG bases, its infrastructure and equipment could fill crucial gaps, especially in maritime surveillance and escort role, in the inshore and off-shore regions, thereby relieving the Navy of part of its responsibility and freeing it to concentrate on the major role of engaging and neutralising adversaries away from the home water.

Maritime Defence Zones

The United States has established Maritime Defence Zones (MDZ) to enhance cooperation between the Navy and the CG, thereby reducing combat deficiencies. It is felt that establishment of these zones in India will help the Navy and the CG to establish standard practices for protecting the ports and the coastal waters.

MDZ are naval commands, headed by CG Area Commanders who report to their respective naval Commanders-in-Chief when activated for operations and for planning and exercise purposes during normal peacetime. MDZ responsibilities include contingency planning, exercising the plan with regular and reserve forces and operational command of designated Naval and CG forces when mobilisation occurs. The MDZ area of operations includes the navigable waterways, port areas, harbour approaches and ocean area up to the limit of EEZ. The MDZ staff is made up of officers from both the Navy and the CG. The forces destined for MDZ operational control when activated include most of the CG ships, aircraft and port security units, naval mine warfare units, inshore undersea warfare units and a limited number of frigates, destroyers and maritime patrol aircraft.

In the Indian context, there is a need to establish five Maritime Defence Zones – two each on the Western and Eastern coasts and one for the Andaman and Nicobar islands. These could be headed by a naval officer of the rank of Rear Admiral or a CG Inspector General. The forces allocated for the MDZ should include almost all the CG ships and aircraft and naval ships earmarked for Local Naval Defence (LND), including minesweepers and missile boats.

The threat with which the MDZ must deal includes the entire spectrum of covert and overt hostile actions that could compromise a port or sink a ship at sea. This ranges from mine and submarine warfare to terrorist attacks to intelligence gathering and special operations. In the face of these challenges, the CG must take advantage of every opportunity and every available resource in peace-time to develop expertise and amass experience doing the kind of things that can readily be applied to MDZ operations in the event of hostilities.

MDZ must ensure that the battle groups, amphibious groups, submarines and support ships deploy unimpeded from Indian ports when hostilities are imminent. It must also ensure that the reinforcement and resupply shipping in support of forward deployments safely departs Indian ports and coastal areas and safe and secure water transportation of economic cargoes continue from Indian ports and coastal areas.

Wartime Role of the Coast Guard

It is imperative that closer ties are established between the CG and the Navy so as to facilitate a smoother transition whenever the CG is required to fight alongside the Navy in times of war. It would be ideal to take a leaf from the US Coast Guard, which "is a military, multi-mission, maritime service..... and one of the nation's five Armed Services". Besides defence of the US coast, the CG ships and aircraft actively participated in the Vietnam War and made sacrifices along with the personnel of other services. According to the US CG policy document it along with the Navy is expected to create "fully interoperable, multidimensional, naval and maritime forces" to meet future maritime challenges. To achieve this "the Navy and Coast Guard must work even more closely". In the Indian context this can be achieved in peace-time by CG participation in joint readiness exercises and multi-service interdiction training and operations. The process has been initiated and would be a catalyst in improving the CG readiness and an asset in improving the professional relations between the Navy and the CG. Coastal defence and coastal law enforcement are complementary. As brought out earlier, with careful planning, a Rupee spent on either of these missions will directly benefit the other. Since 1990 a non statutory forum called the Navy Coast Guard Board (NAVGUARD) has been established to resolve contentious issues and provide solutions to issues of mutual interests, covering the whole gamut from standardisation of equipment to community interactions and welfare measures.

Reality dictates that the CG would always be most useful when it takes on the mission the Navy cannot fulfil. The Navy comprises of a force of large, high technology extremely expensive ships. The CG comprises of essentially low cost ships. It is, therefore, envisaged that the CG would take on the responsibilities where low intensity conflict exists. With the addition of some inexpensive combat systems, these ships will be ideally suited for low intensity conflicts. The CG will provide the platform and personnel and the Navy would provide combat systems for these platforms. While incorporating the combat capability in existing CG platforms, the CG will provide a low coast addition to the national defence resources.

The CG should support the Navy as a general purpose force in being, and for operations in low to high threat environments. Generally, CG units should confine their operations to littoral waters in low threat environments. The wartime tasks of the CG should include defence of off shore installations, local naval defence of ports and harbours, examination services, control of merchant shipping, augmentation of naval resources in amphibious operations, maritime surveillance and Patrol and Logistic Support.

Conclusion

The CG was established to fulfil the long felt need of an organisation to ensure the safety of life and property at sea and for enforcement of national laws in the waters under our jurisdiction. This had become essential from the trends emerging from the preliminary discussions at the Third UN Conference on the Law of the Sea. It was also considered desirable that these predominantly peace-time law enforcement activities should not be undertaken by the Navy, since these will detract from the Navy's operational role and interfere with combat training. Moreover, it would not be cost effective to deploy sophisticated warships and trained manpower of the Navy in a law enforcement role on a continuous basis in peace-time. It was also felt that entrusting these jobs to the Navy would probably require higher defence outlays and cause an uproar in our neighbouring countries.

The CG Act was brought into force on 19 August 1978. This act formally constitutes the CG as an Armed Force of the Union under the Ministry of Defence. The CG is, however, not paid out of defence estimates but its budget is covered under the allocations for the Department of Revenue (Customs). The duties assigned to the CG by this act are mainly maritime law enforcement and marine safety missions. Even though the founders of the CG expected the service to contribute to the maritime defence, no mention of this is made in the CG Act.

The Navy and the CG are two maritime forces operating in the same environment, with overlapping functions and responsibilities in certain areas in peace-time. Indian maritime interests are growing at a tremendous pace and to guard them would be beyond the resources of any one maritime force, especially in view of the resource crunch. Low intensity conflicts have become part and parcel of the scenario evolving around us. Infiltration of arms and explosives from across the maritime boundaries has increased the security threat to Indian maritime assets and the spectre of maritime terrorism is looming large. This requires increased maritime surveillance, which can only come about with close naval and CG cooperation.

In order to enhance cooperation between the two services and to remove the problems likely to arise in their future cooperation, personnel from both the services must be sent on cross-deputation to the other service. The service conditions, rank structure, perks and privileges must be similar for the two services. CG personnel should continue training in naval training establishments and the logistics and maintenance facilities of the two services should complement each other rather than duplicate them. MDZ on the US pattern must be established and a set doctrine must govern joint operations. The requirement of platforms of the two services must be coordinated and as far as possible commonality of equipment must be maintained. CG platforms must be built to naval specifications and must have the capability to stage naval helicopters and to be fitted with naval weapons and sensors. There is also a need to give the CG a representation in HQ IDS. This will not only affirm its identity as an Armed Force but also enable the HQ IDS to get valuable inputs on the maritime zones and CG.

6

Weapon Systems and Air Arm of Indian Navy

SUBMARINE LAUNCHED BALLISTIC MISSILE

AGNI-III

Agni-III is an intermediate-range ballistic missile developed by India as the successor to Agni-II. The ballistic missile has a range of 3,500 km-5500 km, which means that India is capable of engaging targets deep inside neighbouring countries. The missile's Circular Error Probable (CEP) is within 40 meters range, which makes it most sophisticated and accurate ballistic missiles of its range class in the world.

India's Minimum Credible Nuclear Deterrence envisages a triad of nuclear counterstrike capability which required a long range missile to provide robust second strike capability. A missile system that can be dispersed far and wide in the Indian mainland, its far flung islands or its blue water naval assets dispersed across the world's oceans. Following this necessity India developed a larger Agni-III missile, with a heavier payload and a longer range but in a compact configuration, i.e. thicker but shorter length. This development is driven by need for a more assured retaliation that can defeat emerging ABM defenses and countermeasures. Such capability requires a compact missile that can also carry ABM counter-measure payloads along with weapons, in a configuration similar to MIRV, albeit with state of the art decoys.

Description

Agni III an intermediate-range ballistic missile was developed by India as the successor to Agni-II. Designed by the Indian government's Defence Research and Development Organisation, Agni III is intended to be a two-stage ballistic missile that is capable of nuclear weapons delivery.

The Agni-III has two stages with an overall diameter of 2.0 m. The first stage mass is about 32 tonnes and 7.7 m long, the second stage mass is about 10 tonnes and 3.3 m long. The missile is likely to support a wide range of warhead configurations, with a 4,500 km range and a total payload weight of 2490 kg.

The stubby two-stage solid fuel missile is compact and small enough for easy mobility and flexible deployment on various surface/sub-surface platforms.

The missile is equipped with sophisticated navigation, guidance and control systems along with advanced on-board computer systems. The electronic systems are hardened for higher vibration, thermal and acoustic effects. A high performance indigenous ring laser gyro-based navigation system was flight-tested for the first time during the last Agni-III trial.

Propulsion

The Agni-III features two solid fuelled stages and with overall diameter of 2.0 meters. This diameter is compatible with a recently tested Indian sub-surface launch system, which has a 2.3 meter diameter launch tube aperture.

First stage booster

The first stage booster is made of advanced carbon composite materials to provide high mass fraction. It weighs about 32 tonnes, is 7.7 meters long and diameter of 2 meter.

Second stage

The second stage made of maraging steel weighing about 11 tonnes and a length of 3.3 meters. The second stage has flex nozzles, to provide necessary flight trajectory control.

Maneuvering re-entry vehicle: Agni RV-Mk.4

Agni-III supports a wide range of weapons, with total payload weight ranging from ~600 kg to 1,800 kg including decoys and other ABM countermeasures. Instead of conventional bus architecture, the RV (Re-Entry Vehicle) is self-contained with velocity correction package, navigation and re-entry control systems.

Lighter and tougher RV body with all carbon composite re-entry heat shield with multi directional carbon re-entry nose tip and control surfaces, the new lightweight composites can withstand temperatures of up to 6000 degrees Celsius, and capable of greater re-entry velocity.

Agni-III SLBM

The Missile is also called K-X. DRDO is working on a Submarine Launched Version of the Agni-III missile, which will provide India with a credible sea based second strike capability. The SLBM version is a miniaturized version of the Agni-III which is expected to be test fired shortly.

Flight tests

The first test for Agni III was conducted from Wheeler Island off the Bhadrak coast on July 9, 2006. The launch proved to be unsuccessful with the missile falling into the sea off the coast of Orissa, short of reaching the target. According to DRDO, the failure was due to a first stage anomaly that was caused by recirculating hot gases entering the missile-base shroud and damaging the electronic components. Indian Defence Minister Pranab Mukherjee reported it as "partial success" (a trade euphemism to indicate the test generated useful data for diagnosis and correction) as the missile was air-borne for only 5 minutes instead of the expected 15 minutes.

Agni-III was test fired again on April 12, 2007 from the Wheeler Island off the coast of Orissa. This time, the launch was declared as a success. India's Cabinet Committee on Security announced that "This test confirms the extent of India's nuclear reach and India's nuclear deterrence as the missile can accurately hit targets at distance more than 3000 km away".

Already the most powerful and capable in India's missile inventory, the Agni-III is capable of carrying a variety of warheads, including nuclear warheads and can be launched from various platforms giving India intermediate range ballistic missile firepower and greatly extending India's power projection in the region.

Agni III was test fired successfully for third time on May 7, 2008. The missile was launched from Balasore, Orissa.. After a flight of roughly 15 minutes defense scientists confirmed that the test fire was successful and that the missile met all parameters. The missile has a velocity of 5,000 meters per second. Agni-III is a nuclear capable fully solid propellant fueled surface-to-surface missile, and has a range of 3,500 km. A new software for navigation system fitted on the missile, will increase accuracy and lethality. The successful test on May 7, will open door for next generation Indian ICBM Agni-V which will have firing range of 5000-6,000 kilometer.

Agni III was tested successfully for the fourth time from Wheelers Island in Orissa on February 7, 2010. The missile is said to have hit the target with pin point accuracy and met all the mission objectives. Two down range ships located near the target tracked and witnessed the Missile reaching the target accurately. The missile is likely to support a wide range of warhead configurations, with a 3,500 km range and a total payload weight of 2490 kg. The two-stage solid fuel missile is compact and small enough for easy mobility and flexible deployment on various surface/sub-surface platforms. The last development test of Agni III was conducted in August 2009 before being handed over to the army for user trails. The test validated the nuclear triggering mechanism, meaning Agni-III is meant for strategic nuclear deterrence. The test launch is part of pre-induction of the missile into the Indian Army.

In August 2010, the defence minister of India announced that Agni-III is ready for induction.

SAGARIKA

Sagarika (born Sagarika Mukherjee on 4 September 1970) is a popular Indian singer. Before going solo, she was half of a popular Indian duet with her younger brother Shaan with whom she has released albums such as *Q-Funk*, *Roop Inka Mastana* and *Naujawan*.

She released the album *Maa* after Shaan and her went solo. Her album is *It's All About Love* was released in 2006 by Universal Distribution

In 2001 Sagarika married Martin daCosta, who runs an event management company and was closely associated with Shaan and Sagarika for over 8 years. Sagarika and Martin daCosta are partners in Olive Bar and Kitchen chain of restaurants.

She also did a song with a very famous Pakistani Band Strings called "Pal". Which is featured in Strings fourth album Dhaani.

SHIP LAUNCHED BALLISTIC MISSILE

PRITHVI (MISSILE)

Prithvi is a tactical surface-to-surface, short-range ballistic missile (SRBM) developed by DRDO of India under the Integrated Guided Missile Development Program.

Development and History

The Government of India launched the Integrated Guided Missile Development Program in 1983 to achieve self sufficiency in the development and production of wide range of Ballistic Missiles, Surface to Air Missiles etc.

Prithvi was the first missile to be developed under the Program. DRDO attempted to build Surface-to-air Missile under Project devil.

Variants make use of either liquid or both liquid and solid fuels. Developed as a battlefield missile, it could carry a nuclear warhead in its role as a tactical nuclear weapon.

Variants

The Prithvi missile project encompassed developing 3 variants for use by the Indian Army, Indian Air Force and the Indian Navy. The initial project framework of the Integrated

Guided Missile Development Program outlines the variants in the following manner.

- Prithvi I (SS-150)-Army Version (150 km range with a payload of 1,000 kg)
- Prithvi II (SS-250)-Air Force Version (250 km range with a payload of 500 kg)
- Prithvi III (SS-350)-Naval Version (350 km range with a payload of 500 kg)
- Dhanush-Dhanush is reportedly a naval version of Prithvi which can be launched from Ships. Some sources claim that Dhanush is a System consisting of stabilization platform and missiles, which has the capability to launch both Prithvi II and Prithvi III from Ships while others report that Dhanush is a variant of Prithvi-II Ballistic Missile.
-

Over the years these specifications underwent a number of changes. While the *codename* Prithvi stands for any missile inducted by India into its armed forces in this category, the later developmental versions are codenamed as Prithvi II and Prithvi III.

Description

Prithvi I

Prithvi I class was a surface-to-surface missile having a maximum warhead mounting capability of 1,000 kg, with a range of 150 km. It has an accuracy of 10 – 50 metres and can be launched from Transporter erector launchers. This class of Prithvi missile was inducted into the Indian Army in 1994.

Prithvi II

Prithvi II class is also a single stage liquid-fuelled missile having a maximum warhead mounting capability of 1,000 kg, but with an extended range of 250 kilometres. It was developed with the Indian Air Force being the primary user. It was first test-fired on January 27, 1996 and the development stages were completed in 2004. The Prithvi II class of missiles are in the process of induction by the Indian Airforce. In a recent test, the Missile was launched with an extended range of 350 kilometres and improved Aided Inertial Navigation. The missile has the features to deceive Anti Ballistic Missiles. According to news sources the range is now increased to 350kms

Prithvi III

Prithvi III class (*codenamed* Dhanush *meaning* Bow) is a two-stage ship-to-surface missile. The first stage is solid fuelled with a 16 metric ton force (157 kN) thrust motor. The second stage is liquid fuelled. The missile can carry a 1,000 kg warhead to a distance of 350 km and a 500 kg warhead to a distance of 600 kilometres and a 250 kilogram warhead up to a distance of 750 kilometres. Dhanush is a system consisting of a stabilization platform (Bow) and the Missile (Arrow). Supposedly it is a customised version of the Prithvi and that the additional customizations in missile configuration is to certify it for sea worthiness. Dhanush has to be launched from a hydraulically stabilized launch pad. Its low range acts against it and thus it is seen a weapons either to be used to destroy an aircraft carrier or an enemy port. The missile has been tested from the surface ships many times

Prithvi III was first tested in 2000 from INS Subhadra, a Sukanya class patrol craft. The missile was launched from an updated, reinforced helicopter deck of the vessel. The first flight test of the 250 km variant was only partially successful. The full operational testing was completed in 2004. The following year in December an enhanced 350 km version of the missile was tested from the INS Rajput and successfully hit a land based target. The missile was again successfully tested-fired from INS Subhadra anchored about 35 km offshore from the Integrated Test Range at Chandipur on December 13, 2009. It was the sixth test of the missile.

CRUISE/ANTI-SHIP MISSILE

NIRBHAY MISSILE

Nirbhay is a long range, subsonic Stealth cruise missile being developed in India. The missile will have a range of 1,000 km and will arm three services, the Indian Army, Indian Navy and the Indian Air Force. The Nirbhay will be able to be launched from multiple platforms on land, sea and air. The missile is being developed by the Advanced Systems Laboratory, a division of DRDO and after finalizing the design, the technology required for the missile is being developed. The first test flight of the missile is expected in the year 2010. Nirbhay will be a terrain hugging, stealth missile capable of delivering 24 different types of warheads depending on mission requirements and will use an inertial navigation system for guidance. Nirbhay will supplement Brahmos in the sense that it would enable delivery of warheads farther than the 300 km range of Brahmos.

BRAHMOS

BrahMos is a supersonic cruise missile that can be launched from submarines, ships, aircraft or land. It is a joint venture between India's Defence Research and Development Organisation (DRDO) and Russia's NPO Mashinostroeyenia who have together formed BrahMos Aerospace Private Limited.

The name BrahMos is a portmanteau formed from the names of two rivers, the Brahmaputra of India and the Moskva of Russia. It travels at speeds of Mach 2.5 to 2.8. It is about three-and-a-half times faster than the USA's subsonic Harpoon cruise missile. A hypersonic version of the missile is also presently under development (Lab Tested with 5.26 Mach Speed).

Though India had wanted the BrahMos to be based on a mid range cruise missile, namely P-700 Granit, instead Russia opted for the shorter range sister of the missile, P-800 Oniks, in order to comply with MTCR restrictions, to which Russia is a signatory. Its propulsion is based on the Russian missile, and guidance has been developed by BrahMos Corp. The missile is expected to reach total order worth $13 billion

History, Early Development and manufacture

The BrahMos has been developed as a joint venture between the Defence Research and Development Organization (DRDO) of India and the Federal State Unitary Enterprise NPO

Mashinostroyenia (NPOM) of Russia under BrahMos Aerospace. The missile is named after two rivers, the Brahmaputra and the Moskva.

Since late 2004, the missile has undergone several tests from variety of platforms including a land based test from Pokhran desert, in which the 'S' maneuver at Mach 2.8 was demonstrated for the Indian Army and a launch in which the land attack capability from sea was demonstrated.

Keltec, an Indian state owned firm was acquired by Brahmos Corporation in 2008. Approximately ₹ 1,500 crore (US$325.5 million) will be invested in the facility to make Brahmos components and integrate the missile systems. This was necessitated by the increased order book of the missile system, with orders having been placed by both the Indian Army and Navy.

Description

BrahMos claims to have the capability of attacking surface targets as low as 10 meters in altitude. It can gain a speed of Mach 2.8, and has a maximum range of 290 km. The ship-launched and land-based missiles can carry a 200 kg warhead, whereas the aircraft-launched variant (BrahMos A) can carry a 300 kg warhead. It has a two-stage propulsion system, with a solid-propellant rocket for initial acceleration and a liquid-fueled ramjet responsible for sustained supersonic cruise. Air-breathing ramjet propulsion is much more fuel-efficient than rocket propulsion, giving the BrahMos a longer range than a pure rocket-powered missile would achieve.

The high speed of the BrahMos likely gives it better target-penetration characteristics than lighter subsonic cruise-missiles such as the Tomahawk. Being twice as heavy and almost four times faster than the Tomahawk, the BrahMos has almost 32 times the initial kinetic energy of a Tomahawk missile (although it pays for this by having only 3/5 the payload and a fraction of the range despite weighing twice as much, suggesting a different tactical paradigm to achieve the objective).

Although BrahMos is primarily an anti-ship missile, it can also engage land based targets. It can be launched either in a vertical or inclined position and is capable of covering targets over a 360 degree horizon. The BrahMos missile has an identical configuration for land, sea, and sub-sea platforms. The air-launched version has a smaller booster and additional tail fins for added stability during launch. The BrahMos is currently being configured for aerial deployment with the Su-30MKI as its carrier. On September 5, 2010 BrahMos create a record for the first supersonic steep dive.

Variants

- Ship launched, Anti-Ship variant (operational)
- Ship launched, Land attack variant (operational)
- Land launched, Land attack variant (operational)
- Land launched, Anti-Ship variant (existence not confirmed)
- Air launched, Anti-Ship variant (development)
- Air launched, Land attack variant (development)
- Submarine launched, Anti-Ship variant (development)
- Submarine launched, Land attack variant (development)

Operators

India and Russia intend to make 2,000 BrahMos supersonic cruise missiles over the next ten years through their joint venture company, and nearly 50 percent of them are expected to be exported to friendly countries.

Indian Navy

The missile is in service with the Indian Navy. Talwar class frigate and Shivalik class frigate are frigates of the Indian Navy that can fire the BrahMos. INS Tabar and INS Trishul are Talwar class vessels armed with supersonic BrahMos while INS Shivalik was the first vessel of the Shivalik class to incorporate the BrahMos. Other vessels of the Shivalik Class and Talwar Class armed with BrahMos missiles by 2009 and 2010 respectively. In 2007, the navy promised to arm the Godavari class frigates and Brahmaputra class frigates with the BrahMos too. Rajput class destroyers are Destroyers of the Indian Navy that can fire the BrahMos. The INS Rajput, INS

Ranvir (D54) and INS Ranvijay (D55) which are modified versions of Soviet Kashin class destroyers have been fitted with BrahMos Supersonic Cruise Missile systems. The new class of destroyers namely Kolkata Class are also to be fitted with the BrahMos and there are plans to arm the rest of the vessels of the Rajput Class with BrahMos too. On the other hand the Delhi class destroyers are to be modified to incorporate the BrahMos. The first of the Kolkata Class should roll out in 2012 while the Delhi Class and Rajput was armed with the Brahmos by 2009

The submarine launched version of the missile is ready for testing. The missile will be either tested on a Kilo class submarine of the Indian Navy or will be tested in Russia. The land attack version of the missile was fired from Destroyer INS Rajput and the missile hit and destroyed the right target among a group of targets. The vertical launch of Brahmos was conducted on December 18, 2008 from INS Ranvir (D54).

Indian Army

Brahmos Block-I

The missile was successfully tested with new capabilities for the Indian Army in the deserts of Rajasthan, test range near Pokharan (December 2004 & March 2007). It was inducted into the army on June 21, 2007.

Brahmos Block-II

On January 20, 2009, a test of a new BrahMos block II cruise Missile at Pokhran in Rajasthan was conducted with new software. The missile failed to hit the right target among a group of targets. The objective was to hit a small building hidden amongst a group of buildings. According to Brahmos corporation, another test of the new missile will be conducted within one month, which was eventually conducted on 4 March 2009 and was successful.

The latest test conducted on 29 March 2009, was successful. The missile took two and a half minutes to hit the target with precision. According to official sources, "The new seeker is unique and would help us to hit our targets, which are insignificant in terms of size, in a cluster of large buildings. India is now the only nation in the world with this advanced technology" After the third test, Lt Gen Noble Thamburaj, said that the Indian Army wanted the BrahMos to achieve high standards of accuracy and congratulated the scientists on behalf of the Indian Army. The Indian Army confirmed that the test was extremely successful and the army is absolutely satisfied with the missile. The development phase of the Block II version of the missile is over and it is ready for induction.

On September 5, 2010, Defence scientists test fired BrahMos off the Orissa coast and created a world record. It was for the first time that a cruise missile was tested at supersonic speeds in a steep-dive mode. The missile was test-fired from the integrated test rang launching complex-3 (LC-3) at Chandipur around 11.35 am. With this launch, The army's requirement for land attacks with block-II advanced seeker software with target discriminating capabilities has been fully met. BrahMos is the only supersonic cruise missile possessing advanced capability of selection of a particular land target amongst a group of targets, providing an edge to the user with precise hit. The missile can travel at three times the speed of sound and carry a conventional warhead weighing 200-300 kg.

The army has raised one regiment (numbered 861) of the BrahMos Mark I. Now two separate missile regiments of the BrahMos Mark II, which has a seeker that can discriminate and zero in on a small target in an urban clutter, will be raised and are likely to be numbered 862 and 863. Each of the two new BrahMos cruise missile regiments would have between four and six batteries of three to four Mobile Autonomous Launchers that can be connected to a general mobile command post.

Indian Air Force

The air launched version for the Indian Air Force is ready for testing. An expert committee from the DRDO and the Indian Air Force (IAF) has ruled out any structural modification to the advanced Su-30MKI if it is to be fitted with the supersonic BrahMos. January 10, 2009 it was reported that two Indian Air

Force (IAF) Sukhoi-30MKI fighter jets have been sent to Russia for a retrofit program that would enable them to launch the aerial version of the BrahMos supersonic cruise missile.

On October 22, 2008 A. Sivathanu Pillai, chief executive officer and managing director, Brahmos Airspace announced that the Indian Air Force would get its own version of Brahmos by 2012. Trials and tests will be carried out by 2011 and it is expected to be inducted into the IAF by 2012 In addition, India's 5 Il-38 and 8 Tupolev Tu-142 maritime patrol bombers are also to be armed with the missile. Estimated capacity is 6-BrahMos each as per Indian Navy. There are reports of efforts towards adding the capability to fire the Indo-Russian Brahmos cruise missile from these aircraft. Mockups have been displayed with air-launched Brahmos attached to underwing pylons on the Indian Navy aircraft.

On August 8, 2009 Alexander Leonov, Director of the Russian Machine Building Research and Production Center, said "we are ready for test launches." He also said the final development and testing of the air-launched version of the BrahMos supersonic cruise missile will take place soon. A new takeoff engine for launching of the missile in air and at extreme high altitudes had been developed. He said the initial test firing of the missile would be undertaken from the Sukhoi-30 MKI, but did not specify the dates. After testing, the IAF would be the launch customers for the air launched BrahMos cruise missile.

Russian Navy

According to sources the BrahMos could be fitted to the updated Gorshkov class of frigates which will be entering the Russian navy soon. The defense ministry reported that due to the size and hull specifications of the BrahMos, few if any of its new ships will be able to accommodate it.

Export

Brahmos has not been exported to any country however several countries including South Africa, Egypt, Oman, Brunei have expressed interest in the missile. In February 2010, it was reported that India was in "serious negotiations" with Chile, Brazil, South Africa and Indonesia regarding the purchase of the missile. Malaysia is also reported to be considering the purchase of the missile for use on its Kedah class warships.

Future-BrahMos-II/Brahmos Hypersonic

BrahMos II is a hypersonic cruise missile that has been lab tested with a speed of Mach 5.26 that will make it the fastest cruise missile in the world beating Brahmos 1. BrahMos II is expected to be ready by 2013-14 and will arm the Project 15B destroyers of the Indian Navy.

KH-35

The Zvezda Kh-35U is the jet-launched version of a Russian subsonic anti-ship missile. The same missile can also be launched from helicopters, surface ships and coastal defence batteries with the help of a rocket booster, in which case it is known as *Uran* ('uranium';SS-N-25 'Switchblade'; GRAU 3M24) or *Bal* ('whale';SSC-6 'Stooge';GRAU 3K60). It is also nicknamed *Harpoonski* for its similarity to the AGM-84 Boeing Harpoon. It is designed to attack vessels up to 5000 tonnes.

Development

Zvezda started work on the Kh-35 in 1983 as a surface-to-surface missile to replace the SS-N-2 'Styx' for export markets.

Design

The Kh-35 missile is a subsonic vehicle featuring a normal aerodynamic configuration with cruciform wings and fins and a semisubmerged air duct intake. The propulsion unit is a turbofan engine. The missile is guided to its target at the final leg of the trajectory by commands fed from the active radar homing head and the radio altimeter.

Target designation data can be introduced into the missile from the carrier aircraft or external sources. A flight mission data is inserted into the missile control system after input of target coordinates. An inertial system controls the missile in flight, stabilizes it at an assigned altitude and brings it to a target location area. At a certain target range, the homing head is switched on to search for, lock on and track the target. After that, the inertial control system turns the missile toward the target and changes its flight altitude to the extremely low one. At this altitude, the missile continues the process of homing by the data fed from the homing head and the inertial control system until a hit is obtained.

Operational history

The Kh-35U entered service in 1994. The Kh-35U has also been acquired by India.

Variants

- Kh-35U (AS-20 'Kayak', Article 78U)-launched from fast jets.
- Kh-35E *Uran* (SS-N-25 'Switchblade', 3M24)-launched from helicopters, coastal defence batteries, and ships such as the *Neustrashimy* frigates, *Tartarstan/Gepard* frigates and as upgrades to two *Krivak* frigate. It comes in a containerised launcher with four missiles.
- 3M24M *Bal* (SSC-6 'Stooge')-coastal defence version, very similar to Kh-35E
- IC-35-target drone
- Kh-35UE-upgrade with smaller engine allowing increased fuel capacity, and increased range.
- Kh-37 (3M24E1)-proposed upgrade with 250km range and land-attack capability, GPS mid-course guidance and an imaging infrared seeker akin to the Standoff Land Attack Missile (SLAM). Some sources attribute the name *Uran* or *Bal* to this variant.

SUBMARINE-BASED MISSILES

India has a number of foreign-produced cruise missile systems in its arsenal, which includes the Klub (SS-N-27). It also has some indigenous cruise missile systems under development, including the Sagarika and Lakshya variants. The Navy has got the Lakshya PTA. The Sagarika (Oceanic) began development in 1994 as a submarine-launched cruise missile (SLCM) which will have a range of at least 300 km (a few claim 1000 km). Another successful program has been the development of the Yakhont Anti Ship Missile system into the BrahMos, by NPO and India's DRDO. The BrahMos has been tailored to Indian needs and uses a large proportion of Indian designed components and technology, for its fire control systems, Transporter erector launches, to its onboard nav-attack system.

The Navy inducted the Lakshya PTA into service.

INDIAN NAVAL AIR ARM

The Indian Naval Air Arm is part of the Indian Navy which is tasked to provide an aircraft carrier based strike capability, fleet air defence, maritime reconnaissance, and anti-submarine warfare. To undertake these tasks, the Indian Navy employs an aircraft carrier and a variety of manned and unmanned aircraft and helicopters.

The INS Viraat carries a complement of Sea Harrier aircraft and Kamov, Sea King, Chetak and Dhruv helicopters. The Kamov Ka-31 provides AEW support for the fleet. In the anti-submarine role, the Sea King, Ka-28 and the indigenously-built HAL Dhruv are used.

The MARCOS use Sea King and HAL Dhruv helicopters while conducting operations. Reconnaissance operations are carried out by Tupolev Tu-142s, Ilyushin Il-38s, Dornier Do 228s and also by HAL Chetak helicopters. The UAV arm consists of around 30 UAVs, such as Heron and Searcher-IIs, that are operated from ships and shore for better surveillance. The Indian Navy also maintains an aerobatic display team, the Sagar Pawan. The Sagar Pawan team will be replacing the present HJT-16 Kiran with the HJT-36. The HJT-36 will also be used in training pilots.

History

The first naval air station, INS *Garuda*, was inaugurated in Cochin on 11 May 1953. This went hand-in-hand with the commissioning of the No.550 Squadron, utilizing Short Sealand aircraft. and Fairey Firefly aircraft 1960 saw the No.300 White Tigers Squadron, consisting of Sea Hawks aircraft being commissioned.

In the very next year (1961), INS *Vikrant* (formerly HMS *Hercules*) was acquired by the Indian Navy. The *Vikrant's* initial airwing consisted of British Hawker Sea Hawk fighter-bombers and a French Alize anti-submarine aircraft. On May 18, 1961, the first jet landed on board, piloted by Lieutenant (later Admiral) R H Tahiliani. That year, the No.310 Cobras Squadron (consisting of Alize aircraft) was commissioned. After playing an important role in several major Indian military actions, specifically the liberation of Goa and the India-Pakistan war in 1971, she was decommissioned in January 1997 and turned into a museum ship.

In 1976, the Indian Air Force handed over Super Constellation aircraft to the No.312 Albatross Squadron in Dabolim, Goa. Being fairly old aircraft at that point, these were withdrawn from active service by 1983. The No.315 Winged Stallions Squadron was commissioned in 1977 with the Ilyushin Il-38 aircraft.

Operation Vijay

The INS Vikrant participated in Operation Vijay, the liberation of Goa from Portugal. Its role was primarily to deter foreign naval intervention during the 40-hour long military action in December, 1961.

India Pakistan War 1971

The INS Vikrant played a major role in the successful Naval blockade of East Pakistan. Stationed off the Andaman & Nicobar islands along with Indian naval ships, INS Bramhaputra and INS Beas, the Vikrant redeployed towards Chittagong at the outbreak of hostilities. The morning of December 4, 1971, the eight Sea Hawk aircraft on the Vikrant launched an air raid on Cox's Bazaar from 60 nm away. That evening, the air group struck Chittagong harbour. Future strikes targeted Khulna and Mongla. A PTI message is supposed to have read, "Chittagong harbour abalze as ships and aircraft of the (Pakistan) Eastern Naval Fleet bombed and rocketed. Not a single vessel can be put to sea from Chittagong". Air strikes staged from the Vikrant continued till December 10, 1971.

Given naval intelligence that indicated the intent of the Pakistan Navy to break through the Indian Naval blockade using camouflaged merchant ships, the Vikrant's Sea Hawks struck shipping in the Chittagong and Cox's Bazar harbours, sinking or incapacitating most merchant ships there.

The PNS Ghazi submarine was deployed to sink the INS Vikrant. However, she sank off Visakhapatnam harbor under mysterious circumstances.

Aircraft Carrier

INS Viraat was originally commissioned in the Royal Navy as HMS Hermes on November 18, 1959. While in the Royal Navy, Hermes was the flagship carrier during the Falkland Islands campaign. The vessel was acquired by the Indian Navy in April 1986 following an extensive refit at Devonport Dockyard. Another refit followed between 1999 and 2001, which is expected to extend her useful life till 2010. However, there is some uncertainty around this retirement date.. The second refit upgraded propulsion systems, added a package of sensors to sound emergency alerts, and introduced modern communication systems. In addition, long-range surveillance radar, weapon systems, and new hangar with fire curtains was installed. The lift system was revamped to reduce reaction time in the event of an attack and a new flood alarm system was installed. Another year of down time followed while the ship received the Israeli Barak surface-to-air missile system in 2004. In a wartime scenario, the INS Viraat can embark up to 18 combat aircraft. INS Viraat is ideally suited for two missions: supporting amphibious operations and conducting ASW operations. Despite its age and range considerations, INS Viraat can quite effectively project naval and air power anywhere in the South Asia region.

CURRENT INVENTORY OF THE NAVAL AIR ARM

Aircraft

Mikoyan MiG-29K

The MiG-29K program was revived by Russia in response to the decision of the Indian Navy to acquire the Soviet aircraft carrier Admiral Gorshkov. As reported by MiG Bureau, the Indian Navy's association with the MiG-29K began in Apr 2002 when a team led by Commander Gupta reached Moscow to evaluate the MiG-29K prototype for possible induction into the Indian Navy. The Team evaluated the aircraft on ground as well as in the air (the flight evaluation was conducted by a Navy Test Pilot Commander Ahuja).

Some other aircraft were also evaluated but the MiG-29K was chosen. The first 4 of the 16 aircraft contracted for were inducted into the Indian Navy late 2009.

The Indian Navy is likely to buy 29 more of these aircraft. On January 20, 2004, the Indian Navy signed a contract for 12 single-seat MiG-29K and 4 two-seat MiG-29KUB. The first MIG-29K for the Indian Navy took flight on January 22, 2007. Though it is ready it is not yet in service.

First four of the sixteen aircraft was expected to be delivered by September 2008. but has been delayed until the spring of 2009. The fighter plane is different from the MiG-29 flown by Indian Air Force. The aircraft has been made ready for aircraft carrier operation by hardening the undercarriage.

The aircraft also has much better over-the-nose vision to make it easy to land aboard a carrier at high angle of attack. The Naval version also has additional fuel carrying capacity as also a capacity to carry more weapons since there are a total of nine stations as against only seven with the Air Force version. The aircraft also has a full glass cockpit with three large size multi-function displays.

Modifications were made for Indian Navy requirement featured Zhuk-ME radar, RD-33MK engine, combat payload up to 5,500 kg, 13 hardpoints (inclusive of the multi-lock bomb carriers), additional fuel tanks situated in dorsal spine fairing and wing LERXs, increased total fuel capacity by 50% comparing to first variant of MiG-29 and updated 4-channel digital fly-by-wire flight control system. With special coatings MiG-29K radar reflecting surface is 4-5 times smaller than of basic MiG-29. Cockpit displays consist of wide HUD and 3 (7 on MiG-29KUB) colour LCD MFDs and French Sigma-95 satellite GPS module and Topsight E helmet-mounted targeting system. Compatible with the full range of weapons carried by the MiG-29M and MiG-29SMT. The MIG-29 KUB (double seat trainer) is more similar to the MIG-29K but with reduced operational range. The aircraft will be fielded on the aircraft carrier INS Vikramaditya.. A new squadron has been raised & is being christened "Black Panthers". It will get its first batch of four MiG-29K fighters later this year. The squadron will (initially IFTU, will be led by Cdr AD Theophilus, an ex-Sea Harrier pilot)

BAE Sea Harrier

The BAE Sea Harrier operates from the INS Viraat. The BAE Sea Harrier FRS Mk.51/T Mk.60 fly with the INAS 300 and INAS 552 squadrons of the Indian Navy. They were first acquired by the Indian Navy in the mid-1980s. After years of undergoing maintenance in the UK, the Indian Navy launched Project Ashok to set up a maintenance facility in Kochi in 1994. A mid-life upgrade in 1999 for these aircraft was cancelled when the decision was made to purchase MiG-29K air defence fighters, to be deployed aboard the INS Vikramaditya (formerly Admiral Gorshkov). The Sea Harriers are armed with the Matra Magic-II AAM and the Sea Eagle Anti-ship missiles. The aircraft were upgraded with the Elta EL/M-2032 radar and the Rafael Derby BVRAAM missiles. Though the Sea Harriers were expected to remain in service with the Indian Navy till 2012-15, limited upgrades are being performed on these Sea Harriers to extend the life of the aircraft by 15 years, indicating a retirement date of 2023. The upgrades are expected to be performed by Hindustan Aeronautics Limited (HAL).

Tupolev Tu-142

The Indian Navy operates eight Tu-142 aircraft. The aircraft was inducted into service in the year 1988. Upgrading of the aircraft are taking place, which helps to extend the service life of the aircraft by sixteen years. One the upgraded aircraft has been handed over to the Indian Navy. The aircraft operates from INS Rajali and INS Hansa. Two Tu-142 aircraft are being fitted with the air launched version of the Brahmos. The aircraft will be the test platform for the Brahmos cruise missiles. The integration and tests of the missile is expected to be completed by 2010. The eight aircraft will be fitted with the Brahmos cruise missiles.

UAV

The Indian Navy currently has one squadron (INAS 342) that operates the Heron and Searcher Mk-II UAVs. There are plans to have at least three squadron of UAVs. UAVs are operated from ships to increases the range of surveillance. There are plans to introduce rotary UAVs into the Indian Navy. These UAVs will have higher endurance and load carrying capability resulting in better reconnaissance capabilities.

Helicopters

HAL Dhruv Developed by Hindustan Aeronautics Limited with MBB of Germany (now Eurocopter Deutschland), the Navy received its first Dhruvs on 28 March 2002. It is expected to receive a total of 120 units to replace the Chetak helicopters in service. The naval variant is fitted with the Super Vision-2000 maritime radar, capable of detecting targets with low radar cross section at a range of 200 km. The anti-submarine version of the helicopter is fitted with dunking sonar, torpedoes, depth charges. The helicopter may also be fitted with the missiles for anti-ship roles.

Kamov Ka-25 Hormone, Kamov Ka-28 Helix-A, and the Kamov Ka-31 Helix-B: The KA-25 was acquired by the Indian Navy in 1980 for anti-submarine warfare, but had severe technological limitations. The KA-28 were acquired in the mid-80s, and were said to be a quantum leap over their predecessors from an ASW standpoint. The KA-31 takes the Kamov capabilities even further by enabling real-time network-centric warfare for the Indian Navy.

Westland Sea King and the Sikorsky SH-3 Sea King: Used principally for anti-submarine warfare (ASW) and search & rescue roles, the helicopter fleet operate from INS Garuda (Kochi) as well as INS Kunjali-II (Mumbai) air stations. US sanctions on India in response to India's nuclear tests resulted in a large part of the Sea King fleet being grounded for want of spare parts. Seventeen of the Sea King helicopters will be upgraded. The upgrade will feature day and night capability, capability to work in adverse weather conditions, integration of two anti-ship missiles with a range of fifty kilometres and a new radar.

Aérospatiale SA 316 Alouette III: Also known as the Chetak, these choppers have seen active service in the Navy as well as the Coast Guard. They are carried on several combatant as well as non-combatant ships. They are also operated from and maintained at the INS Kunjali-II and INS Utkrosh Naval Air Stations in Mumbai and Port Blair respectively.

FUTURE AIRCRAFT CARRIERS

Vikrant class aircraft carrier:In April 2005, India began construction of a 40,000 tonne *Vikrant* class aircraft carrier at a cost of Rs.40 billion and scheduled to operate 30 aircraft, including Naval LCA, MiG-29K, and Sea Harrier combat aircraft, as well as HAL Dhruv, Ka-31, and Sea King Mk.42 helicopters. Four turbine engines will power the ship. The carrier is being constructed by state-run Cochin Shipyard Limited. and will be commissioned by 2012-13. The Indian Minister of State for Defence, Pallam Raju, went on record in September 2006 stating that the aircraft carrier is likely to be commissioned by 2011. There are plans to build more Indigenous aircraft carriers.

INS Vikramaditya: On January 20, 2004, after years of negotiations, Russia and India signed a deal for the sale of the ship, the then-Admiral Gorshkov. The ship was free, while India will pay US$800 million for upgrade and refit of the ship, as well as at least an additional $1bn for the aircraft and weapons systems. The Navy looked at equipping the carrier with the E-2D, but decided not to. The deal also includes the purchase of 12 single-seat MiG-29K 'Fulcrum-D' (Product 9.41) and 4 dual-seat MiG-29KUB aircraft (with an option for 14 more aircraft)$1bn, 6 Kamov Ka-31 "Helix" reconnaissance and anti-submarine helicopters, torpedo tubes, missile systems, and artillery units. Facilities and procedures for training pilots and technical staff, delivery of simulators, spare parts, and establishment maintenance on Indian Navy facilities are also part of the contract.

The announced delivery date for INS Vikramaditya was August 2008, an ambitious schedule, but one that would allow the carrier to enter service in 2009, around the time as light carrier INS Viraat (formerly HMS Hermes, last of the Centaur class) was scheduled to retire. The new ship will berth at the new Indian Navy facility in Karwar, on India's west coast. The INS Viraat's retirement is now set for 2010-2012. The sea trials of INS Vikramaditya are expected to begin by 2010 and delivery is expected by 2012.

Aircraft Under Development and Future Aircraft

- HAL Tejas:The naval variant of the Tejas will have strengthened landing gear and other necessary modifications for service on an aircraft carrier. Two Naval prototypes will be built, the NP-1 (Naval Prototype-1) which will be a two seat variant and NP-2 (Naval Prototype-2), a single seat variant for carrier operations. The Tejas is expected to be delivered before 2012. The first flight of NP-1 is expected to take place by the end of 2008 but the carrier trials was delayed due to the delay in the delivery schedule of INS Vikramaditya. Hence the trials will have to be carried out at the SBTF (Shore-based Test Facility) under construction at the naval airbase INS Hansa in Goa. Indian Navy plans to operate two squadrons (40 aircraft) of carrier borne Tejas aircraft from the two aircraft carries. Indian navy has placed an order for six Naval LCAs. At an approximate cost of Rs 150 crore per aircraft, that will provide a Rs 900 crore infusion into the Naval LCA programme. The Navy has a requirement of 50 Tejas aircraft. The first Naval prototype NP-1, was rolled out in July 2010.
- Additional Fighter Aircraft:Indian Navy has issued RFI to various fighter aircraft manufacturers including Boeing for F-18 Super Hornet & Dassault for its Rafale fighters.These aircraft will be used for supplements to

MIG29K's operating from Indigenous & Vikramaditya class aircraft carriers. These are ordered in order to reduce the delays in the procurement of fighter aircraft. Unknown number of fighters will be procured.

- Long Range Maritime Patrol Aircraft: The Indian Navy issued an RFP for eight maritime patrol aircraft. The plan is to induct up to thirty new maritime patrol aircraft by 2020. Out of all the bidders the P-8I Poseidon has won the contract. New Delhi and Boeing have inked a lucrative, $2.1 billion contract for the delivery of eight P-8 Poseidon sub hunters. The new aircraft will replace a fleet of outdated Russian-manufactured Tupolev-142M planes.
- Medium Range Maritime Reconnaissance Aircraft: The Indian Navy issued an RFP for six medium-range maritime reconnaissance (MRMR) aircraft. Contenders are ATR-72MP/ATR-42MP, EADS C-295MPA/C-235MPA, Dassault's Falcon 900MPA and Embraer P-99A platforms.
- E-2D Advanced Hawkeye
- 17 Hawk Trainer
- HAL HJT-36
- 20 ASW Helicopters (to replace Sea King) Extended to 60 helos
- 15 NAL Saras aircraft have been ordered, mostly to replace the Dornier Do-228.
- 40 Unmanned helicopters. This helicopter is under development and will be based on the HAL-built Cheetah helicopters.
- Rustom UAV
- 50 Light Helicopers

Personnel and Structure

The 5000-person Naval Air Arm is headed by Rear Admiral Vijay Shankar, Assistant Chief of Naval Staff (Air). The current Chief of Naval Staff, Admiral Nirmal Verma PVSM, AVSM, ADC .

Western Command

Established in 1986, the Flag Officer Naval Aviation (FONA) is headquartered in Goa, and is responsible for all naval aviation aspects. The Directorate of Naval Air Staff at Naval HQ has centralized functions like laying down the general principles of operational deployment, organisation, administration and operational/training standards for the flying units. On the other hand, FONA controls training, maintenance and other functions of naval aviation. Aircraft yards at Kochi, Kerala and Dabolim, Goa are responsible for maintaining the fleet's air arm. An exclusive base, INS Shikra for helicopters was commissioned in Mumbai.

Eastern Command

To protect and preserve India's growing trade with Southeast Asia and offer a bulwark against Chinese dominance in the Bay of Bengal, a new naval base is being built near Visakhapatnam. It is expected to be capable of harboring two aircraft carriers, including the new Vikrant-class aircraft carrier that is being planned.

Southern Command

It has at least one airfield.

Andaman & Nicobar Command

A fighter squadron is expected to be based in Port Blair in the future, to bolster the strength of the squadron of Mi-8 helicopters currently operating there.

Muscat (Oman)

A new airbase will be setup in Muscat, Oman to tackle piracy in the Gulf of Aden.

7

The Indian Navy in 2020

Modernisation" of a Navy is a continuous process-and each major upgradation takes time and needs to be planned well in advance. The "Great White Fleet" which circum-navigated the globe in 1908-09, and announced to the world that the USA had arrived on the world scene, took twenty years to build. It took the FSU, under the dynamic leadership of Admiral of the Fleet Gorshkov, almost 25 years to build the Soviet Navy to a level where it could challenge the western allies.

The Indian Navy of 2010-20 is already being built – the Air Defence Ship at Kochi, the Vikramaditya (Ex Gorshkov) at Russia, along with its complement of MiG 29K, the Naval LCA at Bangalore, the Scorpene submarines at MDL, and at last count about 22 Destroyers, Frigates, corvettes, LSTs, OPVs, and FACs at various shipyards around the country. We must, therefore, look at what is needed, and what is possible, for the time frame of 2020-2030, and what else is needed to fill the voids prior to 2020. In arriving at the final figures we must take into account the probable security challenges and maritime threats that we will need to counter and the maritime interests that we will need to protect, preserve and indeed promote; India's stature and position in the comity of nations; our economic potential; and finally our design, industrial and ship-building capability.

A little "crystal ball gazing" is, therefore, an essential part of the planning process – never an easy thing to do at the best of times.

Security Environment and Challenges Geo-strategic Location. Geography, they say is the handmaiden of strategy– and geography has indeed been very kind to us. It has bestowed on India many strategic opportunities, options and indeed advantages some of which are:-

- A coastline of 7516 Km, which includes the mainland as also the Island territories.
- 12 major, 21 intermediate and 164 minor ports.
- A total of 1197 Islands, which provide Defence in Depth and also give us a huge EEZ. At 2.01 million sq km our EEZ is 2/3rds of our land area. After demarcation of the continental shelf our EEZ is likely to be 2.54 million sq km.
- A very favourable geo-strategic location astride the vital East-West trade routes, which enables us to control, when necessary, this energy/trade lifeline. Position matters – on land as on the Sea.
- Moreover, the ocean that laps our shores is itself unique. Unlike other oceans, it is not "open-ended". It is closed to the North by the Indian sub-continent and has a few "choke points" that afford entry into it.

Unregulated Ocean Space. Speaking to the press at Singapore on 12 Nov 2003, the Oceans as "the largest unregulated space in the world", a quote that has appeared in the editorial of the 2005 edition of "Jane's Fighting Ships".

As the editorial points out, this may seem strange considering that the UN Convention on the Laws of the Sea is now in place. But the fact is that while the UNCLOS has given various rights to nations, the right to freedom of navigation has not changed, nor have the attributes and essential characteristics of the oceans that constitute 70% of the surface of the globe. These attributes are:-

- Large parts of the Oceans remain Unowned. While nations have sovereign rights over their territorial seas and commercial rights to all the resources in their EEZ, no nation "Owns" the "High Seas".

- Because the High seas are largely unowned, they are uncontrolled. It's a case of "No Policeman-No Law". On the high seas there is nobody, but nobody, to control your movements.
- Because the High Seas are unowned, there are No Boundaries at Sea. This is what makes the Navy different to all other Services, which work within the confines of national boundaries. The Navy works in an International arena on a daily basis. Twelve miles out of port and we are in International waters.
- Because of these attributes of the Oceans, the Sea is One.

Thus, all nations with a coastline are maritime neighbours.

Maritime Terrorism. The new scourge of terrorism has taken the world by storm. So far major acts of terrorism have by and large been restricted to land areas. But as security on land is tightened, the ease of access and movement across the world's ocean areas will tempt terrorists to take their "trade" to sea. The war on terror at sea cannot be fought by individual nations. It will have to be a worldwide effort that will require Navies of the world to work together – as countries are doing ashore.

Nuclear Backdrop. We are now a declared nuclear weapon state (NWS) and, after some hiccups, the world has accepted this reality. Our nuclear doctrine clearly states that we will maintain a "Credible Minimum Deterrent" based on a triad of weapon delivery systems. We are also a declared "No First Use" (NFU) NWS. Any country with an NFU policy must ensure that it has an assured second-strike capability. Missile silos, airfields and aircraft are easily detected by satellites and are hence easy targets. A nuclear submarine is very, very difficult to detect. Even if detected, it is extremely difficult to target, as it is constantly on the move at speeds of twenty knots or more.

Territorialisation of the Seas. Maritime powers have always wanted (as they still do) as much freedom of the seas, as possible; whereas non-maritime powers want as much ownership of the seas, as possible. With the UNCLOS, both have got much of what they wanted. Almost 40% of the ocean areas have become the Exclusive Economic zones of countries. The full claims for the world's EEZ have yet to be submitted by many countries and agreed to by the UN, and more important, by neighbouring states. Earlier we had neighbours and boundaries only on land. Now we have them at sea as well. The more the neighbours, the more are the problems. The larger the EEZ, the greater is the area of responsibility of the maritime Services.

Global Governance. Globalisation has made countries more inter-dependent and States will increasingly work together to ensure their economic development, as also to promote peace, stability and combat common threats. In future, therefore, one sees a form of "Global Governance" slowly but surely creeping to seaward to ensure that the "Freedom of the Seas", that the west holds so dear, is not misused by terrorists. The ISPS code, the Container Security Initiative and the Proliferation Security Initiative are manifestations of this trend. This will require the Indian Navy to patrol its area of interest, and work with other Navies, much more than it has done in the past.

Strategic Frontiers. What then is The Indian Navy's "area of interest"? Our land frontiers are well known. So also are our maritime boundaries with our immediate maritime neighbours. But our current area of interest lies far, far beyond our territorial sea and the EEZ. It extends all the way to the choke points that afford entry into the North Indian Ocean as shown in the map below.

Extra-Regional Presence. Any nation with the capability can traverse the Oceans and arrive in force at the doorstep of another maritime state-no matter how distant it may be. Powerful Navies have indulged in "Gun Boat Diplomacy" in the past. While the phrase may be out of fashion these days, Navies continue to be used for the same purpose, by whatever name it may be called. It is well known that the strategic focus of the world has once again shifted to the North Indian Ocean, due to a combination of Terrorism and world energy reserves. The presence of extra-regional powers in the Indian Ocean is bound to last well into the foreseeable future. The Indian Navy consequently has to operate in the same waters as are being patrolled by the world's most technologically advanced nations.

Defence of Trade. Trade is the lifeblood of any economy– and so it is with India. Our economy is booming and this trade will continue to soar. Today 90% of the crude oil we use comes from across the oceans – be it imported or produced in our offshore oil fields. Our dependence on natural gas is increasing by the day. Over 95% of our trade by volume comes across the oceans. Any disruption of this trade lifeline, particularly any disruption in the flow of oil, will endanger the economic prosperity and security of the country. Defence of trade has always been a major mission of the Navy and this will continue to be so.

Maritime Diplomacy. The Navy works very closely with the External Affairs Ministry to further the interests of the country around the world. Towards this end it sends ships on overseas deployments to show the flag and build "Bridges of Friendship" – which was also the theme of the Navy's very successful International Fleet Review in 2001. Towards this end the Navy also trains a considerable number of foreign Naval personnel in its many training institutions. With many small nations on the Indian Ocean rim now getting huge EEZs there is a growing demand for assistance and suitable vessels to patrol these areas. It is in India's interest to meet these demands and supply equipment as and when requested. Since many of these countries cannot afford to buy such vessels we must be willing and ready to supply them at short notice, and free of cost. Budgetary provisions must be regularly made for such assistance.

Regional Naval Expansion. The Naval development plans of maritime states in the Asia-Pacific region clearly indicate that all are giving greater importance to maritime security then ever before – a trend that we must take note of.

The immediate threat is well known, always desisted from identifying others because "to name an enemy is to make one". But more important is the fact that in this respect the Navy has to think and plan differently than the other two services, which can clearly identify the threat across our borders. Because of the unregulated ocean space, ease of access and movement a threat can develop from the sea very quickly. So, unlike the other two Services, Navies are not built purely to counter known threats but to protect maritime interests. The larger a country's dependence on the oceans, and the larger its interests at sea, the larger its Navy has got to be.

FLEET MODERNISATION

Availability of Funds. The Navy is a capital intensive Service and it takes a long time to design, develop and build ships. The larger the ship, the longer is the time taken to design and build it. Taking a typical destroyer/frigate (The work horses of any Navy) it takes around 10 to twelve years from Government approval to commissioning, if the ship is to be designed and built in India. Assured funding over three plan periods (i.e. 15 years) is absolutely essential for any planned modernisation. Historically, the fate of Navies has been linked to the fate of their country's economy. Fortunately for us the Indian economy is doing very well and modernisation of the Navy (and indeed of the Armed Forces) can be easily funded over the next three plan periods in particular, and for the future in general. This statement is supported by published/stated figures for the Indian economy and the assumptions at sub-paras (d) and (e) below:-

- The GDP in 2004-05 was around Rs 2658750 Crores.
- The GDP has been growing at an average rate of 6.35% and very recently the PM announced that this year it will grow at 7% (for the first time the GDP growth in the first half of the fiscal year has been over 8%) and there is every possibility that it could touch 10% in the future.
- The percentage of GDP allocated for Defence during the latter 1980s varied from 3.08 to 4.24%. Since then this has gradually dropped, and from 1991 to 2005 the percentage has varied from 2.77 to 2.24. This was quite inadequate to fund the modernisation of the armed forces.
- We have been able to afford 3 to 4% of GDP for defence in the past and we can easily do so in the future. It must

become stated Government policy that we will spend 3% to 4% of GDP for defence;

Besides making adequate money available for defence, it will also enable planned modernisation which has not really been possible in the past as, more often than not, the Budget has driven the "Plan" rather than the Plan driving the Budget. Assuming a modest 6.35% growth rate, the expected GDP at five yearly intervals is likely to be:

- 10-10 Rs 36,17,137 Crores
- 15-15 Rs 49,20,989 Crores
- 20-20 Rs 66,94,835 Crores
- 25-25 Rs 91,08,091 Crores
- 30-30 Rs 123,91,243 Crores

Share of the Defence Cake. How much each Service should get from the allocations for Defence has always been somewhat contentious. The Navy being the smallest of the three Services, has always received the least. As early as in 1988, General Sundarji had stated that by 2000 the Navy should get 20% of the Defence budget. He realized the value of a Navy in World affairs. Regrettably, this has not happened and it was only in 2002-03 that the Navy crossed the 15% mark and received the highest ever allocation of 17.6% in 2003-04.

Since then it has hovered around the 17% mark and this should gradually be increased to 20% as India will certainly need a powerful Blue Water Navy as it takes up greater responsibility in world affairs. The peace process currently underway will ultimately give us a Peace Dividend that will allow us to reduce troops on the border. (Sub-continental Armies are perhaps the only ones that are amassed on the borders. The rest of the world takes boundaries for granted and respects them) For planning purposes, however, let us assume an allocation of 17%. Even with this, the expected allocations to the Navy as shown below (assuming only 3% of GDP is allocated for Defence) would be adequate to fund the projects/ modernization being recommended:

- XI Plan 2007-08 to 2011-12 Rs 92586 Crores

- XII Plan 2012-13 to 2016-17 Rs 125960 Crores
- XIII Plan 2017-18 to 2021-22 Rs 171366 Crores

Aircraft Carriers. For many years now the Indian Navy has been stating that it needs a minimum of three aircraft carriers to fulfill its missions. One is required to be operational on each coast and the third will normally be under maintenance. After much delay (it took over 15 years!), the Government finally approved the construction of the Air Defence Ship to replace the INS Vikrant, which was phased out in 1997. It took 8 years to get government approval to induct the Ex-Gorshkov (now christened Vikramaditya), which will replace Viraat in 2008/09. It is time now to place the order for the third carrier, which should really be a repeat of the ADS.

Batch building of ships and standardization greatly reduce the life cycle costs of a ship. Moreover, for the third carrier we will not have to invest in a separate carrier air wing, as the intention and requirement is to have only two carriers operational at any one time. If approved now, we will have three carriers in the 2020s.

Strategic Forces. Now that India is a declared Nuclear Weapon state with a No First Use Policy it is absolutely essential that we put our second strike capability in Nuclear Submarines as soon as possible.

There are many advantages in doing so and the actions of existing NW States are good indicators of the direction in which we should go. The Government should approve, start and fund such a programme at the earliest, as it is vital for the security of the country. The ultimate aim should be to have at least four such submarines so that at least one, if not two, are on patrol at all times.

Destroyers and Frigates. These ships are really the workhorses of the Navy, both in peace and war. Today, we have 11 destroyers and 11 frigates, which are far too few. In fact, after the 1962 war a study had recommended that the Navy should have 28 such warships – a target that the Navy has never been able to achieve. Forty years down the line much has changed and the responsibility of the Navy has increased manifold. In the next 20 years this figure must go upto at least 20 of each type. Five Leander Class frigates are already well past their prime and need immediate replacement. (One was earlier decommissioned without a replacement) Three project 17 Frigates under construction will replace the first three Leanders.

The three Godavri class frigates will need to be replaced between 2010 and 2015 by which time they will be between 25 to 30 yrs old. Thus there is an immediate need to place orders for at least six more P17 frigates, just to maintain the current force levels of Frigates. Additional orders will need to be placed on MDL and GRSE to take the frigate numbers to twenty by 2025.

As far as destroyers are concerned, the first of the Kashin class destroyers will be 25 years old this year and the youngest (Ranvijai) will be 17 years. They will all need to be replaced between 2010 and 2020. Three Project 15A destroyers are already on order and it would be cost effective to increase this order to five so that they replace the five Kashins.

It will thus be seen that Mazagon Docks, the shipyard building both the P17 Frigates and the P 15A Destroyers, must deliver 9 x P 17 frigates and 5 x P15A destroyers between now and 2020 i.e. almost one ship a year – assuming that orders are placed well in time and no delays are introduced. Going by their past performance they will not be able to meet this target and so the only option to maintain present force levels will be to exercise the import option and a repeat order for the Talwar class destroyers recently imported from Russia is a very attractive option. A minimum of four should be immediately ordered to maintain force levels. Additional orders for the Talwar class and/or the Delhi Class must be placed a little later to take the destroyer fleet upto 20 by 2025.

Submarines. Submarines are a vital part of the Naval Fleet and ideal for dissuasion and sea denial operations, particularly against a vastly superior Navy. Their operational value in the Indian Ocean is much greater than in the other oceans as the hydrological conditions in our waters afford the submarine many advantages. Some years ago the Navy had 18 operation.

INDIA'S FUTURE AIRCRAFT CARRIER FORCE AND THE NEED FOR STRATEGIC FLEXIBILITY

A Three Carrier Fleet by 2020

India has long striven for a three carrier fleet comprised of one carrier battle group stationed on each seaboard, and a third carrier held in reserve. This would enable Delhi, by rotating ships, to continuously protect both its flanks, since aircraft carriers regularly require long periods of maintenance at berth. The struggles and travails that the Indian Navy has encountered while doggedly pursuing this goal, what with the seemingly interminable negotiations surrounding the purchase and modernization of the ex-Admiral Gorshkov, and the chronic delays in construction of the IAC, or indigenous aircraft carrier, have become somewhat emblematic of the sometimes frustratingly ponderous rhythm of India's naval expansion.

It would seem now, however, that Delhi's long-sought quest for a three carrier force is at last edging towards fruition. Indeed, it was announced earlier this year, shortly before Prime Minister Vladimir Putin's visit, that a price finalization for the future Vikramaditya had finally been reached. The 44,500 ton ex-Soviet vessel, which is undergoing an extensive modernization, (70 per cent of the structure will be completely renewed) will carry 16 new MiG-29K aircraft, as well as an assortment of Kamov-28 and Kamov-31 helicopters. Now that the price has been finalized, the Vikramaditya is expected to arrive in late 2012 or early 2013.

It will be joined, hopefully little more than a year later, by India's first indigenously built aircraft carrier, a 37,000 ton ship, which, like the Vikramaditya, will be equipped with a STOBAR (short-takeoff, barrier-arrested design) and is slated to field a slightly smaller air wing of 12 MiG-29K Aircraft. Both aircraft carriers will also in time carry India's indigenously designed LCA, or light combat aircraft. The IAC project, which will embody a significant milestone in India's shipbuilding capacities once completed, has been plagued by difficulties from the outset, be it due to budget-related quibbling over its tonnage, insufficient quantities of high quality steel for the hull, or, some say, Cochin Shipyard Limited's struggle to adopt a modern modular assembling technique to speed up construction. Recent reports, however, seem to indicate that the IAC is back on track, and that there is a good chance that it will be launched later this year, and commissioned in 2014/2015.

Following its launch, the Indian Navy is expected to officially out its plans for a second home-built aircraft carrier, the ubiquitously named IAC-II, which will be both larger and more formidable than its predecessor. Details surrounding the vessel were long murky at best, but information has now begun to surface, although many aspects remain somewhat sketchy. The Chief of Naval Staff, Admiral Nirmal Verma, indicated in December 2009 that the IAC-II would be sizeably larger than the IAC-I, with a displacement of 50,000 tons. It would also have a more modern launch system, either via steam catapult or, as some as yet unconfirmed rumours have suggested, an EMALS (Electromagnetic Aircraft System). It is also unclear whether the carrier will be conventionally or nuclear-propelled. In any case, its larger size and more efficient launch system will enable it to field an aircraft wing that is superior both in size and diversity. An RFI (Request for Information) has thus been issued for 40 new multi-role fighters. It is hoped that Cochin Shipyard, having already run through all the hoops while constructing the first IAC, will be able to deliver the second carrier with greater alacrity. If this is indeed the case, one can fully expect the Indian Navy to boast three operational carrier groups by 2020 at the latest.

What would be the strategic ramifications of such a quantum leap in India's naval capabilities? Over the years so much time and energy has been devoted to the pursuit of this "constabulary" blue-water force, that scant attention has actually been paid to the tactical options and possibilities proffered by India's new carrier fleet. Here follows an attempt to briefly summarize the panorama of uses India's carrier force could serve in future contingencies, be they wartime or during peace, as well as the need to protect what some sceptics have termed the "white elephants" of modern naval warfare.

STRENGTHENING THE ELEPHANT'S HIDE: PROTECTING INDIA'S AIRCRAFT CARRIERS

An aircraft carrier is undoubtedly one of the most potent symbols of national power. This symbolic potency, however, can rapidly morph into a disadvantage, if the fear of its loss irreversibly damaging the nation's morale prevents it from fulfilling its full spectrum of wartime capabilities. In the past, an unsavoury blend of political indecisiveness and inappropriate threat assessments have frequently stunted Indian aircraft carriers' tactical flexibility in times of conflict. During Operation Vijay, for example, which was conducted in 1961 to successfully wrest Goa from Portugal, the INS Vikrant was instructed to keep clear of the embattled enclave when a foreign submarine was detected. Similarly, in 1965, fears related to the INS Vikrant's severe deficiencies in terms of anti-submarine warfare played a part in the decision to maintain her under refit. In 1971, the Vikrant was able to operate relatively unimpeded off the Bay of Bengal only because the Pakistani submarine PNS Ghazi had already been sunk. In 2002-2003, during Operation Parakram, the INS Viraat was hastily retrofitted with the Israeli Barak Anti-Missile System once it dawned on Naval Headquarters that it would be particularly vulnerable to submarine-launched Harpoon missiles.

The most recent existential threat to India's carrier force takes the form of China's newly inducted anti-ship ballistic missile, the DF-21, which can reportedly hit a moving target while travelling at a speed of Mach 10. Whereas before it would have been extremely difficult to locate and target a fast-moving carrier, China's progress in the field of ISR, notably via satellite surveillance, has rendered such a feat increasingly possible. It would seem, however, that the Indian Navy is determined to break a historical pattern of being more reactive than proactive when it comes to dealing with threats to its carriers, and it was recently reported that Lockheed Martin had held talks with Indian authorities regarding a potential collaboration with the DRDO, which would result in an integration of the future Prithvi Air Defence Shield (PADS) with the firm's celebrated phased array AEGIS missile defence system. Although it is not yet certain whether the AEGIS system could ward off a DF-21 strike, it would certainly provide the Indian fleet with a greater degree of anti-missile protection. An abiding concern however remains the prohibitive cost of such a system, as it is estimated that equipping a Kolkata class destroyer with an AEGIS defence system would more than triple its cost.

Preparing for Diverse Combat Contingencies

India's Maritime Strategy lays out a wide gamut of roles for the Indian Navy in times of war. It is stated, for example, that it will be expected to perform operations ranging from "*distant credible sea denial over large areas of the Indian Ocean*" to "*distant sea control in selected areas of the Indian Ocean to protect economic interests and mercantile traffic,*" to conducting "phased operations" which will result in the use of maritime power to support land or air-borne strikes. India's carrier fleet will therefore have to display a high degree of tactical flexibility. This can be accomplished in part by reconfiguring the vessels' air wings depending on the nature of the crisis at hand. A flotilla of Chinese submarines could be met by an eastern carrier fleet more heavily geared towards anti-submarine warfare, with a flight deck comprising a greater number of maritime patrol aircraft or Seaking and Kamov ASW helicopters. An anti-piracy operation in a large body of water may require less strike aircraft and more maritime surveillance capabilities in the shape of patrol aircraft or UAVs. MARCOS commando strikes could be facilitated by increasing the number of helicopters aboard, or by adding specific Special Forces ammunition and equipment modules on board.

In the course of the next two to three decades, China's string of pearls, which is still very much in its embryonic phase for the time being, may gradually take on a more decidedly military nature. This would require Indian naval practitioners to develop a capacity for opposed amphibious landings. The fleet's amphibious component has received a considerable boost over the past few years with the induction of the 17,000 ton INS Jalashwa in 2007, as well several smaller landing ships. Direct amphibious assaults may become less feasible in time, however, as the gradual proliferation of medium and long-range anti-ship missiles renders landing craft ever more vulnerable to a devastating hit which would obliterate not only the ship but also the precious amphibious strike force it hosts. Aircraft carriers can play an important role by providing a first over-the-horizon attack, either by air strike or by the air-borne insertion of special forces. This would serve to isolate and soften up the beachhead before engaging in a full heliborne assault, supplemented by the landing craft and LSTs ferrying in reinforcements.

Vital Humanitarian Platforms

Aircraft carriers can prove to be extremely valuable assets when responding to humanitarian emergencies or engaging in NEOs (non-combatant evacuation operations). A carrier can provide a self-generating supply of fresh water, medical assistance or engineering expertise to populations in dire need, and have revealed themselves time and time again to be vital humanitarian platforms. The participation of the INS Viraat in the 2004 tsunami relief effort comes to mind, as does the recent action of the USS Carl Vinson off the coast of Haiti. Much can be done, nevertheless, to further bolster a carrier's humanitarian response skills. First, the air wing can be reconfigured in order to field more helicopters, as well as vertical lift aircraft, such as the recently upgraded Sea Harriers, which can gain access to rough terrain. Secondly, medical modular facilities can be installed on board in order to enhance the carrier's medical responsiveness. Finally, a command centre can be set up so that key government personnel and civil response teams can coordinate their efforts via the carrier's communication systems. This could be extremely useful, for example, in the event of disruption of landlines or the destruction of government offices.

In less than a decade, India's naval force structure will have undergone a seismic shift, able to continuously deploy carrier groups on both seaboards. In order for the Indian Navy to efficiently project both hard and soft power throughout the Indian Ocean Region, its commanders will need to display a degree of strategic flexibility by learning how to leverage the many uses of Indian's new aircraft carriers. Only this way will they prove themselves to be the formidable force multipliers, both in peace and war, required to lead the Indian Navy into the 21st century.

INDIAN NAVY LIE IN SUBMARINES OR AIRCRAFT CARRIERS?

A increasingly apparent reason for the Ministry of Defence's slow decision-making on a second submarine production line for the Indian Navy is the deep divisions within the navy over India's submarine force. A debate rages between the submarine arm and the surface navy — particularly the dominant aviation wing — on whether the future lies in submarines or aircraft carriers. The navy's submariners, meanwhile, debate the merits of conventional versus nuclear-powered submarines.

Slowed by these internal debates, India's 30-Year Submarine Construction Plan, which the government approved in 1999, has languished. The 30-Year plan envisioned building 24 conventional submarines in India. Six were to be built from western technology and six with Russian collaboration; then Indian designers, having absorbed the best of both worlds, would build 12 submarines indigenously.

A senior retired admiral, reflecting the views of the submarine arm, blames the navy's "aircraft carrier lobby" for the delay in building submarines. He alleges: "The last two naval chiefs (Admirals Arun Prakash and Sureesh Mehta) were aviators, who had no interest in using the navy's limited budget for building submarines. So they exploited the division of opinion amongst submariners — the nuclear-powered versus conventional submarine debate — to push submarine building into the future."

Nuclear-powered submarines are of two types: ballistic missile submarines (called SSBNs) and attack submarines (referred to as SSNs). Both are propelled by power from a miniature on-board reactor, but SSBNs also fire nuclear-tipped ballistic missiles. SSBNs are not a part of the fighting navy; they constitute a country's nuclear deterrent and fire their nuclear-tipped missiles on orders from the national leadership. SSNs operate as part of a naval fleet, moving under nuclear power and sinking surface warships with conventional torpedoes and missiles.

Votaries of nuclear submarines, such as Rear Admiral (Retired) Raja Menon, argue that nuclear-powered submarines have a crucial advantage over conventional ones: endurance. While conventional (diesel-electric) submarines are more quiet and harder to detect while submerged, they are easily picked up when they surface to charge their batteries.

Furthermore, they move slowly underwater, unlike nuclear submarines, which can remain submerged almost indefinitely. This allows a single nuclear submarine — travelling underwater to its patrol station and remaining there, undetected, for months— to do the job of multiple conventional submarines, which give their position away when they surface at regular intervals.

Admiral Menon explains, “A single SSN can dominate an area 1,000 nautical miles (1,850 km) away as effectively as three conventional submarines, which require one submarine on station, another transiting to relieve it, and a third transiting back to refuel. If the patrol area is farther than 1,000 nautical miles, a single SSN does the job of five conventional submarines. That is why the US Navy fields an all-nuclear force.”

But Menon accepts that the Indian Navy would always need conventional submarines. India’s coastal waters are so shallow that SSNs, which typically weigh 4,000-5,000 tonnes, run the risk of scraping the bottom. Conventional submarines, which normally weigh around 1,500 tonnes, are needed for dominating the coastal areas.

But the complexities of a nuclear submarine programme are evident from China’s current difficulties. China relies on its four primitive Han-class attack submarines (Type 091), having decided to close construction of the newer Shen-class (Type 093). Currently, China is grappling with a newer Type 095 SSN; five of these could be added “in the coming years”. Meanwhile, China shifted focus to a newer Jin-class (Type 094), of which the first SSBN “appears ready”, with four more under construction. (From Business Standard)

A BLUEPRINT FOR A FUTURE INDIAN NAVY

Navies are meant to project power, protect sea lanes and defend the country fair distances away from the coastline. They can serve to blockade enemies in their offensive role and platforms to land forces. India has no territorial ambitions and is currently interested in being a regional power with no present intentions beyond the Bay of Bengal, Indian Ocean and the sea lanes from the Straits of Hormuz to the Straits of Malacca, through which traverse its own energy supplies and those of its potential allies and opponents. The first step in defense planning is to determine the most likely nations which may wage a war against our nation. In India's case these are Pakistan, China and Bangladesh in descending order. Of these Pakistan and Bangladesh have adjacent maritime boundaries.

Bangladesh Navy is mainly a coast guard with few ocean going frigates and no submarines. Thus our aging carrier Viraat and a few frigates with a small reconnaissance and anti-ship warfare capable air-arm and two submarines would suffice to blockade and have complete domination over the waters of the Bay of Bengal. Air and naval bases at Vishakhapatnam and Andaman islands could be expanded and modernized to fulfill that role. A war with Bangladesh is a remote possibility, but it is best to be prepared for a coming world, where oil and water are likely to be the reason for future wars.

A much more likely scenario is war with Pakistan. Its newer Agosta submarines and P3C Orion anti-submarine and anti-ship warfare capabilities require the Gorshkov-Vikramaditya and a large force of submarines, ASW frigates, destroyers and an air-arm with the equivalence of P3C Orion or Nimrod planes. Our aircraft carrier, a billion plus dollar equipment needs a support group of ASW ships, ship based helicopters, missile frigates, destroyers and submarines. This is one of the main reasons that bigger powers like Russia and China have not fielded aircraft carriers. These assets are very difficult to protect against hunter-killer and attack submarines and cruise missiles. Thus the use of an aircraft carrier to project power is only feasible against Pakistan and foolhardy or impossible against China, Russia, France, Germany, UK or the US. Except for China, the rest are unlikely opponents and even China is unlikely to go to war with us again. Nevertheless, all possibilities must be considered and the way to deal with superior or stronger powers is to retain the capability of severe punishing retaliatory damage to inhibit misadventures by pre-emptive aggressors.

The next factor to be considered is the cost benefit ratio. Aircraft carriers even like the Gorshkov and its aircraft and the support vessels to protect it, would cost two billion dollars for one carrier group. Thus two aircraft carriers should suffice. They would be unusable against any major power and are likely to lose their effectiveness even against Pakistan with time, as it acquires more sophisticated submarines, planes and missiles. On the other hand missile and ASW frigates or destroyers and ASW and air to ship missile carrying aircraft and newer quiet diesel submarines can be built or purchased for 25 to 100 million dollars per piece. India's 7500 kilometer shoreline permits two or three naval air-arm bases with one or two squadrons of reconnaissance, rescue and attack aircraft at three coastal areas from Gujarat coast to Kerala coast, and two from Kanyakumari to Kolkata because of the bases at Andamans and Vishakhapatnam.

Thus the top priority is a buildup of blue water ships, quiet submarines and a substantial and independent air-arm for the Indian Navy. The big bucks spending should be for a nuclear powered submarine with sea-based ballistic nuclear missiles of long ranges to serve as retaliatory deterrent. Twenty-four modern submarines, Thirty blue water navy frigates and destroyers armed with missiles, helicopters and ABMs, about 100 land based naval aircraft for reconnaissance, rescue, Anti-Submarine Warfare and equipped to attack ships and submarines, and two nuclear powered submarines with nuclear missiles would ensure India's safety. It needs considerable time to build up navies, so foresight, planning and adequate funding are essential for India's security. Unlikely though the scenario may be, in the event of a war with China, there must be sufficient naval power and assets to blockade the Straits of Malacca, the bottleneck of oil transit to China.

8

The Indian Navy: A Military Power at a Political Crossroads

INTRODUCTION

The Indian Navy stands at an important juncture in its history. Long considered a "blue water" navy, many of its major vessels are nearing the end of their useful service lives, and will soon require replacement. Unfortunately, the country has chosen to devote the majority of its fiscal resources toward other pursuits, primarily business-related ones. Tenuous military procurement relationships with both the east and the west, coupled with an indigenous shipbuilding program which is struggling to achieve an acceptable level of productivity, portend for a future that is unclear at best. Nevertheless, India is expected to enter the 21st Century with a smaller, but still formidable, regional naval presence. This paper will review the growth of the Indian Navy over its relatively short history, examine in detail its current tasking, organization and capabilities, and venture an estimation of what the immediate future may hold for this proud, but aging force.

NAVAL HERITAGE

Prior to examining the Indian Navy in detail, it is important to establish a historical framework upon which the current capabilities are built. Although India's maritime history is not often well-remembered, sea-faring traditions date back to Vedic times, from 2000 to 500 B.C., when the ancestors of modern

India recognized their unique geographic position, and exploited the surrounding sea, using it as an "avenue" of trade to both the east and the west (incidentally, the Indian Ocean is the only body of water its size that draws its name from a country).

At the height of its early maritime activity, India's culture and religion "traveled" peacefully with its trade and influence. From the coming of the Moghuls in the 1500s, and on up through the more modern colonial period of the 1900s, India largely relinquished its maritime heritage and supremacy to the European powers, instead focusing its fears of (and defense against) aggression by the peoples of the Asian land mass to the north. Even after independence from colonial rule was achieved in 1947, Indian involvement in wars with Pakistan in 1948 and 1965, as well as with China in 1962, kept national attention focused on the security of the country's land frontiers to the north. Although an Indian Navy emerged following the period of colonial rule, and contributed to the 1965 victory over Pakistan, it was not until 1971 that the "watershed event" for the modern Indian Navy occurred.

In mid-December 1971, a United States naval task force, led by the nuclear-powered aircraft carrier USS Enterprise, entered the Bay of Bengal, ostensibly to evacuate Americans from war-torn East Pakistan. The carrier's deployment, at the height of the third Indo-Pakistani War, also coincided with the presence of several (additional) Soviet warships in the Indian Ocean. Although the initial State Department public release declared the intent of the mission to be "a show of force by the United States for the benefit of both India and the Soviet Union," President Nixon later clarified the event to be a gesture of support for Pakistan and China in light of the increased Soviet naval presence, in addition to the more obvious evacuation efforts. Both India and the Soviet Union lashed out at the American presence, the Soviets labelling it "gunboat diplomacy and gross blackmail against India."

For the second time in a decade, India had been embarrassed by a major world power. In 1962, they had been defeated quickly and handily at the hands of the Chinese Army, prompting an "obsessive" build-up of their land forces. Now, despite the absence of direct conflict, a major naval power had sailed into "their" contiguous international waters with relative impunity, causing them to recognize that even had they wanted to resist such an "incursion," they were relatively powerless (militarily) to do so. Consequently, since 1971, the Indians have sought to improve and modernize their Navy, much as they did with their army starting in 1962.

Despite competing national interests over the last 25 years, which have limited the funds available, both to the defense forces in general and the Navy in particular, the Indian Navy has been transformed from a small, "brown water" coastal defense force into formidable, comparatively-modern "blue water" fleet. Unlike the Indian Navy of 1971, the modern-day force is capable of projecting Indian military force throughout the Indian Ocean and South Asia, while protecting the country's national security interests.

NAVAL ROLES AND MISSIONS

Since 1971, India has sought to ensure its maritime safety and security by achieving and maintaining a "powerful, well-balanced, multi-purpose 'blue water' fleet." This fact is reflected in a mural on the outer walls of the Indian Navy's dockyard in Bombay, which depicts a naval force composed of surface ships, submarines, and aircraft, and bears the caption: "Three-Dimensional Navy." This Navy is charged with a number of imperatives. In general, it must protect the nation's almost 8,000 km of coastline, more than 300 island possessions, two million square kilometers of Exclusive Economic Zone (EEZ), and important sea lanes of communication, or SLOC's, which account for 97% of the country's external trade. Each of these taskings warrants discussion in additional detail.

The Indian coastline is not only home to the numerous seaports through which the country's life blood passes, but the western coast (in particular) contains vast oil fields, which account for about two-thirds of India's domestic oil production. The Indian island territories are of both strategic and economic importance to the country; their location is near vital major sea lanes (read trade routes), and they provide an advanced site from which the country can project its military power (if required) well beyond the shores of the Indian sub-continent. Also, the coral reefs adjacent to the Indian island chains contain fertile fishing grounds, which satisfy domestic food needs, while serving as a valuable source of foreign income. Both the oilfields and the fishing grounds lie well inside India's EEZ, as do other rich mineral deposits.

Also, the importance of maintaining free access along the SLOC's cannot be overstated. Although the dominant naval power in the region, the Indian Navy maintains that its role is not to dominate the Indian Ocean. Nevertheless, India feels a responsibility for ensuring free and unencumbered passage for ships of all nations throughout the world's third largest ocean, from the west coast of Africa to the Straits of Mallaca. The Indian Ocean represents one-fifth of the world's water mass, is bounded on its littoral shores by 47 countries, and serves as the transport route for 65 percent of the world's oil supply. By protecting the Indian Ocean's SLOC's, India can not only further its own national strategic national interests (i.e., free trade in support of a growing market economy), but can also help guarantee similar benefits for its littoral neighbors. In addition to providing a "persuasive deterrent" to superpower intervention in the Indian Ocean, India sees its Navy as a means of countering other specific, formidable threats to maritime security in the region. These include Pakistani attacks on Indian oil platforms in the Arabian Sea, the growing influence of China in the South Asia region, including the establishment of a surveillance station in the Bay of Bengal (located on the islands of Myanmar) and an expanding naval presence in the Indian Ocean, and attempted aggression in or against friendly littoral nations, which could threaten Indian influence in the region. Two examples of the latter, in which India played a suppression role, were an attempted coup in the Maldives in 1988, and a similar occurrence in nearby Sri Lanka.

The Indian Navy has also played an important role in the ecological well-being of the region, such as efforts to quickly contain a 40,000-ton oil spill in the Andaman Sea in 1989 which, without the quick intervention of Indian naval and

Coast Guard units, could have destroyed wildlife as far away as Malaysia, Thailand and Indonesia. Only recently has the Indian Navy shown signs of relaxing its isolationist philosophy in certain areas. India and the United States have conducted two major, joint naval exercises in the 1990's, and a third one is scheduled for 1996.

These are apparently the first significant joint naval exercises that India has ever engaged in with a major navy, and have helped open the door for similar exercises with other countries. Ironically, despite the strong Soviet influence evident in Indian Navy hardware, the two countries have apparently never engaged in a major naval exercise. A senior representative of the Indian Navy summarized this change in philosophy: "the situation with the United States has changed; we are no longer at arm's length, are trying to understand each other, and will be together in certain fights in the future."

NAVAL ORGANIZATION

The Indian Navy, under the command of the Chief of Naval Staff (CNS), located in New Delhi, is the world's seventh largest navy. It consists of two fleets, the Eastern Fleet, homeported primarily in Visakhapatnam, on the Bay of Bengal, and the Western Fleet, homeported primarily in Bombay, on the Arabian Sea. The Eastern Fleet tends to be composed primarily of older, former eastern block vessels, while the Western Fleet tends to be mostly newer, more capable ships, acquired primarily from western nations. In addition, to simplifying maintenance requirements by grouping like-class ships geographically, this postures the Indian Navy's most formidable weapons platforms closest to its most likely threat, Pakistan.

Regionally, there are three principal commands, each also commanded by a flag officer. These are the Eastern, Southern, and Western Naval Commands, located in Visakhapatnam, Cochin (on the southwestern coast), and Bombay. In addition to the principal commands, flag officers direct three large sub-commands: Naval Aviation and Goa Area (in Goa, on the western coast between Bombay and Cochin), Submarines (in Visakhapatnam), and the "Fortress" in the Andaman and

Nicobar Islands (Port Blair), located in the southeastern Bay of Bengal.

NAVAL FACILITIES

Each of the areas which is home to a principal command is also the location of a variety of naval and naval support facilities. On the east coast of India, the Visakhapatnam area includes a submarine base and the Navy's submarine school, several naval air facilities (including one well to the south, in Madras), the Navy's new recruit training facility, and a major dockyard (which was built with Soviet support, and is still being expanded). Other facilities in the region include the submarine VLF broadcast transmission facility, at Vijayaraghavapuram, and shipyard facilities further to the north in the Calcutta area, where frigates, corvettes, amphibious ships, and auxiliaries are constructed.

On India's west coast, the Cochin area is home to a naval air station, a ship repair yard, and the naval training command's professional schools. Further to the north, Goa is the site of the Indian Naval Academy (which may eventually be moved), various naval air facilities, as well as a shipyard which constructs some of the Navy's smaller vessels, including patrol and landing craft. Nearby Karwar has been selected as the site for a new naval base, which has been delayed, like many other projects, due to funding constraints. When complete, it will include "alongside berthing" for an aircraft carrier, and a new naval air station.

In the north, Bombay's naval facilities include a barracks and main dockyard with one aircraft carrier dock, submarine pens, the Navy's supply school, and a shipyard, where submarines, destroyers, frigates, and corvettes are constructed. Aside from those facilities located on the mainland of the Indian sub-continent, the Indian Navy maintains a distinct presence in each of its major island territories. At Lakshadweep, in the Laccadive Islands (about two hundred miles off of the southwest coast), there is a patrol craft base. Six to seven hundred miles to the southeast of Visakhapatnam, the Andaman and Nicobar Islands have their own respective limited support facilities, including a floating dock. Port Blair, in the northernmost of the two island chains, the Andaman's, is home to a naval air station.

NAVAL FORCES

Like most modern military arms, the Indian Navy's most important asset is its people. The Indian Navy numbers some 55,000 and is a professional, well-trained, allvolunteer force. Of the 55,000 officers and enlisted personnel, some 5,000 are members of the naval air arm, and another 1,000 are members of the relatively new Marine commando force, which was formed in 1986. The Indian Navy's amphibious mission is primarily in support of the Army (vice the Marines).

In fulfilling its roles and missions, the Indian Navy employs a variety of capable ships and aircraft acquired from both the east and the west, as well as an increasing number of indigenously-built platforms.

Because the naval portion of the defense budget has been in decline, fleet operational readiness has suffered. The latest edition of *Jane's Fighting Ships* reports that only about half of the country's aging fleet is "fully operational," with the remainder of the Indian Navy's ships considered only "seaworthy."

In addition to the varying "lineage" of the Navy's vessels, most can be considered "technological melting pots" in and of themselves, owing to the diverse producers of their various weapons and support systems.

Some vessels contain integrated systems from as many as eight different nations. The design source nation breakdown among Indian Navy ships' systems as of 1993 was as follows: Russia-41, Great Britain-35, India-27 (minimum), Germany and Holland-six each, and Sweden, Canada, France, Italy, and the United States—three each. To the credit of the Indian naval engineers, and not without the expenditure of significant time and expense, they have managed to satisfactorily resolve most compatibility problems among the various systems, and are able to send formidable warfighting platforms to sea with some regularity.

AIRCRAFT CARRIERS

The backbone of India's Navy is its carrier force, which consists of the INS Vikrant and the INS Viraat. The Vikrant (ex-Glory), with a range of 12,000 miles, was acquired from the United Kingdom in 1957, and the Viraat (ex-Hermes), with a more-restricted range of 6,500 miles, followed in 1986.

Both carriers routinely embark six Sea Harrier Vertical/ Short Takeoff and Landing (V/STOL) fighters and approximately eight Sea King Anti-Submarine Warfare (ASW) helicopters. In a wartime scenario, the carriers can embark 22 and 18 combat aircraft, respectively. Both carriers are ideally suited for two missions: supporting amphibious operations and conducting ASW.

Despite their age and range considerations, either carrier can effectively project naval and air power anywhere in the South Asia region. In that only the United States, Britain, France, Australia, and Russia possess one or more aircraft carriers, these two Indian ships may be viewed by other nations, especially their Indian Ocean neighbours, as much diplomatic tools as military ones.

Since Vikrant is expected to reach the end of its service life prior to the turn of the century, and Viraat is some 40 years old, India is reportedly pursuing procurement of at least one additional carrier of similar size. According to a senior representative of the Indian Navy, "the Indian Navy would like to have a total of two to four carriers; the question is just mastering the resources."

SUBMARINES

The Indian Navy has a highly formidable submarine force, consisting of 18 dieselpowered submarines, most of which are of Soviet origin. The most modern ships of the force are the four Shishumar (209) Class submarines, early-1980s vintage, Germandesigned ships, the first two of which were built in West Germany, with the latter two being built in Bombay. The primary advantages inherent in this class of ship are its long range, and higher speed. Also impressive are the Navy's eight, late-1980s vintage, quiet, Soviet-built Kilo Class submarines, perhaps the first class of submarines from any nation to possess a limited surface-to-air missile capability.

Finally, there are six, 1970s vintage, Soviet-built Foxtrot Class submarines, one of which is already being used as a "spare parts bin" for the other ships of the class, and all of which are due to be retired shortly. While all of the Navy's classes of submarines are ASW-capable, and carry both torpedoes and/or mines, all lack an anti-shipping missile capability, equivalent to that enjoyed by the Pakistani Navy.

Although the Indian Navy continues to show an interest in the development of a nuclear propulsion capability within its submarine force, and leased two Soviet Charlie Class SSGNs from 1988 to 1991, realization of an indigenously built, nuclear-powered attack submarine appears to be years away. Nonetheless, the importance of the submarine to India's future naval strategy was underscored in a statement by the Navy's former commander, Admiral S. N. Kohli, who stated, "India cannot be content to have the nuclear submarines of other countries prowling around the Indian Ocean and not be able to deter them in any way.

The presence of an Indian attack submarine would make them think twice before undertaking such a deployment." The strong emphasis on submarine warfare is also logical given the fact that the acoustic conditions in the Indian Ocean (varying and unpredictable thermal gradients and layers of varying salinity) favour submarine concealment.

MAJOR SURFACE COMBATANTS

In addition to its two carriers, the Indian Navy possesses 23 operational major surface combatants, five of which are destroyers, and the balance frigates. The most powerful escorts are the modern, Soviet-built, Rajput (Kashin II) Class destroyers, which have a formidable surface-to-surface, surface-to-air, and ASW capability. The most capable of the smaller frigates are the three, indigenously-built Godavari Class ships, which represent half of the total planned class; this is one of the classes which exploits a mix of technologies from various countries, and completion of the three follow-on vessels has been delayed by Russian equipment supply problems. Fielding the same basic warfighting capabilities of the Rajput Class, one advantage of the Godavari Class is its ability to carry two ASW helicopters, vice the standard one.

Combining the best of both classes in a larger, more capable vessel is another indigenously-built class of ship, the Delhi Class destroyer, which has not yet become operational due to a breakdown in the central control of Russian export equipment. The ship is being fitted with a combination of Russian and Indian weapons, though delays in obtaining the Russian systems may drive the Indians to seek technological relief from the west in outfitting future ships of the class.

Other classes of principal surface combatants include the Soviet-built Petya II Class frigate, the British-designed, Indian-built Nilgiri (Leander) Class frigate, and the modern, Indian-built Khukri Class corvette; all of these classes of ships have primarily an ASW role.

Smaller Combatants

Because of the very long coastline and island territories which it is responsible for patrolling, the Indian Navy has wisely built a capable contingent of 41 patrol and coastal combatants, primarily small corvettes (17), but also including missile craft (6) and inshore (11) and offshore (7) patrol craft. Most of the smaller vessels are less than 20 years old and most of the larger vessels are less than 10 years old.

The majority of the larger vessels are of Soviet design and manufacture, while the smaller vessels are indigenously built; the Sukanya Class offshore patrol ships represent an exception, having been designed and built (initially) in South Korea. Almost all of the larger vessels have at least a limited surface-to-surface and surface-to-air missile capability.

Amphibious Warfare Ships

The Indian Navy's amphibious arm (excluding the aforementioned role of the carriers) is only nine ships strong, namely one indigenously-built Magar Class LST (another ship of this class is planned) and eight Polish-built Polnochny Class LSMs. Both vessels have a range of over 2500 miles, and can carry several hundred troops.

While the Magar is less than ten years old and generally-reliable, some of the older, Polnochny Class vessels are almost 20 years old, and the entire class is under operational restrictions due to the lack of spare parts. While the Navy's amphibious capability has significantly-improved since 1971, having effectively supported the nation's regional peacekeeping interventions in the 1980's, given the material condition of many of its ships, its long-term reliability is questionable, as is its force projection effectiveness over great distances.

Auxiliary and Support Vessels

Of the 43 remaining ships in the Indian Navy, almost half (20) are Mine Countermeasures ships, mostly of Soviet origin, and are believed to be more than capable of keeping the waters surrounding India's major ports accessible in time of conflict.

Of the remaining vessels, there are only two large tankers, five small tankers, and one ex-Soviet submarine tender; the balance of the vessels is tugs and oceanographic research ships. It is this distinct shortage of replenishment vessels which has caused many to question the true extent of India's long-range power projection aspirations with a critical eye.

NAVAL AIRCRAFT

The naval air arm includes 68 combat aircraft and 75 armed helicopters. In addition to the carrier-borne Sea Harrier aircraft and Sea King helicopters, the shipborne naval air order of battle also includes several other highly-capable rotary-wing aircraft, including the Soviet-built Kamov KA-27 "Helix 'A'" ASW helicopter, which may also eventually carry anti-shipping missiles.

The Indian Navy also includes a substantial landbased maritime aircraft contingent, including the Soviet-built Illyushin IL-38 "May" ASW maritime patrol aircraft (3800+ nautical mile range) and the Tupelov TU-142M "Bear 'F'" long-range (6700+ nautical mile range) surveillance and ASW aircraft. Both aircraft carry extensive weapons and sensor suites. The Navy also has a Maritime strike squadron of 12 SEPECAT/HAL Jaguar International fighter/bombers, capable of employing anti-ship missiles, and is considering another Russian fighter, the SU-27 "Flanker," for future purchase if the budget permits.

INDIA'S NAVAL FUTURE

Over the past 25 years, India has frequently demonstrated the commitment to exercising unsurpassed naval leadership within the Indian Ocean and South Asia regions. However, how well this record and vision will translate to future success remains to be foreseen. Two significant areas warrant special attention, with the common potential stumbling block being budget constraints.

Readiness

The operational readiness of the fleet is reported to be as low as 50 percent. Various factors play into this problem. There are aging ships, previously purchased from countries such as the Soviet Union, for which repair parts are not readily available. Those parts which are available, especially in the case of the Russian suppliers, are generally provided on a "cash and carry" basis, due to severe economic problems in Russia. The competing interests, not only within India as a whole, but also within the Indian Navy, mean that not all material problems can be promptly resolved.

Contributing to this problem is the difficulty of system compatibility between parts produced in different countries. In other words, although a similar component may be available more cheaply, or on credit, from another supplier, it may ultimately be more expensive, both in time and money, to purchase that part, and then have to "re-engineer" it to make it compatible with the existing system. On a larger scale, this compatibility problem also exists on newer, indigenously-built ships, where the procurement of suitable sensors or weapons systems from various suppliers is only half the battle—making them work together effectively as a system of systems is often even more costly than buying them all from a common source.

Procurement is not the only material readiness problem the Indian Navy faces. Both the quality, and in some cases, the integrity, of workmanship have come into question. The Indian shipbuilders have proven a lack of technical expertise in accomplishing difficult tasks, such as the welding of the high-tensile steel in submarine hulls, or the potential manufacture of glass-reinforced plastic (GRP) for minesweeper hulls. Also, there have been accusations that former dockyard officers of middle rank, who started small civilian companies to do naval contract work, supplied substandard materials with the intent of winning follow-on contracts.

A secondary aim of India's indigenous shipbuilding program has been to boost the country's economy through exports. The cost overruns and suspect products for which problems such as these bode are not likely to foster confidence among, or sales to, interested countries. Also, much as material readiness has directly affected operational readiness, it is conceivable that fiscal limitations could also start to directly affect training readiness; upon reflection, it is inevitable that training readiness has already been indirectly affected by the inability of many crews to get underway and gain valuable atsea operating proficiency, for which there is no true substitute in the shore training environment.

At the "macro" level, the question of readiness can be extended to the discussion of whether or not a service's assets, given that they can get underway on-demand, and are trained proficiently to accomplish their mission, are really "ready" if they are limited by such factors as endurance and capacity. As previously discussed, the Indian Navy probably lacks the auxiliary support assets to effectively and continuously engage in a prolonged conflict distant to its continental shores. Depending on the location and the nature of the conflict, amphibious lift could also prove to be constraining.

Modernization

The importance of India's aircraft carriers as both political and military instruments has been highlighted, as has been the fact that both are growing "weary." This is perhaps the best example of the imperative to modernize which the Indian Navy faces. At the systems-level, the most glaring need of the Indian Navy is to upgrade its surface-tosurface missile capability, both with respect to range and survivability, in order to meet the current threat presented by other powers in the region.

In 1992, Chief of Naval Staff L. Ramdas mandated a re-balancing of India's naval forces from two-thirds small and medium-sized ships, to 60 percent larger, sea control ships. percent small combatants, thereby precipitating the country's ambitious, indigenous shipbuilding program. The long-term commitment to an indigenous shipbuilding program was reiterated more recently by a senior representative of the Indian Navy, who acknowledged that although it may be cheaper to purchase ships abroad, "India must be willing to pay the price to stand on its 'own two feet.'"

It is becoming apparent, however, for the reasons discussed in the previous section, that indigenous production will probably not meet all of India's near term shipreplacement needs, especially in the areas of modern, missile-armed vessels and a replacement or additional aircraft carrier. It is vital that this be recognized, and key decisions be addressed regarding the direction of the Navy's modernization program. Specifically, if India is not willing to settle for "less" in both quantity and quality from a sub-optimal indigenous shipbuilding program, then perhaps the government should be willing to spend the money to meet the military shortfall elsewhere. If the future decision to import ships is made, India must then make some hard political choices regarding its future alliances, and whether its commitments should be toward the east or the west. One commitment that seems, at least "on the surface" (no pun intended), to have remained reasonably firm throughout the past decade is India's desire to someday indigenously produce a nuclear-powered attack submarine. The cognizant program, alluded to earlier in the force capabilities section, is best known as the Advanced Technology Vessel (ATV) program. The model for the ATV is the Russian Charlie Class SSGN, two of which the Indians operated for three years. The 2500-ton Indian vessel will be a Russian-designed ship with an Indian pressurized-water reactor (PWR). There is thought to be a land-based prototype of the PWR already in existence. According to speculation in open sources, laydown is anticipated in 1997 in Visakhapatnam, with the Russians providing technical assistance during the building process. The ATV is expected to be outfitted with the Indian Sargarika cruise missile, also currently under development. Currently, the ATV Program is thought to have priority over the procurement of an additional (or replacement) aircraft carrier.

When questioned about the prognosis for the ATV program, and specifically, when India could be expected to have an operational, nuclear-powered submarine, a senior representative of the Indian Navy responded that he was "not authorized to comment on the subject." This fuels speculation by other sources that a nuclear-powered submarine is not in India's immediate naval future.

SUMMARY

This chapter has reviewed the history of the Indian Navy, detailed its current roles and capabilities, and examined its future course. For it to remain a credible force, maximum readiness and an aggressive modernization program must become top priorities of not only this proud, professional force, but more importantly, the Indian government. The bottom line is simple: "everything has its price." At a time when the Indian defense budget as a whole is dwindling in favour of other national interests, and the Navy has the smallest portion of the three major services to begin with, a significant financial commitment is required to effect the required improvements. This paper has detailed some of the key decisions which Indian politicians must realistically (and quickly) face if the "ship is to remain on course." The outcome of those decisions will significantly impact the future of a service, if not ultimately, the destiny of an aspiring nation and its sea-faring people.

TRENDS IN NAVAL POWER IN SOUTH ASIA AND THE INDIAN OCEAN

During the past year (1995), there was no change in the order of naval forces in South Asia and the Indian Ocean, in terms of the strengths of their principal combatants (Table I). Amongst the twelve indigenous navies of the region possessing major surface and sub-surface combatants, India continued to remain the largest, followed by Pakistan, Australia, Indonesia, Iran, and Thailand. In view of the number and nature of major warships planned to be acquired in the near future by countries such as Australia, Thailand, and Singapore, the position of naval forces is expected to change next year.

The most notable will be that of the Royal Thai Navy, which is planning to launch its first aircraft carrier early this year. The 11,500-tonne carrier, presently being built in Spain, is scheduled to be commissioned into the Thai Navy in July 1997. This will result in the possession of carriers by two countries of the Indian Ocean littoral. The most significant aspect of the expansion/modernisation of South Asian and Indian Ocean navies last year was in terms of submarine forces. As clearly evident from Table I, major submarine acquisitions have been planned, and are presently being implemented. In effect, a dramatic increase is expected to take place in the number of patrol submarines operated by the littoral states of the Indian Ocean within the next six or seven years.

The maritime reconnaissance/strike capabilities of the navies in South Asia and the Indian Ocean also underwent major developments during the past year. This was primarily in relation to the formalisation of the new international Law of the Sea in late 1994. During the past year, China continued to maintain a keen interest in the seas around India. The nature and extent of Chinese activities in Myanmar could lead to a Chinese naval presence in the Indian Ocean in the near future.

Amongst the extra-regional naval forces in the Indian Ocean, the most important development last year was the creation, for the first time ever, of a permanently deployed American fleet for a part of the Indian Ocean. These developments have serious implications for Indian security and the Indian Navy. Simply put, the declining force levels of the Indian Navy are clearly in contradiction to the major trends apparent for naval forces in the Indian Ocean.

MAJOR INDIGENOUS NAVAL FORCES IN SOUTH ASIA AND THE INDIAN OCEAN

Country	*Carriers*	*Patrol Subs*	*Destroyers*	*Frigates*	*Copters*	*Aircraft*	*Manpower*
INDIA	2	16(2)	5(3)	14(3)	63	68	54000
PAKISTAN	0	6(3)	3	8(?)	13	15	22800
AUSTRALIA	0	3(6)	3	8(8)	29	129	13670
INDONESIA	0	2(2)	0	17	47	43	30000
IRAN	0(1)	2(1)	2	3	32	11	18000
THAILAND	0	0	0	12(3)	33	33	43000
SAUDI ARABIA	0	0	0	4(2)	42	0	12000
BANGLADESH	0	0	0	4(1)	0	0	8050
MALAYSIA	0	0	0	2(2)	12	4	12000
SOUTH AFRICA	0	3	0	0	10	20	5034
IRAQ	0	0	0	1	0	0	2000
SINGAPORE	0	0(1)	0	0	0	8	4000

Note: Figures in brackets denote warships planned.

TRENDS IN SUBMARINE FORCES

During the past year, significant developments have taken place to enhance submarine capabilities in the Indian Ocean. These relate to the modernisation and expansion of existing submarine forces, as well as the acquisition of submarines by navies of the region for the first time.

In effect, a dramatic increase is expected to take place in the number of patrol submarines operated by the littoral states of the Indian Ocean within the next six or seven years (Table II). At present, six Indian Ocean littoral states maintain active submarine arms in their navies. The largest is that of the Indian Navy, which consists of sixteen diesel-electric submarines. This is followed by the six conventional submarines of the Pakistani Navy, and those of Australia (3), South Africa (3), Indonesia (2), and Iran (2).

Amongst these navies, Pakistan and Australia maintained active submarine construction programmes in 1995, while South Africa carried out a major upgrade programme. Meanwhile, Singapore finally decided to start a submarine arm for its navy, and India planned to build additional submarines in the country.

Pakistan's submarine construction programme was the result of a substantial naval arms agreement with France in late September 1994, worth about a billion U.S. dollars. This contracted for the construction of three advanced technology Agosta 90-B diesel-electric submarines for Pakistan. These new 1,700-tonne boats are to possess a vast amount of sophisticated technology, including a closed-cycle steam turbine MESMA Air Independent Propulsion (AIP) system to enhance the submerged endurance of the submarine, as well as a number of lethal Exocet SM-39 underwater launched anti-ship missiles. Both the AIP system and the anti-ship missiles are to be exported by France for the first time.

In terms of the agreement, the first submarine is to be built in France, the second will be built in France but assembled in Pakistan, while the third boat will be built in Pakistan with the transfer of a substantial technology package. The keel of the first submarine was laid at the DCN shipyard in Cherbourg in France in the autumn of 1995. The boat, yet to be named, is scheduled to be launched in late 1997, and commissioned about a year later. Meanwhile, the Karachi Shipyard and Engineering Works (KSEW) also began making preparations for the work to be carried out on the second and third submarines. This will entail building considerable specialised infrastructure for submarine assembly and construction. The second and third submarines was commissioned into the Pakistani Navy in 1999 and 2002. By this time its four old Daphne-class submarines would have begun to decommission.

During 1995, Australia launched the second of its planned six Collins-class submarines, and continued to carry out the sea trials of the first boat of this class. The commissioning of this 3,000-tonne submarine, launched in August 1993, has been delayed from November 1995 to early 1996. Although it is believed to have performed well in the trials conducted so far, difficulties relating to the software of its highly sophisticated combat system have been reported. The construction of these Swedish Kockums Type 471 submarines in Australia, as a replacement for the ageing Oberon-class boats, was the result of a major naval arms agreement in June 1987. All the six submarines, to be armed with torpedoes and anti-ship missiles, are expected to be commissioned into the Australian Navy by the end of the decade. This would coincide with the decomissioning of the Navy's three remaining Oberon submarines.

During 1995, the South African Navy carried out a major upgrade programme to improve the combat effectiveness of its three Oberon-class submarines. In the wake of the 1988 upgrade programme, which focused on electronic systems, the 1995 programme emphasised the full integration of the boats' system, as well as improved supportability.

The upgrade programme underway emphasises the use of software-driven systems as well as commercial off-the-shelf components. This includes the total revamp of the sonar system, the modernisation of the search and attack periscopes, and extensive work on the Electronic Support Measures (ESM) sub-system. In addition, new action information systems, navigation systems, and communications suite, have been acquired for the submarines. The first completely upgraded system in the Navy's Oberon-class submarine continues to undergo operational test and evaluation. They are expected to keep the three submarines operational through the year 2005, by which time replacement submarines are expected to be commissioned.

Over the years, Singapore's plans for the acquisition of submarines appeared to be the most ambitious amongst the Indian Ocean littoral states of South-east Asia. At various times in the past, it had conveyed an interest in leasing two small 800-tonne boats, in addition to buying four larger new construction boats, by the end of the decade. Finally, in late September 1995, Singapore decided to purchase a second hand 1200-tonne diesel electric submarine from Sweden. This is the first time that Singapore will be operating a submarine in its navy. The Kockums Type A-12 submarine, launched in 1967, is armed only with torpedoes, not anti-ship missiles. In view of this decision, Singapore is not expected to acquire any German HDW Type 206 submarines for the time being.

Meanwhile, in January 1995 the Thai government came close to giving final approval to a programme for the purchase of two or three modern submarines for the Navy. Quite unexpectedly, this proposal ran into some difficulty, with the budgetary request being delayed in Cabinet. Later in the year, the proposal for the submarines appeared to be ready for approval. In this respect, at least four European submarine builders had submitted bids to the Royal Thai Navy by the end of the year. These comprised DCN of France, HDW of Germany, Kockums of Sweden, and RDM-VSEL of the Netherlands and Britain. In addition, Russia's Kilo-class submarines are also expected to compete for the order. Moreover, the submarines finally chosen are expected to be equipped with American technologies and sub-systems. In January 1995, the American administration eased restrictions on American companies seeking to provide such items to South-East Asia. As a result, companies like the Loral Corporation have already begun to market submarine fire control and navigation systems to Thailand.

During the past year, Iran continued to wait in vain for the delivery of its third Kilo-class submarine ordered from Russia. Although it officially maintained that the transfer could be expected any time, it does not appear likely to take place due to heightened American sensitivities over the deal. Nonetheless, Iran proved it had overcome the problems associated with its submarine batteries by carrying out major naval exercise during the year involving the Kilo-class boats.

Although the Malaysian government approved the acquisition of four patrol submarines for its navy-two new construction and two older boats-as early as 1990, its decision remained to be implemented in 1995.

The delivery of two additional submarines for Indonesia from Germany also did not take place last year.

At the annual Navy Day press conference held towards the end of last year, the Chief of the Indian Navy, Admiral V.S. Shekhawat, stated that the construction of two additional HDW submarines would commence soon at the country's Mazagon shipyard in Bombay. This would, in effect, complete the abruptly concluded 1981 order with HDW for six submarines (in view of the financial scandal which erupted in the late 1980s). According to the United Nations Conventional Arms Register, a full submarine kit had already been tranferred from Germany to India in 1992. This decision of the government will rejuvenate submarine construction facilities at the shipyard, lying idle for nearly four years, since the launch of the second indigenously-constructed HDW submarine in 1992. As the year ended, considerable speculation remained over the transfer of possibly two, but as many as six, additional Kilo-class Type 636 submarines from Russia to India.

In view of the diesel-electric submarines planned (including those currently being built) or those projected, some 24-30 boats were commissioned into the navies of the Indian Ocean littoral by the year 2002-2003. This could increase to 53 the number of submarines operated by these countries alone, from the 32 at present.

TRENDS IN SUBMARINE FORCES

Figures are for Conventional Diesel Powered Submarines

COUNTRY	*1995*	**Planned / Projected*	***Total in 2002-03*
INDIA	16	2	14
PAKISTAN	6	3	5
AUSTRALIA	3	6	6
SOUTH AFRICA	3	0	3
INDONESIA	2	3	5
IRAN	2	1	2(3)
SINGAPORE	0	4 to 6	4(6)
THAILAND	0	3	3
MALAYSIA	0	2 to 4	2(4)
SAUDI ARABIA	0	2 to 4	2(4)
TOTAL	32	26 to 32	46(53)

** SSKs Planned (and Projected) by the Year 2002/3*

*** SSKs in 2002-03*

TRENDS IN MARITIME RECONNAISSANCE/STRIKE CAPABILITIES

The past year was one of the most important in the tumultuous thirteen year history of the Law of the Sea. It was during this period that the International Seabed Authority (ISA) came into existence, and the maritime zones of littoral countries could be further extended in less than ten years to 300 nautical miles from the 200 nautical miles delineated so far.

These developments came in the wake of the formalisation of the international law of the Sea in late 1994. The ISA was of special importance to India as it was the only littoral country of the Indian Ocean to have marked a 150,000 sq. km. site in the area, off Cochin, for the exploitation of polymetallic nodules from the seabed in the future. On the other hand, the potential extension of a country's Exclusive Economic Zone (EEZ) by 100 nautical miles, on the basis of a preliminary exploration of the additional zone, focused considerable attention on the maritime reconnaissance/strike (MR/S) capabilities of a number of countries of the Indian Ocean region. At present, eight littoral states of the Indian Ocean maintain dedicated MR/S capabilities in their Air Force or Navy. The largest is that of Australia, which operates a fleet of 19 Lockheed P-3C Orion Maritime Patrol Aircraft (MPA), armed with lethal anti-ship missiles, in its Air Force. This is followed by the maritime strike capabilities of the Pakistani Navy, the Royal Thai Navy, and the Iranian Navy.

Other countries possessing maritime reconnaissance/Anti-Submarine Warfare (ASW) capabilities, include the Indian Navy, the Indonesian Navy, the Malaysian Navy, and the Sri Lankan Navy. Amongst these countries, both Pakistan and Thailand expanded their maritime MR/S capabilities in 1995, while Australia prepared for an extensive refurbishment of its Orion MPAs. The Pakistani Navy's MR/S force of four Dassault Breguet Atlantic aircraft since late 1988, expanded in 1995 through the order for French submarines, as well as the passage of the Hank Brown Amendment in the American Congress. In a bid to induce Pakistan to acquire French submarines in late

1994, France agreed to supply three additional Atlantic aircraft to Pakistan. Although these aircraft were ostensibly to be used for spares for the Atlantics already in the Pakistani Navy, it appears that this did not take place. Reports in 1995 indicated that the aircraft were in store and available for use when required.

In addition, the most important and lethal of the American arms and equipment provided to Pakistan through the Brown Amendment in late 1995, consisted of three P-3C-II Orion MPAs, along with their complement of Harpoon anti-ship missiles. Pakistani pilots have already been trained on this aircraft prior to 1990, when their transfer was barred in view of the Pressler Amendment. It is expected, therefore, that these aircraft will commence patrolling the Arabian Sea soon after transfer. In effect, Pakistan's MR/S capability more than doubled in 1995, from a force of four aircraft to that of ten. Moreover, the Orions provide major advantages over the Atlantics in terms of both reach and strike capability.

These factors essentially enable the Pakistani Navy to conduct offensive maritime air operations on a far greater scale and depth than ever before. During 1995, the Royal Thai Navy also acquired two more P-3A Orion MPAs for its naval air force. This brought the total number of Orions in the Thai navy to five. Meanwhile, the Australian Air Force began preparing for a major avionics and structural upgrade of all its P-3C Orion MPAs. This would be carried out in batches from 1997 to about the year 2001, and is expected to extend the life of the force till at least the year 2015. The programme also includes the purchase of associated ground-based facilities, and three ex-U.S. Navy P-3Bs that are being converted to training aircraft. The upgrade programme will involve the employment of a new radar; a modern acoustic processing system; and a new data management system.

THE CHINESE NAVY IN THE INDIAN OCEAN

During the past year, warships of the People's Liberation Army-Navy (PLA Navy) did not venture into the Indian Ocean, nor pay goodwill visits to ports in the area, which they had done twice in the recent past-in 1986-1987 and 1993. Nonetheless, other developments in the region continued to indicate increased Chinese interest in the seas around India, which could lead to sustained Chinese naval activity in the area in the near future. These developments essentially focus on China's assistance in the construction and use of naval facilities in Myanmar. These facilities would augment considerably the ability of the PLA Navy to operate in the Indian Ocean.

They could permit shipping in the area to be monitored, and provide Chinese warships docking, resupply, and maintenance facilities, thereby enhancing their combat capability in the Indian Ocean. Since the middle of 1992, reports have persistently indicated Chinese assistance in the construction of naval and electronic facilities in Myanmar. These essentially relate to the construction of deep-water facilities and additional infrastructure at the naval base on Hianggyi island at the mouth of the Bassein river, the modernisation of existing naval facilities at Akyab and Mergui, and the establishment and operation of a Signals Intelligence (SIGINT) station at Great Coco island. Although early assessments indicate that the Hianggyi base, when finally completed, will be too small to host Chinese surface warships of the size required for effective operations in the Indian Ocean, it may just be too soon to reach such a conclusion.

Moreover, the activities being carried out could be used to support diesel-electric submarines being transferred from Russia in a major naval arms agreement finalised last year. In terms of the agreement, China initially plans to acquire four, but possibly as many as ten, Kilo-class submarines at a rate of one to two boats a year. The first submarine of this type was transferred to China last year, with the second to be delivered early this year. Chinese activities on the strategically located Great Coco island, at a distance of only some 30 nautical miles from the Indian Andaman chain of islands, is of particular concer. In 1993, some 70 Chinese naval and engineering personnel are believed to have arrived on the island to assist in the installation of a new radar facility. This could enable

China to monitor Indian naval communications in the area, and possibly even India's missile tests off its eastern coast. China is also upgrading Myanmarese naval facilities at Akyab, and port facilities at Mergui.

In addition, Myanmar has agreed to the presence of Chinese military instructors on its territory to provide training to its armed forces personnel. The strong defence relationship between the two countries can also be seen from the nature and extent of Chinese arms transfers to Myanmar recently. The initial 1 billion U.S. dollar arms deal in 1992 was followed by a further deal of 400 million U.S. dollars in 1994. This new agreement includes six Hainan-class patrol ships and a number of small gunboats for its Navy. Myanmar already operates 10 ex-Chinese Hainan-class ships, and is reportedly negotiating with China for the purchase of two missile-armed Jianghu-class frigates. If this naval transfer does come through, it will represent the first time that Myanmar will operate warships of this size and nature.

Intensification of Chinese activity in the Andaman Sea can also be seen from the success of the Indian Coast Guard in August 1994, when it apprehended three Chinese trawlers, flying the Myanmarese flag, in Indian waters off Narcondam island. Aboard the trawlers were several detailed charts clearly identifying hydrographic details of the waters around the Andaman islands. The trawlers were believed to have been heading towards the Great Coco island. It is clearly not perceived that China will be granted exclusive control over the naval base in Hanggyi or the SIGINT facility on Great Coco island. However, in view of its military relationship with Myanmar, it is expected to be granted some sort of access to the former, and receive data from the latter. The extent to which Myanmar at present is sharing India-related intelligence data with China is not known.

THE U.S. FIFTH FLEET IN THE INDIAN OCEAN

The establishment last year of an independent U.S. fleet for operations in the Persian Gulf is of considerable strategic importance to the naval balance in the Indian Ocean. This is the first time ever that the U.S. has especially created a permanently deployed fleet for any part of the Indian Ocean. The force levels and capabilities of the Fifth fleet, along with associated infrastructure and logistical support facilities, will clearly increase American naval and military presence in the area. Since the end of the Second World War, warships drawn from both the Second Fleet in the Mediterranean Sea, and the Seventh Fleet in the Pacific Ocean, have been deployed for operations in the Indian Ocean. During the 1971 Indo-Pakistani war, for instance, the American aircraft-carrier led naval task force which entered the Bay of Bengal was drawn from the Seventh Fleet.

The American naval presence in the Indian Ocean has now been reinforced by the Fifth Fleet for the Persian Gulf, warships of the Seventh Fleet deployed in the Indian Ocean, additional rotationally deployed forces, and forward stationed forces in the area. The Fifth fleet created last year is quite different from the fleet of the same name which operated in the Pacific Ocean, but was disbanded soon after the conclusion of the Second World War.

The new Fifth fleet was activated in July 1995, with its headquarters located at Mina Sulman in Bahrain. It will come under the operational jurisdiction of the Commander of U.S. Naval Forces, Central Command, Vice-Admiral John S. Redd. Its area of responsibility includes the Red Sea, the Gulf of Aden, and the western part of the Indian Ocean. The United States has officially justified the creation of the fleet on the basis that it is essentially symbolic in nature, to reinforce America's long-term military commitment to the region. It is stated, therefore, that American military force levels in the region will not increase, but simply be consolidated. However, in view of American naval strategy and shifting force levels, this explanation does not appear credible. A major aim of American policy, as enunciated in the February 1995 document on "U.S. National Security Strategy of Engagement and Enlargement", is to enhance the security of the country, to be achieved by the maintenance of a strong defence capability and the promotion of cooperative security measures.

In this endeavour, American naval doctrine in the post-Cold War world has undergone a dramatic transformation. From its focus on open-ocean war fighting on the sea, it has increasingly shifted to one of power projection and the employment of naval forces from the sea, in order to influence events in the littoral regions of the world. This strategic concept has been further expanded to encompass the employment of naval expeditionary forces and joint operation missions. In essence, therefore, the creation of the Fifth fleet represents this fundamental aspect of American naval policy, and ought not to be seen simply as a symbolic act. This is especially true for the two countries in the region with which it has hostile relations, Iraq and Iran.

Moreover, the nature and extent of the force level associated with the Fifth fleet has not been clearly defined. In effect, over the years there has been a major increase in the number of warships and naval aircraft associated with Central Command in the Persian Gulf. While the U.S. Central Command, with Headquarters at MacDill Air Force Base in Florida, clearly did not have a fleet under its command till less than a year ago, it used to take over command of naval forces deployed in the region. On average, this comprised a single carrier battle group, consisting of five principal surface combatants (including an aircraft carrier), two nuclear-powered submarines, and one support ship. On the activation of the Fifth fleet in July 1995, it comprised 15 warships including the aircraft carrier USS Abraham Lincoln. By early September, this force had doubled to comprise 31 ships. This increase was due partly to the arrival of seven military sealift vessels, which arrived in the Gulf at the end of August as part of the US deployment. They carried heavy weapons and equipment for a 17,000 man Marine expeditionary force and 5,000 man mechanised army brigade.

Furthermore, by the middle of September, American naval forces in the Gulf had increased to some 43 warships, including support ships; albeit on a temporary basis, in view of the joint exercises held with Kuwaiti forces. The departure of the single American aircraft carrier from the Persian Gulf in the middle of October, for just over a two month period, was compensated for by the deployment of an additional five warships in the area, along with under 30 fighter and transport aircraft at Sheik Eissa airbase in southern Bahrain. Moreover, the inherent firepower of the warships in the Gulf, in terms of their capability to launch guided weapons such as the Tomahawk cruise missile, had increased by 200% since the end of the Gulf war in 1991, according to an official statement of the U.S. Navy issued in late 1995.

IMPLICATIONS FOR THE INDIAN NAVY

During the past year, the only major ship acquired by the Indian Navy was an old Leander-class frigate from Britain for training purposes. This appeared consistent with the pattern of naval acquisitions in the past few years. For the past eight years, since the beginning of 1988, the Navy has not acquired a single principal surface combatant, either from abroad or the shipyards within the country. In terms of the sub-surface force, only four submarines have been commissioned into the Navy in the past six years. This situation is due primarily to the severe budgetary crisis faced by the armed forces, and particularly the Navy, since about 1990-1991. This will result in a massive decrease in the number of principal combatants of the Navy in the near future. According to a reliable estimate, this could be as much as a fifth of the total force of principal combatants; from 37 at present to 29 in the next four years by the year 2000, if no major warships are acquired from abroad.

Moreover, the scheduled decommissioning of the two aircraft carriers (the first towards the end of the year, and the second in six or seven years) in the absence of any replacement in place, will effectively end the Navy's balanced force structure, and capacity for blue water operations. In effect, a major change in naval doctrine and tactics will have to be thought out, prior to a major compensatory programme of naval acquisitions. The major trends in submarines and maritime reconnaissance/strike forces in the Indian Ocean point to the need to maintain a carrier arm in the Indian Navy for effective Anti-Submarine Warfare (ASW) and naval air operations. The modernization of the submarine arm is clearly another priority concer. While the recent statement of the naval chief is welcomed, it needs to be taken much further, in view especially of the emerging challenges to be faced from the Chinese Navy.

The interest displayed by China in the Indian Ocean, especially in terms of the construction and use of naval facilities in Myanmar, indicates the possibility of a Chinese naval presence in the area in the near future. Initially, the Indian Navy would primarily need to be prepared to deal with Chinese submarines in the Bay of Bengal. In the absence of any effective carrier-launched ASW force, this task would assume nightmarish proportions. The U.S. Fifth fleet in the Indian Ocean will remain a potential source of concern to the Indian Navy. While it may not directly attempt to influence Indian naval operations, the permanency of its presence signifies highly sophisticated weapon sytems and far superior firepower in proximity to Indian waters. The nature of the political relationship between the two countries will determine the level of rhetoric to which the Fifth fleet will periodically be subjected to in public. Nonetheless, further developments in relation to it need to be watched carefully in India.

Transparency in the number and nature of warships in the fleet should be encouraged, and would be welcomed by the Indian Navy. The year ahead promises to be far more important for the Indian Navy than the past year. Notwithstanding the general elections scheduled for the year, major acqusitions for the Navy are expected to be decided, including that of a replacement aircraft carrier. The naval budget for 1996-1997 is correspondingly expected to rise even further in real terms than the budget provided the previous year. More important, the decisions taken during the year will have a critical bearing on the size and nature of the Indian Navy in the early part of the next century.

THE STRATEGIC VISION OF INDIAN NAVY

Indian Maritime Doctrine was formally announced in April-2004. However, the year-2006 'Navy Day' is considered to be as the day, once Indian Navy actually started, "transforming itself from a 'brown water' coastal defense force to a formidable 'blue water' fleet." Blue water navy has indeed two connotations:

the technical and the political. Technically, a naval force having the capability to operate 200 nautical miles (320 km) from its sea shore into the deep sea on the longer ranges can be graded as the blue water navy. However, politically, it is the long range extension of the state's presence, as the former Indian Navy Chief of Staff, Admiral Jayant Nadkarni once said that, "legitimate use…of a Blue Water navy is power projection which is necessary" for a "power like India."

Indeed, India started expanding its naval fleet in early 1990s after conceiving the concept of blue water navy. Since 1998, India is regularly improving its naval doctrine. In 1998, Indian Navy issued; "The Maritime Dimension-A Naval Vision." This document set the mission for Indian Navy as, a force capable to operate in the open seas.

In April 2004, a formal Indian Maritime Doctrine of 148 pages was proclaimed. The doctrine clearly lay dawn the future strategic vision of the Indian Navy with the subtitle as; The Maritime Dimension-A Naval Vision. Through the Vision Statement, Indian Navy gave a Roadmap to Transformation in October 2006. In 2007, with the mission to 'Freedom to Use the Seas': India's Maritime Military Strategy (IMMS) was issued. Since 1998, an Indian maritime vision has the dedicated support including the enhanced budget allocation from the successive governments; initially the NDA Government under BJP and later the Congress lead UPA Government.

Indeed, the Indian Maritime Doctrine-2004 has been formulated on the basis of strategic concept given by US Navy Admiral Mahan, to the United States President Roosevelt for the domination of oceans especially the Pacific Ocean to gain the status of a major power.

Admiral Mahan had a vision that domination of Pacific would give US an edge over the other states geopolitically as well as geo-economically. According to Mahan, "the convergence there of so many ships…will constitute a centre of commerce, inter-oceanic encounters between states. It was one whose approaches will be watched jealously, and whose relations to the other centres of the Pacific by the (maritime) lines joining it to them must be examined carefully."

In the historical perspective, what Admiral Mahan had visualized for US Navy in the Pacific towards the end of 19th century, Indian Navy desires to achieve through the domination of Indian Ocean and surrounding waters by the end of first quarter of 21st century. India in fact desires the Indian Ocean to become 'India Ocean' and the way US entered the club of global powers in the beginning of the 20th century; India does the same in 21st century. Otherwise India considered the Indian Ocean as the part of its extended neighbourhood, where Indian Navy will safeguard its "diplomatic, security and economic interests".

Salient features of the Indian Maritime Doctrine-2004 include, controlling the choke points, significant islands and trade routes in the Indian Ocean, Arabian Sea and in the Bay of Bengal. The doctrine further lays down limits of the vision for the Indian Navy for the first quarter of 21st century as to; "look at the arc from the Persian Gulf to the Straits of Malacca as a legitimate area of interest." The doctrine also highlighted the Indian Navy as the "three-dimensional blue water force", having the potential to undertake significant assignments and roles "on the surface, underwater, and in the air." During the peace time, Indian navy will have to undertake the naval diplomatic assignments for the promotion of its cause. However, the proactive role of the Indian Navy would be the projection of its power beyond the limits of Indian shores. It has to counter the "distant emerging threats and protect extended 'Sea Lines of Communication' through and from the Indian Ocean."

In the regional perspective, as perceived Indian Navy has to operate against the navies of Pakistan and China. The doctrine however, "calls for a stronger deterrent capability against foreign intervention by non-littoral navies, not limited to China and Pakistan only. This strategic reach indeed call for procurement of more sophisticated diesel and nuclear capable submarines, establishing aircraft carrier and developing new cruise missiles. Indian Navy, currently operating in area of over 3.5 million square kilometres (extending from the Arabian Sea through Indian Ocean to the Bay of Bengal) is being modernized through the procurement of modern submarines, frigates and other naval vessels in collaboration with its Western allies, US, Israel and Russia.

With respect to the strategic designs of the Indian Navy, as 'Oceanic Navy', it has assumed for itself, "the primary responsibility lying on the Indian Navy to guard the steel ring created by Singapore, Ceylon, Mauritius and Socotra...the Indian Ocean must therefore remain truly Indian." With this strategic thought, the Indian Navy Vision Statement (2006), clearly laid down the role for Indian Navy as, "of safeguarding our maritime interests on the high seas and projecting combat power across (and around) the (Indian Ocean) littoral." Covering these wide ranging naval interests of India, Indian Premier Dr. Manmohan Singh said that, "our strategic footprint covers...to the far reaches of the Indian Ocean. Awareness of this reality should inform and animate our strategic thinking and defence planning."

In order to meet its energy needs and for its burgeoning economic drive as a great power status, securing the extended sea lines of communication from the Gulf to Southeast Asia is essential for the Indian Navy. In the wording of former Indian Naval Chief, Admiral Sureesh Mehta; "we are not only looking at countering threats but to protect the country's economic and energy interests.

This task has extended our area of operations. This might necessitate our operating in distant waters. As the Indian economy grows, the country is making increasing investments in distant places to ensure the availability of energy flow to maintain this growth. This is gradually defining what may be called our secondary area of maritime interest."

Through yet another revised Maritime Doctrine of 2009, Indian Navy has made major changes in its 2004 doctrine. Indian Navy has revamped its existing policies to factor in maritime terrorism, piracy and coastal security as the matter of great strategic significance. The strategic designs of India as the blue water navy, capable to operate in the open seas, to pursue and safeguard Indian oceanic interests raise the question of "how far India has got the naval capability, the capacity, to match such strategic intentions".

INDIAN NAVY: CHALLENGES BEYOND THE HORIZON

The Currency of Power

In the mid-1980s many commentators predicted the end of the role of military force as the "currency of power". Subsequent decades were however marked by global changes that significantly altered the distribution of international power. Radical shifts in the status of erstwhile subjugated states, the empowerment of newly developed and developing nations, and the displacement of totalitarian regimes across Europe, have altered the perception of the influence of military power in determining the course of global events.

The freeing up of economies, which became the norm by the mid-1990s, resulted in a rise in expectations in many parts of the world. The spread of information made the disparities in living standards more glaring and national, political or ethnic groupings became assertive of their right to a share of the global wealth.

As changing tectonic conditions result in periodic earthquakes which enable the earth's crust to adjust to the altered conditions, this instability created violent upheavals involving the use of military force to realign political or economic power. Predictions of the demise of military force as a currency of power were thus belied by the unilateral exercise of the military option in Central Europe and in West Asia. Far from the imagined era of stability (which is largely interpreted as the maintenance of the status quo) and the much vaunted "end of history" theory, the last two decades have been the most violent in history.

Apart from its being used as a means of forcibly redistributing political power within and between nations, military power is also being applied to further economic interests. The attack on Iraq by the US, and the current imbroglio in that unhappy country, had as much to do with the perceived energy requirements of the US as with any real or imaginary weapons of mass destruction. Similarly, it has been argued that Iraq's plans to trade its oil wealth in euros threatened the primacy of the dollar as the global currency, and the attack on Iraq was a measure to safeguard vital US economic interests.

It is apparent therefore, that far from becoming irrelevant, or even waning in importance, military power is still considered a legitimate and viable option by countries that wish to impose their vision of the international order on recalcitrant lesser states. It is equally an unavoidable conclusion that states that wish to retain their freedom of manoevre in global affairs, must possess a sound economy, backed by a robust (even if defensive) military capability. Clearly the age has not yet arrived when nations can dispense with their armed forces. If anything, recent events would indicate the opposite – that failure to invest in national defence capability could cost a country dear.

THE NATURE OF FUTURE WARS

While it is fairly clear that nation states will continue to resort to military force, and we will need to maintain armed forces for the foreseeable future, it is much less clear, what size and shape and capabilities those forces will need to have. Warfare has begun to evolve away from the historical pattern, and massive wars on a global scale between evenly matched and industrialised opponents are generally accepted to be a phenomena of the past. Major influences on the nature of future warfare will be exerted by three main factors-economic interdependence and globalisation, redistribution and realignments of international power, and technology.

With the collapse of the USSR, socialist economic doctrines were rapidly discarded by all countries and they have embraced the free market philosophies of the West. The resultant free flow of capital, the increase in global movement of labour, and the offshoring of industrial production have bound countries together in a variety of ways-economic, social and cultural. It would be impossible under these conditions for a country to inflict severe or lasting damage to another with which it has close economic ties without itself suffering in the process. Globalisation has thus curtailed the freedom of the more powerful nations to act with impunity against weaker nations with well-developed economies, and with which they have economic relationships. The nature of conflict between such countries would necessarily be of brief durations and be focused on the achievement of narrow and specific (mainly economic) objectives.

The changed distribution and alignment of international power has various facets. The US, and under its leadership NATO, have resorted to military actions decisively against several countries in the last two decades.

The object states of these actions are countries that are characterised by poor economic levels, political instability, and the absence of democratic forms of government. It is hard to see similar actions being taken against countries with a stable and democratic system in place, and which have well developed economic, social and cultural international linkages. Although the US has emerged as the sole superpower, it has been forced to become increasingly heedful to international opinion. Thus, while the end of the Cold War resulted in the emergence of a single super power, the economic globalisation that followed has swung the pendulum slightly back, resulting in a moderation of the superpower status.

The spread of satellite television brought distant wars to the homes of viewers, and the developed countries are finding it increasingly difficult to justify the loss of human life. The political cost of casualties in war has increased to the point where risk avoidance has become an important factor that impinges on war tactics in Western countries.

These factors permit the following conclusions:

- Wars of the future are likely to brief and focused on economic objectives.
- They will be more in the nature of specific operations against unequal and weak states with poorly developed and insular economic and political systems.
- They will not be waged with equally industrialised or advanced countries.
- They will be increasingly subject to world opinion and approval.

- Risk avoidance will result in the use of long range weapons and aerial bombardment with precision weapons.

THE REVOLUTION IN MILITARY AFFAIRS

The factors discussed above will have a profound effect on the framework and rules by which wars will be fought. They will determine under what circumstances nations, even powerful ones, will resort to military action against other states, and with the passage of time, will increasingly circumscribe the kind of targets that will be acceptable for attack. In contrast, the third factor, i.e. technology, will have its greatest impact on the means and methods in which future wars will be fought, and on the weapon systems and platforms of military and naval forces.

In the mid-1990s it was realised that the rapid growth of information technology and digital communications made possible the transmission of huge amounts of battle theatre data in real time.

This happened at a time when the demise of the Soviet Union suddenly knocked out the core of the US Navy's strategy, which was centred on tracking, outmaneuvering and pre-empting the Russian forces at sea.

The US Navy was quick to recognise the need to shift its strategy to one based on joint operations with other forces, on and over land. This shift was only possible because of the emergence of technology to back it up.

The new concept of operations is based on data being uploaded on to a network which can be accessed by all combatant commanders, and the scenario perceived by individual units can be integrated in real time to give all commanders a total perspective on the overall operational scenario. It has thus become possible for a unit to bring to bear its fire power on a target, even if it does not even have it on its radar or other sensors.

Western military scholars define a revolution in military affairs as a rapid change in the warfare paradigm brought about by technology or new concepts, which are usually accompanied by new organisational structures.

Unlike earlier such revolutions in naval warfare in the past such as the advent of steam, the invention of the submarine, the invention of the radar, the development of the aircraft carrier and nuclear power, the current RMA is different in that it is likely to affect not only one service and its combat methods, but will have its impact on all armed forces and their operational doctrines.

The Future Navy

Specifically for the Navy, the current RMA will impinge on one of its basic traditional characteristics – the isolation of the naval commander at sea and the corresponding degree of freedom he had to make operational and tactical decisions.

The published opinion is that the new scenario will enable rapid dissemination of operational information and decentralise decision-making, but there is another aspect which may have the opposite effect; the operational commander's superior too will have the total picture and will in a sense be alongside the fleet commander, which will considerably curtail his initiative!

Notwithstanding these areas of uncertainty, it seems inevitable that net-based war or network-centric warfare is the way naval warfare is headed, and our planners and designers will have to factor this into their template for the Navy of the future.

The US and NATO have recognised this and have embarked seriously on a programme of "transformation" of their Navies to make them conform to the new roles and warfighting trends. New organisations have been set up with the specific task of conceptualizing and implementing the process of transformation and many decisions have already been taken to make the force structure of the future navy correspond to its predicted role and missions.

It goes without saying that the strategic imperatives of all countries vary, and notwithstanding recent writings and pronouncements about shared strategic interests and natural strategic partners, those of the US and Western powers are bound to be at divergence with several aspects of our own strategic perceptions.

It is necessary for the current trends to be seen through the prism of national self-interest, and to make plans for the future structure of the Navy accordingly. One fact does seem evident – there is a need for transforming the Navy to one that will meet our requirements of the future.

The Indian Navy has no time to lose in instituting such a process. The concept of network-centric warfare has already been studied for several years, but the task of making the navy of the future capable of it has to be addressed now if the current discourse is not to remain an academic one. A few major thrust areas could be:

- Design and production of an indigenous net platform on which the network-centric operations will be based. This would have two or three versions with differing capabilities for different classes of ships.
- Commonalisation of procedures between the Air Force and the Navy to enable joint operations followed by standardization of communication and sensor systems for networking compatibility.
- Reduction in the number of types of warships, to reduce logistic complexity and improve ship availability. The Quadrennial Defence Review of 2006 for the US Navy envisages four types of ships for a total of 143 major surface combatants. In contrast, the 21 principal surface combatants we have in the Navy today belong to seven different types.
- Institution of a programme for integration of the submarine force into the network; this will require a major effort to equip submarines with real time communication systems with minimal loss of stealth. It will also require a changed mindset in the operating philosophy of submarines wherein submarines are given the minimum essential operational intelligence and directives before deployment and thereafter left pretty

much to themselves for the duration of hostilities.

- Institution of a development programme for precision guided weapons.
- Development of a modern and interoperable radar system network between all combatant units.

This is probably a minimalist approach, and it has not considered the major efforts required in associated areas, particularly in education and training. But the point to be emphasised is an often-stated truism: it takes a lifetime to build a Navy, and if we are to transform the Navy of today into one that meets the task of (say) 2025, then the time to act is already upon us.

It is interesting to observe that in the US context, two of the most ship innovative design decisions, the Littoral Control Ship and the conversion of the Ohio class, were thrust from above upon the US Navy. The Indian scene is different, and the Navy will have to wage a long struggle to get approval for its every proposal. The scenario is complicated by the fact that technology is advancing at an exponential rate, and this increases the cost of upgradations, and brings in its wake the spectre of rapid obsolescence.

The preparation of a blueprint for the future Navy, the setting in motion of the development of the technologies required, and the steering of the concept and its implementation will require a dedicated organisation at a high level. Such an organisation will need to study the problem in a comprehensive manner, and cover the entire range of issues from the analysis of technology to finance and design, construction and training. More importantly they will have to convince the Government and many within the Service itself of not only the need, but also the urgency of such measures.

Conclusion

Modernisation of warfare strategies and techniques, and adoption of technologically advanced concepts are futile exercises if the basic structure of the Navy is not given the timely attention that is due. The creation of a balanced maritime defence force is an essential aspect of any modernisation, and the shortfall in our fleet units and submarines has to be made good by the political commitment to a sustained building programme rather than by sporadic inductions.

In conclusion it needs to be said that the entire premise in this article has been that the equipment and system needed for net-based warfare will be developed and built in India, as dependence on foreign sources for such crucial systems will create an unacceptable vulnerability.

It has also been based on the hope that the process of production and acquisition and for obtaining government approvals will also be modernised along with the equipment and systems for the armed forces.

9

Historical Perspective of Indian Maritime

INDIAN OCEAN

The Indian Ocean, is named after peninsular India which juts into its centre and occupies a unique position. These vast waters wash the shores of the entire East Coast of Africa, the South. Coast of Arabia, the Southern shores of Iran and Baluchistan, the Malaysian Peninsula and Indonesia's Sumatra. The ingress and egress of the ocean are through the eastern and western waterways at the Straits of Malacca and Bab-el-Mandeb. The former lead to the Indonesian Archipelago, the South China Sea, the Far East and the vast expanse of the Pacific Ocean while the latter control the entrance to the Red Sea. Commanding the gateway to the landlocked Persian Gulf in the northwest is Hormuz formerly known as Ormuz. For ages, Aden, at the Southern tip of Arabia, was the home and main base of the Arab corsairs. Two off-shoots of this Ocean are the Arabian Sea and the Bay of Bengal which wash the 5600-kilometre-long shores of the Indian peninsula, Pakistan, Bangladesh, Burma and the island of Sri Lanka which is separated from India by the Palk Strait.

Because of its unique features, the Indian Ocean has always been regarded as an area of great geopolitical significance and India has been regarded as its centre of gravity. Sardar K.M. Panikkar, has said: In spite of the vastness of its surface and the oceanic character of its current and winds, the Indian

Ocean has some of the features of a land-locked sea. The Arctic and the Antarctic, circling the Poles have but little connection with inhabited land. The Pacific and the Atlantic lie from the north to the south like gigantic highways. They have no land roof, no vast land area jutting out into their expanse. The Indian Ocean is walled off on three sides by land, with the southern side of Asia forming a roof over it. The continent of Africa constitutes the western wall and Burma, Malaya and the insular continuations protect the eastern side. But the vital feature which differentiates the Indian Ocean from the Pacific or the Atlantic is not the two sides but the subcontinent of India which juts out far into the sea for a thousand miles to its tapering end at Kanya Kumari. It is the geographical position of India that changes the character of the Indian Ocean.

The islands in the Indian Ocean area are neither as numerous nor as evenly spread out as those in the Pacific. The major islands in the region *Mxe* Sri Lanka and Malagasy while the minor ones are Socotra near the Arab Coast. Zanzibar and Seychelles off the African Coast, Mauritius and Reunionon the Tropic of Capricorn, Lakshadweep and the Maldives near the West Coast of India, the Bahrain group near the Persian Gulf, the Andamans and the Nicobars in the Bay of Bengal and the Diego Garcia group in the Chagos Archipelago. Considerable geopolitical significance is also attached to the bays, gulfs and bights of the Ocean. The Persian Gulf which is virtually a land-locked sea with its choke point at Hormuz, the Arabian Sea which separates the Indian and Arabian peninsulas, the Gulf of Aden entry to which is controlled by the island of Socotra, the Red Sea whose gate-post is at Bab-el-Mandeb, the Bay of Bengal separating the Indian and Malaysian peninsulas and the Gulf of Malacca with Singapore commanding entry into it, have all played a significant role in the maritime history of the region.

Because of the unique feature of the monsoons and the development of the nucleus of civilisation around this Ocean, oceanic activity and traditions developed in this region before any other place. Centuries before the development of seafaring activities in the Aegean Sea, the littoral states of peninsular

India had already built up their oceanic traditions. The strategic, naval and geopolitical importance of land-locked countries establishing links with the seas by acquiring sovereignty over waterways or even land corridors has been appreciated by politico-military thinkers for centuries. For instance, the potential of their presence in the Indian Ocean or even in its seas, bays and straits prompted some super powers of today to make attempts to gain access to this ocean over land even in the last century. The British appreciation of the balance of power in and around Asia after World War II and its future plans made during the forties also catered to these contingencies.

What is most striking and little known is the fact that Maharaja Ranjit Singh, the great ruler of the Punjab, had also realised the importance of establishing a link with the sea after his victory over the Pathans and Afghans during the third decade of the last century. To quote a historian, "If the Punjabi empire was to expand any further, it could only be across the Sindh desert to the sea or across the Sutlej to India." (The portion of India then held by the British.) The British were clever enough to persuade the Maharaja to sign a commercial treaty in December 1832 and abandon his plans to extend his empire to the sea. These facts and today's rivalry between the super powers over their presence in the Indian Ocean confirm the wisdom of the observation made by Khaireddin Barbarosa, the Egyptian Admiral centuries ago, "He who rules on the sea will shortly rule on the land also."

Another fact that emerges from a careful analysis of the sequence of events in India's maritime past is that during the last five millennia, those who came over land from other parts of the world, mainly using the mountain passes in the northwest, did rule some parts of the Indian subcontinent for a while but were eventually absorbed in the mainstream of Indian culture and traditions and, over the centuries, became an integral part of the Indian milieu. Some of these were the Aryans, Pathans, Moghuls, Afghans, Sakas and even the Huns. But those who came by sea during the last two millennia, the Portuguese, Dutch, French, British, Germans, Danes, Flemish, Armenians and the Jews, did not lose their identity and came to stay for hundreds of years, some of them holding sway over larger areas and for longer periods. India's maritime history can be broadly divided into five distinct periods— the Hindu period extending from the hoary past to the middle of the 15th century A.D., the Portuguese period from the closing years of the 15th century to the end of the 16th century; two British periods—from 1612 to 1830 and from 1830 to 1947; and the Indian period which commenced on August 15, 1947. The British period is divided into two parts because in 1830, the East India Company's Navy in India underwent two major changes; it was constituted as a combatant service and given the name Indian Navy and the first ship of the Service to sail under steam, the 411-ton *Hugh Lindsay,* covered the distance from Bombay to Suez in 21 days thus ushering in the conversion from sail to steam.

The Vedas, Buddhist Jatakas, Sanskrit, Pali and Persian literature, Indian folklore and mythology and even the Old Testament bear testimony to the fact that as far back as the days of Mohen-jo-Daro, Lothal and Harappa (3,000 to 2,000 B.C.), i.e., the Indus Valley Civilisation, there was considerable maritime activity between India and the countries in Africa, Southern Europe, Western Asia and the Far East. Seals and potsherd portraying anchors and tools and kitchen implements made of coral and mussel-shell have been found at these places and Java, Sumatra, Indo-China, Sri Lanka and Egypt. A recently unearthed huge drydock at Lothal in Gujarat further confirms the existence of India's seaborne trade with these countries, especially Sumer, Egypt, Crete and countries in Central Asia and Persia at that time. Late Professor Buhler, the well-known German orientalist, expressed the view that "there are passages in ancient Indian works which prove the early existence of navigation of the Indian Ocean and the somewhat later occur rences of trading voyages undertaken by Hindu merchants to the shores of the Persian Gulf and its rivers."

This fact is further borne out by available works in the languages of the littoral states of the region; such as Sindhi, Gujarati, Marathi, Konkani, Kannada, Malayalam, Tamil, Telugu, Oriya and Bengali; the writings of foreign travellers and historians—Chinese, Arabic and Persian—which contain observations on Indian subjects; the evidence available from archaeology— epigraphic, monumental and numismatic; and Indian and foreign art and foreign literature—English, Greek, Portuguese, French, Dutch, Persian, Chinese, Japanese, Arabic, Malay, Thai, Burmese and Sinhalese.

Some of the little-known facts about the extent of commercial and cultural influence of India and sea-borne trade using ships built in India during the Hindu period (pre-Christian era to the middle of the 15th Century A.D.) are: The Matsya Yantra (the fish machine), an iron fish floating on oil Qitig to the north serving as a primitive compass used by Indian sea-farers for several millennia (as per Hindu mythology, Matsya was the first incarnation of Lord Vishnu).

— The names of some of the places in Southern and southeast Asia such as Socotra which is a derivative of Sukhadhara (container or island of happiness); Sri Lanka which originally was Swarna Alankar (gold ornament), Nicobar which was derived from Nak-Dweep (the island of the naked) and Calicut which originally was Kallikote (in Kannada a stone-fort);

— Reference to Indians as Klings in Thailand and Telangs in some parts of Burma because of the conquests of these countries by the Kalingas and Andhras several millennia ago;

— The similarity between the Thai and Oriya scripts due to the long Kalinga rule over Thailand;

— The scriptures in a Buddhist temple in Japan which are recited by the monks every morning even today being in the 6th Century A.D. Bengali script; and

— The transfer by sea of the weary, tired and demoralised army of Alexander the Great from the mouth of the Indus to the shores of the Persian Gulf in 323 B.C. in about 800 Indian-built sailing vessels.

During this period, while the Arabian Sea and the Indian Ocean were used mainly for purposes of maritime trade, the Bay of Bengal provided a highway for the countries on the Eastern seaboard to embark on proselytising, cultural and colonising missions to Sri Lanka and countries as far as the East Indies and Japan.

During the Hindu period, considerable maritime activity took place in the waters around India. As described by Megasthenes,6 the royal shipyards of the Mauryas built seagoing ships of various classes. The War Office of Emperor Chandragupta had, as one of its six boards, a Nav Parishad (Board of Admiralty) which controlled national shipping. During the days of Emperor Ashoka in the 3rd century B.C., his sister, Princess Sanghamitra sailed from Tamralipta in Bengal to Sri Lanka on her historic mission of spreading Buddhism there. Ashoka also had a strong seagoing fleet and regular commercial intercourse with Syria, Egypt, Cyrene, Macedonia and Epirus/ Between 200 B.C. and A.D. 250, the Andhras carried out maritime trade with Western Asia, Greece, Rome, Egypt, China and some other Eastern countries and had even set up embassies in some of these countries. Roman coins discovered in India, especially in the South, establish the existence of trade between these countries even before the Christian era. Persecution at the hands of the Romans forced some Jews to flee Rome and take refuge in Malabar in A.D. 68. Larger sailing vessels built by the Cholas, Pandyas and the Keralas of South India and the Kalingas of Orissa were used for trade, passenger traffic and nava l warfare. These ships were considered excellent for navigation across the oceans as their lower parts were reinforced with triple planks in order to enable them to withstand the force of tempests.

Some of the leading communities in organising sea-bferne commerce were the Manigramrftan Chetties, Namdasis, Valangais and Elangais of South India. It is a fact of history that during the first decade of the seventh century, a ruler of Gujarat who was faced with defeat at the hands of his enemy, sent his son with thousands of followers comprising cultiva tors, artisans, warriors, physicians and writers in over 100 vessels to Java where they laid the foundation of a new civilisation whose contribution to the world is the temple and sculptures of Borobudur. The Cholas (A.D. 985-1054) maintained a strong naval fleet on the Coro-mandel Coast. The Chola emperors Rajaraja I and Rajendra I had strong armadas which were used to capture Sri Lanka and in A.D. 1007 the Cholas launched an expedition against the Sri Vijayas, who at that time ruled the Malayan Peninsula, Java, Sumatra and some neighbouring islands and the sea areas continguous to them, and defeated them to establish Chola power in the Malayan Peninsula.

Evidence from various sources confirms the existence of trade in various commodities between India and Europe for at least three millennia. India maintained trade relations with the Phoenicians, Jews, Assyrians, Greeks, Egyptians and Romans during the earlier centuries and with the Turks, Venetians, Portuguese, Dutch and English during the later part of the period. While India imported few items such as tin, lead, glass, amber, steel for arms, coral and medicinal drugs from Europe and West Asia, Arabia supplied frankincense to India for use in her temples. The items exported to Europe, North Africa and West Asia included wool from the fleeces of sheep bred on the northwestern mountain ranges, armour, onyx, chalcedony, lapis lazuli, jasper, resinous gum, furs, asafoetida, musk, balm, myrrh, embroidered woollen fabrics, coloured carpets, silk (considered most valuable and exchanged by weight with gold), various types of cotton cloth ranging from coarse canvas and calicoes to muslins of the finest texture, peacocks, apes, oils, brassware, ivory, ebony, pearls, sugar cane extracts, salt, indigo, drugs, dyes, rice, sandalwood, timber for building ships, aromatics, pepper, cinna mon and edible spices which were, during the later years, mainly traded for precious metals, especially gold.

Interrelation is further confirmed by the fact that the word for peacock is "tuki" in Hebrew and "tokei" in Tamil and by the adoption of Tamil words by the Greeks and vice-versa. There was considerable sea-borne commercial intercourse between Greece and South India during the Hindu period affirmed by the fact that the words for rice, ginger, cinnamon and foreign merchants in Greek and Tamil respectively are ryza and arisi, zingibar and inchivar, karpion and karava and Iaones and Yavana. In April A.D. 800, as described in the 199th Chapter of the Japanese document Ruijukokushi, an Inglian was cast up on the shores of Japan and some seeds of the cotton-plant, so far unknown to that country, were found on his ship and sown in the provinces of Kii, Awaji, Sanuki, Jyo, Tosa and Kyushu. Thus cotton was introduced into Japan.

There is evidence of Herodotus (450 B.C.) who wrote about the (cotton) worn by the Indian contingent of Xerxes Army which had been woven from "the wool which certain mild trees in India bear instead of fruit that in beauty and quality excels that of sheep." Thus, it was India that introduced the use of cotton to Europe, West Asia and the Far East.

One of the most sensational discoveries that helped maintain trade between India and the West was that of the regularity of the seasonal winds of the southwest monsoon by a Greek named Hippalus in A.D. 45. His discovery helped him in finding a direct route to Malabar which was far shorter than the older coast-hugging route.

Toward the end of the summer months, "ships used to depart from the mouth of the Arabian Gulf or Kane on the coast of Arabia Felix and sail straight in 40 days to Muziris (modern Kodungallur) on the West Coast qf India. They began their homeward voyage in December by sailing with the North-East Wind, enter the Arabian Gulf, meet with a South or South-West Wind and thus complete the voyage by using the trade winds throughout the period." The discovery of the directions and regularity of the monsoon air current was a major contributing factor towards the continuance of maritime trade between India and the Western countries over the centuries.

That oceanic navigation was well advanced during the earlier centuries of the Christian era is further borne out by the writings of the celebrated Chinese monk, Fa Hien who came to India overland to study Buddhism at Bodhgaya, Sarnath and Varanasi in A.D. 413. On his way back to his home land he sailed from Tamralipta in Bengal and 14 days later reached Sri Lanka where he embarked for Java and called at the Nicobars before passing through the Straits of Malacca to reach the pacific.

Hindu supremacy over the Eastern waters reached its zenith during the period of 5th to 12th centuries when the Sri Vijaya Empire ruled the entire sea area between India's eastern seaboard and the. Far East. The Sri Vijayas' cultural and colonising expedition took them to such farflung areas as Sumatra, Burma, the Malayan Peninsula, Java, Thailand and Indo-China.

Besides spreading Hindu culture, they maintained regular political and commercial intercourse with the Cholas, Pandyas and Keralas. As a result of jealousy between the Cholas, the Tamil Kings, and the Sri Vijayas, however, a series of sea battles were fought between their navies toward the end of the 10th century A.D. resulting in the weakening of these empires and opening the way for Arab supremacy in the region. About the same time, the rulers of Gujarat and Calicut also maintained large fleets of sailing vessels for commercial purposes which sailed with cargoes of silk carpets, precious stones, pearls, ivory, spices and other valuable goods to Europe and West Asia. With the weakening of the Indian rulers, their sea-borne trade routes passed into the hands of the Arabs who became great intermediaries of maritime commercial intercourse between the two regions.

During this period the Arabs acted as a link between the East and Europe and used to pass the Indian merchandise to the Venetians who supplied the Indian goods to the European markets where they were in great demand. The Venetians soon became immensely prosperous which aroused the jea-lousy and cupidity of the seafarers of the Iberian nations, i.e., Spain, Portugal and other Mediterranean countries, and the quest for a direct passage to India began.

For several millennia ships had been traversing the Indian Ocean carrying valuable merchandise and cultural emissaries between India and the West. Cities that directly engaged in the maritime trade or stood on the ancient trade routes continued to grow in importance and prosperity. Some of these centres of commerce were ancient Chaldea, Babylon, Nineveh, Ophir, Tad-more and the ports in the Mediterranean, Persian Gulf and the Red Sea. The Phoenicians had for some years arrogated to themselves a major share in the Mediterranean trade but were later driven out of it by the Assyrians, Greeks and Romans but the Arabs continued to hold away over the Red Sea, Persian Gulf, Indian Ocean and the Arabian Sea.

Egypt, during the days of the Ptolemies, developed Alexandria into the most important port in the world. One of the Ptolemies, Ptolemy Philadel-phus was planning to construct a canal between the Red Sea and the Nile, a hundred cubits wide and thirty cubits in depth, in order to transport Indian goods to Alexandria wholly by water but, for reasons not known, this project was never undertaken and hence a new port called Berenike was developed on the Western shore of the Red Sea. Ships from India carried merchandise, sailing from Tatta at the head of the lower delta of the Indus or other ports on the West Coast to the coast of Persia and after following the Arabian shore to Berenike. From Berenike, the goods were carried overland to the city of Koptos, which was very close to the Nile, where they were loaded into ships which navigated along a canal to Alexandria. Carthe-gian merchants carried Indian goods to all Mediterranean ports. During the period of Egyptian supremacy, the northern countries of Europe received Indian goods which were carried overland from India to Oxus from where they went to the regions bordering the Caspian Sea and the Black Sea.

After its conquest of Carthage, Egypt and Syria, the Roman Empire monopolised trade with India for many years and Alexandria continued to be the principal port for Indian merchandise. The conquest of Persia and Egypt by the Mohammedans later, however, deprived the European countries of the use of Alexandria for trade and access to Indian merchandise. Basra was founded at the head of the Persian Gulf and became as important a trading centre as Alexandria, controlling the movement of merchandise in both the easterly and westerly directions. The Arabs later gained control of the trade routes and stopped supplying Indian goods to the sea ports of the Mediterranean but the overland route to Constantinople provided the alternative for carrying Indian products to the European trade centres. In fact, Constantinople became the focal point for the movement of merchandise between Europe and India.

The rise and fall of the Venetians, Genoans and Pisans, the bitter struggle between Venice and Genoa over the eastern trade and the Venetian supremacy over this trade for some time form but a small chapter in terms of time in our maritime history. With the annexation of Constantinople and trading routes to India by the Turks towards the end of the 15th century and with the continued piracy on the Alexandrian trade route by the Egyptians, a new pattern of rivalry involving South European, North African and West Asian countries over trade with the East emerged. Since mastery over these trade routes had a direct bearing on the power and prosperity of these nations, an alternative route to India was sought to be established by some of these countries which already had centuries of seafaring experience and expertise.

The quest for an alternative route hugging the coasts of Africa and Asia led to the sailing down the West Coast of Africa by the Portuguese Navigator, Bartholemy Diaz in 1487 and the discovery of the Cape of Tempests, later to be renamed the Cape of Good Hope. Vasco da Gama was deputed by King Manoel of Portugal in July 1497, five years after the discovery of the West Indies by Columbus, to complete the work done by Diaz. The King's astrologer, Abraham Ben Zakut, having studied his horoscope and having found it favourable for the discovery of the sea route to India, there were high hopes of success in the venture. Four ships, the *Sao Gabriel* (120 tons) commanded by Vasco da Gama, the *Sao Raphael* (100 tons) commanded by his brother Paulo da Gama, the *Berrio* (50 tons) under the command of Nicolas Coelho and a 200-ton store ship set sail from Belem on March 25, 1497. A violent storm was encountered while rounding the Cape and the crew, which wanted to go back, plotted a mutiny but Vasco da Gama succeeded in suppressing the mutiny by arresting the ring-leaders and threatening to throw them overboard. In March 1498, *Sao Gabriel* and *Sao Raphael* reached Mozambique, the store ship having returned to Portugal after transferring her stores and the *Berrio* having been found not seaworthy and broken up to repair the other ships. Vasco da Gama now needed a pilot to take him across the Indian Ocean and Arabian Sea to India and found one in the Moorish Broker, Davane, from Gujarat who was an experienced pilot and knew the seas contiguous to Africa, West Asia and India very well. His expert pilotage not only provided security from the jealous Arabs but also helped Vasco da Gama to proceed to Melinde from where the ships sailed on August 26, 1498. Had Davane not assisted Vasco da Gama, the Portuguese would not have reached India for some more decades which probably would have changed the course of India's maritime history.

MARITIME TRADE

While the discovery of the sea route to India by da Gama was of no great significance, especially when compared to the feats of Columbus and Magellan, the importance of his achievement lies in the fact that while the seas were regarded by the Arabs as a pathway for carrying out maritime trade, the Portuguese were the first to lay claim to sovereignty over these waters and using them as an instrument for the projection of their national policy. This claim was further sanctified by the Bull of Pope Calixtus III which considered the seas they sailed to be their possession. The Portuguese thus began considering themselves to be lords of the seas and thought they

Were justified in confiscating the merchandise of all ships that sailed without their authority. K.M. Panikkar is fully justified in saying, "It may truly be said that India never lost her independence till she lost command of the sea in the first decade of the 16th century."

The Portuguese claim to sovereignty of the seas and da Gama's strong attitude at the Court of the Zamorin of Calicut displeased the latter and the challenge to the ruler's limited sea power led to a series of indecisive skir mishes and sea battles off the coast of Malabar in the years that followed. The Portuguese intruders were detested by the Arab traders who joined hands with the Zamorin and in 1500 when Admiral Pedro Cabral bombarded Calicut, 80 ships of the Zamorin, manned by 1500 intrepid sailors and reinforced by the ships of a rich Arab trader, Khoja Amber, drove him away to Cochin. Two indecisive battles were fought off Cochin in 1503 and off Chaul in 1508. In 1509 the next battle of importance was fought off Diu when ships of the Zamorin, under the command of the courageous Kassim and reinforced by an Egyptian fleet under Admiral Mir Hussain, fought against a strong Portuguese force led by Den Francesco d'Almeida. This battle also produced no decisive result because of the treachery of the Sultan of Gujarat which led to the Egyptian fleet sailing away in disgust. The Indian Ocean was thereafter dominated by the Portuguese, and Albuquerque, the great commercial empire-builder and statesman, helped in firmly establishing Portuguese supremacy over the area.

Mention must be made here of the outstanding role played by the Zamo-rin's fleet which, under the leadership of the AH Marakkars, gave valiant battle to the Portuguese for well over 90 years. The Marakkars who had their headquarters at Ponnani, a natural harbour South of Calicut, held sway over the waters around Calicut. The most illustrious name in the family of the Ali Maraklcars was that of Kunjali Marakkar II who sank a number of Portuguese ships (the tally in a particular year being 50) and struck terror in the hearts of the Portuguese forces. For some reasons, however, Kunjali III (Mohammed Kunjali Marakkar) who was the last of the Kunjali Admirals and had won many a battle against the Portuguese, fell out with the Zamorin. This led to the weakening of the Zamorin's fleet and its capitulation to the Portuguese. The main contribution of the Kunjalis during the 16th century was that for over 90 years they kept the Portuguese at bay and harassed their fleet thus preventing them from carrying out incursions into the land areas of the subcontinent.

Having failed to defeat the Zamorin, Albuquerque seized Goa and its surrounding areas in 1510. Operating from Goa which occupied a commanding position in the prevailing scenario, Albuquerque hounded the Arab traders out of their favourite haunt, subdued the Sultan of Ormuz and relegated him to the level of a vassal of the Portuguese ruler, developed Socotra into a powerful naval base with a well-defended fort, established a strong government in Cochin after bypassing the Zamorin and brought immense power and wealth to his country by exercising mastery over the Arabian Sea. In 1513, he mustered a strong naval force and seized and fortified the Straits of Malacca. He also established amicable relations with the ruler of Pegu, who controlled the Arakan Coast, after prolonged negotiations with him.

Portuguese supremacy over the waters around India was thus established and reached its zenith during the days of Albuquerque. But in 1580, when Portugal joined hands with Spain and the Spanish Armada suffered a crushing defeat, it changed the course of events around the globe, one of its off shoots being the decline of Portuguese supremacy in the Indian region. It is a moot point that if the Spanish Armada had triumphed, the United States could in all probability have become a Latin American country and India a Portuguese dominion!

The sudden change in the power equation was first exploited by the Dutch and the Dutch East India Company was formed at Amsterdam in 1592. The first merchant fleet of the Dutch reached India in 1595 but they did not challenge the Portuguese supremacy. Instead, they occupied Java and established a naval base at Batavia. Meanwhile, the British and the French also decided to benefit from fishing in our troubled waters and came to India during the earlier years of the 17th Century. It is thus apparent that while the Hindus controlled the trade routes until the beginning of the 15th Century, the Arabs took over the main bulk of it from them for a while with a short period of overlap. But supremacy over these routes passed into Portuguese hands towards the end of the 15th Century. The Portuguese then reigned unchallenged for nearly a century till the defeat of the Spanish Armada and then the sun of the British maritime power rose over Indian horizons and the Indian Ocean during the first decade of the 17th Century.

The Mughal ruler, Akbar had a fairly strong Navy but its main component was a fleet of ships and craft based at Dacca which were used for operations in rivers and creeks for the protection of deltaic South Bengal from the *Magh* (Burmese) and *Feringhee* (half-caste) pirates who had the support of the Arakan rulers. He had an Admiralty which looked after the supply of ships and smaller craft, recruitment of suitable personnel for the ships and craft, security of rivers and waterways and collection of port revenue. The Mughals, however, did not appreciate the importance of building up a blue-water navy and developing sea-borne trade and commerce. Shipping and shipbuilding, ocean-going and riverine, however, flourished during the Mughal days in various parts of India such as Bengal, Kashmir, Lahore and Surat and there is evidence available to establish the high standard of technology maintained in the construction of these ships and craft.

Aurangzeb's navy was superior in size and efficiency to that of Akbar. Besides naval ships, he had four ships at Surat for carrying Haj pilgrims free of cost to Mecca but the lack of adequate sea-going naval ships caused the loss of some of his bigger ships to British pirates.

By a Royal Charter of Queen Elizabeth I, the Honourable Company of the Merchants Trading to the East Indies, better known as the East India Company, was founded by the British on December 31, 1600 and a ship of the Company, the *Hector,* with Captain Hawkins as the Commanding Officer, arrived in Surat bringing a letter to Emperor Jehangir requesting for permission to trade with India. Hawkins reached Agra on April 16, 1610 and permission was duly granted and trading facilities promised by the Emperor but the Portuguese did not appreciate the British encroachment on their trade preserves. The British sensed this and sent a squadron of warships, the *Dragon, Osiender, James* and *Solomon,* under the overall command of Captain Thomas Best, which reached Swally, the roadstead of Surat, on September 5, 1612. This date is regarded by the British as the foundation day of the Royal Indian Navy, as the first arrival of their warships in India and the formation of the Indian Marine took place on this day. A very interesting fact "discovered" by the late Commander (special) G.E. Walker, who was the Judge Advocate General of the RIN immediately before Independence, is that the Jack flown by the Indian Marine in 1612 was the flag worn by ships on the American side during the War of Independence when they rejected the Union Jack. The Jack of the Indian Marine was thus the first flag of the U.S.A. which over the years developed into the stars and stripes. The Indian Marine Jack had seven red and six white stripes and in the position occupied by the stars today, was displayed the St. George's Cross. This flag forms a part of the insignia of the existing RIN Association in the U.K.

Their monopoly over trade in the region having been challenged by the British, the Portuguese attacked the ships of the Indian Marine on October 29, 1612 with four galleons and forty other craft but had to admit defeat after a protracted battle. They then withdrew leaving the British as masters of the land and sea area around Surat who set up factories and formed a fleet of Indian small craft known as Ghurabs (the British called them Grabs) and Galivats for the protection of their sea-borne commerce from the Portuguese. The sobriquet "The Grab Service" by which the British Indian Navy was known for many years does not necessarily bracket it with the pirates of various nationalities who infested the Indian waters at that time.

INDIAN MARINE

The nucleus of the Indian Marine consisted at that time mainly of some warships built in England and a larger number of vessels built in India. The Ghurabs were heavy beamy vessels (about 300 tons) of shallow draft and were armed with six 9 to 12-pouiider guns while the Galivats were smaller craft (about 70 tons) mounting half-a-dozen 2 to 4-pounders. The crews of these craft consisted mainly of Hindu fishermen from the Konkan Coast.

The second major battle with the Portuguese took place in 1614 in which the Indian Marine emerged victorious and the East India Company was granted further trading rights by Jehangir. In the following year, Sir Thomas Roe was appointed Ambassador from King James I to the Moghul Courts. Merchandise manufactured at the Surat factories started moving by sea to the West for trade with the Persian Gulf ports in 1618. Having had the monopoly of trade in these ports for nearly a century, the Portuguese tried to block the passage of these ships across the Arabian Sea but were successfully thwarted from doing so by the British who annexed Ormuz from the Portuguese in 1622 and thus began their uninterrupted trade with Persia. This, however, did not deter the Portuguese from seeking another battle at Swally in 1630 where they were defeated once again and a truce was declared leading to the opening of some of the Portuguese ports to the East India Company's ships.

The Dutch had been keeping an eye on the balance of power in this region and in their efforts to consolidate their base at Batavia (now known as Jakarta), they captured the Straits of Malacca in 1641 and drove the Portuguese away from the Eastern gateway to the Indian Ocean. Realising the strategic importance of Colombo as a naval base for operation for the annexation of the Indian mainland, the Dutch then befriended the ruler of Sri Lanka which helped in driving the Portuguese away from Colombo also in 1654. Soon thereafter, they made inroads into the Portuguese bastions on the Malabar Coast. This was rendered even more effective by the main base of the Dutch at Batavia, their control of the Straits of Malacca and the advanced operational base at Colombo. Cochin was captured in 1663. This was further made possible by the British preoccupation with other problems but their friendly relations with Emperor Shahjahan prevented the Dutch from making any forays into the waters around Surat where the British factories were situated. A year later, however, Shivaji, the Maratha ruler, attacked Surat by land but the Britishers repulsed his attack.

Meanwhile, King Charles II of England had married Infanta Catherina of Braganza, the Portuguese princess, in 1662 and Bombay was ceded to him as a part of his dowry. The official version of the transfer document described the gift as "the Port and Island of Bombay in the East Indies, together with all the rights, profit, territories and appurtenances thereof whatsover." Since, however, it was virtually impossible for King Charles II to administer Bombay successfully from England, he transferred it to the East India Company at an annual rental off 10 in

1668—one of the most significant events in the history of Bombay.

Despite the advice of his counsellors to the contrary, Sir John Child who was appointed the Admiral of the East India Company's land and sea forces between the Persian Gulf and Kanya Kumari in 1685, decided to adopt an aggressive policy towards the Moghuls. Having taken on afar superior force, Child suffered an ignominious defeat at the hands of the Moghuls who, with the support of the Sidis' fleet, captured most of Bombay island and besieged Child in the Bombay Castle which is now known as the Naval Barracks. Peace was, however, restored by redeeming Bombay on the payment of £ 15,000 in 1690 and some kind of a reconciliation having been effected between Aurangzeb and the Company. Meanwhile, in 1685 the Indian Marine Headquarters were shifted to Bombay and a year later the Service was rechristened the Bombay Marine.

In 1698, the Danes appeared on the scene and set up their trade after obtaining the permission of Prince Azimus-shan, grandson of Emperor Aurangzeb. By 1755, they had set up a factory and had hoisted the Danish flag at Serampore. In 1801, the British authorities forcibly seized Serampore but restored it immediately. In 1808, however, a detachment of British troops from Barrackpore occupied Serampore. The Danish East India Company recovered it later but in 1844 transferred all its assets to the British Government and left the country.

The beginning of the 18th century saw the emergence of an Admiral of Shivaji's Maratha Fleet, Kanhoji Angre, whose name became a legend during these years and whose exploits are written in letters of gold in the annals of the navies of India. Shivaji was a firm believer in the doctrine "Jalaim Jasya, Valaim Tasya" (he who rules the sea is all-powerful) and Tukoji Angre, his Admiral and son, Kanhoji Angre and his descendents, put it to practice. In 1706 the fleet of Kanhoji, menaced and considerably reduced British trade between Bombay and the lower Malabar Coast and captured Colaba from the Sidis. A year later, maritime trade in the Indian Ocean was threatened by Arab pirates operating from Muscat who plundered a large number of ships. Equipped with a fleet of 10 Ghurabs and 50

Gali-vats, the Maratha Fleet, under the command of Kanhoji Angre, challenged the Arab fleet and drove it away from the Indian Ocean. Thereafter, Kanhoji began establishing mastery over the Konkan Coast by fortifying his base at Gheria (Vijaydurg). This fortress was manned by a specially trained garrison which had been armed and provisioned to withstand severe attacks from land and sea and prolonged periods of blockade. This was further reinforced by a dockyard built on a river front behind the fortress which was equipped to build bigger, stronger and better sea-going vessels for his navy.

The Portuguese by this time having been reduced to an insignificant sea power, along with the Sidis and the British faced a strong challenge from the Maratha Fleet. The size, manouvreability and fire-power of the Maratha Fleet continued to grow and hence the British Council decided to build corvettes for the Bombay Marine which would escort the merchant ships of the Company and protect them from Angre's wrath. This went on for some time and the Governor of Bombay, Charles Boone, decided to attack Gheria in 1717 with a strong fleet under the command of Captain Barleu. A bitter engagement followed and the Marathas forced the Company's ships to beat a hasty retreat after inflicting severe damage on their ships and killing a large number of the Company's soldiers and sailors. Uuderred by the near-catastrophe, Charles Boone carried out another attack, this time a surprise one, on Gheria on November 5,1718 and succeeded in silencing many Maratha guns after a ship-shore artillery engagement. The next day, however, when his forces landed, the Maratha guns which had been strategically positioned to cover the entire beachhead, mowed them down. The British fleet, with the handful of survivors hastily withdrew.

On receiving a petition from the Governor of Bombay for naval reinforcement, the King of England sent four warships under Commodore Mathews to provide support to the fleet of the Bombay Marine. British and Portuguese ships carried out an attack on Colaba, five miles from Gheria, in October 1722 but even this attempt was successfully repulsed by the Marathas and the attacking forces withdrew after having suffered severe losses of men, guns and ammunition.. Angered by the capture of some of their ships by the Maratha Fleet, the Dutch attacked Gheria in 1724 with a powerful squadron of seven men-of-war, each mounting 30 to 50 guns, but they suffered heavy losses and were beaten back.

The success of the Maratha Fleet against bigger and better equipped ships of England, Portugal and Hollalid and those of the Moghuls and the Arabs stretching over several decades was mainly due to Kanhoji's tactics of using a large number of light, strong and fast craft, adequately equipped, which surrounded the heavier vessels of the enemy and simultaneously attacked them from all sides "thus overwhelming the crews of the enemy ships and then boarding them and putting them out of action by scuttling them or setting them on fire. Having had the unique distinction of maintaining naval supremacy over the sea area off the Konkan Coast for many years, Kanhoji suddenly passed away in 1729, survived by his sons, Sekhoji Angre and Sambhaji Angre.

The British treaty of alliance with the Sidi's to fight the Angres in 1733 was followed by Sambhaji's capture of some British merchant ships on December 16, 1735 which was a heavy blow on British trade. The Peshwas of Poona who were not quite friendly with the Angres, were then wooed by the British and a treaty was signed in 1739. By this time, Maratha control of the seas had extended from Kutch to Cochin and had severely hampered British trade. Meanwhile, in order *to* build ships at a site closer to the scene of action, the British had set up a naval dockyard at Bombay in 1735.

A combined operation by the British and the Peshwas by land and sea, led by Admiral Watson with his ships and 1400 sailors and Colonel Robert Clive with his army contingent, besieged Gheria and were successful in capturing it and reducing Maratha sea power to nought. It may not be out of place to mention here that Admiral Watson and 50 sailors of the Marine assisted Clive in the Battle of Plassey in 1757.

Some merchants from Ostend, Antwerp and other Flemish towns arrived in Bengal on board a ship laden with merchandise during the second decade of the 18th Century. The Ostend Company was set up in 1722 with the blessings of Nawab Murshid Kuli Khan and a factory was set up in Banki Bazar, south of Chandernagore. They, however, faced considerable opposition from the other European trading communities and the Nawab's Charter was withdrawn in 1727 as a result. Soon thereafter, a naval engagement took place between the Flemish and Nawab's forces and the Flemish merchants, having been defeated, withdrew from India.

Entering the scene to challenge British sea power in the region in 1740 were the French and they began their operations by capturing Mauritius and converting it into a strong naval base and then sending a strong fleet into the Bay of Bengal to intercept and capture British merchant ships. The war of Austrian succession in Europe in 1744 saw the British and the French in opposing camps and Dupleix, the French Governor of Pondicherry, decided to act. Having already decided to capture the entire South Indian region, he used the French Fleet, which was under the command of La Bourdon-nais, to launch an attack on the British Fleet which was led by Captain Peyton. The French Fleet succeeded in driving the British Fleet up the Hooghly and then, after a brief resistance, captured Madras.

Dupleix, however, did not appreciate the importance of sea power as an essential factor in maintaining supremacy over land areas continguous to the sea. La Bourdonnais was thus allowed to return to France in 1747 and the British regained the command of the seas around India once again. They also brought six powerful ships and several small craft of Boscawan's Fleet to the Bay of Bengal in 1748 and beseiged Pondicherry. This siege, however, was not successful but the British continued to make their presence felt by annexing strategic and important regions. One of these was Chandernagore, a French possession, which was captured by Admiral Watson, assisted by Clive, in 1756. Watson died in 1757 and the British Fleet, under the command of Admiral Pocock, attacked Madras. Despite some reverses suffered at the hands of the French, the British land forces took the offensive and defeated them in the Carnatic War while Admiral Pocock defeated the French Fleet under

D'Ache which was driven away from the sea leaving the British as the masters of the entire sea area around India.

Peace was, however, short-lived for after a few years of the British annexation of Pondicherry, Admiral Suffren, a redoubtable naval tactician, appeared on the scene with a reinforced French Fleet and attacked the British Fleet which was under the command of Admiral Sir Edward Hughes. A series of encounters ensued but following a treaty between England and France, Admiral Suffren and his Fleet left the area, converting the Indian Ocean into a British lake. The later half of the 18th century saw the extinction of Portuguese power in India, the British seizure of the island of Sal-setta and other Portuguese holdings in India and the British victory over Haider Ali's navy at Honavar and Mangalore.

Both Hyder Ali and Tipu Sultan had maintained a fleet mainly to support their operations on land and protect their trade interests abroad. They were formidable adversaries who inflicted a severe defeat on the British and came near to breaking the power of the East India Company. But they were confined to the south and did not directly affect the fortunes of India as a whole. Haider Ali was a remarkable man and one of the notable figures in Indian history.

He had some kind of a national ideal and possessed the qualities of a leader with vision. Continually suffering from a painful disease, his self-discipline and capacity for hard work were astonishing. He realised, long before others did the importance of sea power and the growing menace of the British based on naval strength. He tried to organise a joint effort to drive them out and, for this purpose, sent envoys to the Marathas, the Nizam, and Shuja-ud-Dowla of Oudh. But nothing came of this. He started building his own navy and, capturing the Maldive Islands, made them his headquarters for shipbuilding and naval activities. He died by the wayside as he was marching with his army. His son Tipu continued to strengthen his navy. Tipu also sent messages to Napoleon and to the Sultan in Constantinople. Haider Ali had, however, lamented that he could beat the English on land, but he could not dry up the sea.

One of the other little-known facts of our maritime history is that, over two centuries ago, the Germans too made an attempt to establish a footing in Bengal. In 1753, some merchants from Empden, atown in Germany, founded a company, popularly known at that time as the Bengal Company of Empden or the Royal Prussian Bengal Company. The British, the French, the Dutch and the Danes, who had already set up factories on the banks of the Hooghly, combined against the newcomers and orders were issued forbidding their pilots, masters and mates to render any assistance to the Germans. The Moghul Nawab also issued orders to these foreigners asking them to prevent the setting up of a German establishment.

The German ships, the largest of them being the Prince Henry of Prussia, however, arrived and set up a factory near Chandernagore and succeeded in getting the Nawab's approval for carrying on their trade after paying a "nazrana" (gift) on Rs. 5,000 to him.

Faced with bitter hostility from the other European competitors, the Germans failed to expand their trade and could not make any headway toward constructing buildings and warehouses for the purpose. They decided, therefore, to wind up their trade and by 1760, returned to Germany.

Lord Nelson, when he was only 16, visited Bombay and Calcutta while on board the *Seahorse,* a twenty-gun ship, during its voyage to the 'East Indies' in 1775. The ship reached Bombay on the morning of August 17, 1775 and later visited Calcutta when Nelson contracted some "distressing illness and fevers." He was sent home on board the frigate, *Dolphin* and completely recovered before reaching England.

The details of his journey from the Hooghly to Portsmouth are recorded in the book *Nelson* written by Carola Oman. The shipbuilding yard at Surat had been setup in 1635 during which year the East India Company built four pinnaces and other larger vessels, this being the first record of any of their shipbuilding activities in India. The shift to Bombay in 1735 was necessitated by its being safer and closer to the scenes of action. It was Lowjee Nusserwanjee Wadia, ancestor of along line of famous Parsi master-builders of ships, naval and commercial, who selected the site for the Naval Dockyard which during the course of the next 100 years, proceeded to build not less than 115 war vessels and 144 merchant ships including 84 gun-ships of a total tonnage of over 2,000 for the Royal Navy. The quality of construction of these ships was of such a high order that they were acclaimed by shipbuilding nations around the globe.

It was the Wadias who proved to the world that Indian-built Malabar teak ships were far superior in seaworthiness and withstanding the detrimental effects of the elements than Britishbuilt oaken ships. *HMS Trincomalee*^ which was built by the Bombay Naval Dockyard in 1817 for the Royal Navy and which saw many battles during the period of her commission, is still in use at Portsmouth as *TS Foudroyant* for training school and college students in seamanship arid navigation and is the oldest sail-driven warship afloat today. Her Malabar teak hull and superstructure, despite several major modifications, damages suffered during battles and storms and continuous use for training purposes, is still as good as new and to quote a well-known shipbuilder, "good for another 300 years".

The earlier decades of the 19th century saw the arrival in the Indian waters of pirates belonging to an Arab tribe called the Joasmis. They operated from the Arab side of the Persian Gulf covering the coast from Bahrain to Cape Mussendon and, with their headquarters at Ras-el-Khaima, they held sway over the entire Persian Gulf. Originally merchants and pearl-fishers, they now took to piracy. For many years they left the ships of the East India Company alone and attacked only small craft but since the Company ships took no action against the Arab pirates plundering ships and craft belonging to the others, this was interpreted by the Joasmis as a sign of weakness and later they stopped sparing the Company ships.

A fleet of 12 ships of the Bombay Marine, carrying 4,000 men and under the command of Captain Seaton, attacked Ras-el-Khaima in 1809 and bombarded this focal point of the Joasmis' operations but were beaten back by the well-entrenched Joasmi forces. The squadron of ships had, therefore, to return to Bombay and the Arab pirates continued to seize and plunder the

Company's ships. Under the command of Captain Collier, the Company later despatched another fleet of II ships with 6,000 men under Major General Sir William Grant Keir.

They blockaded the town of Ras-el-Khaima for four days as a result of which Sardar Hasan Bin Rehman, the Joasmi Chief, gave himself up and admitted defeat. The Arabs guaranteed safe passage to British ships in a treaty in 1820 and the East India Company was not subjected to harassment by the Arabs any further.

An interesting fact recorded is that the Punjab Regiment of the Indian Army is probably the only example in the world of a land-based force, having a naval craft as its cap-badge with the motto "Sthal-wa-Jal" (earlier "Khushki-wa-Tari"). This regiment was permitted to adopt the galley as an emblem because it took part in many military expeditions overseas between 1796 and 1824.

Two important events took place in 1829. The Bombay Marine was assigned the new nomenclature, the Bombay Marine Corps, and *Hugh Lindsay,* a ship of the East India Company, was the first to be fitted with a steam engine. *Hugh Lindsay, a. 411-ton* ship of the Bombay Marine Corps, steamed out of Bombay on March 20, 1830 and reached the Suez after 21 days of actual steaming averaging a trifle under six knots. Thus began the gradual conversion of the Company's ships from sail to steam which was completed during the next 15 years. The year 1830 also saw another change in the name of the Service—this time to the Indian Navy.

All went well for seven years thereafter when in 1837 a pilgrim ship of the East India Company, whilst on passage to Mecca, with a number of rich pilgrims on board, was seized and plundered near Aden. A squadron of the Indian Navy's men-of-war, led by Commander Haines, was then sent to attack Aden but since the Sultan of Aden was in a repentant mood and ready to pay an indemnity of Rs. 3 lakhs, the ships spared Aden and returned to Bombay in 1838. The indemnity promised was, however, never paid by the Sultan and hence the ships returned to Aden in the same year and captured it.

In 1848, during the Anglo-Sikh War, the Indian Navy provided a contingent of 100 ratings and seven officers with their guns to participate in the siege of Multan. This would appear to be the second occasion when the Navy was actively employed for land operations.

In 1852 a strong fleet of the Indian Navy, under the command of Captain Lynch, attacked and captured Rangoon. The Raja of Burma had refused to be cowed down by the naval might of Lord Dalhousie who was Viceroy of India and his defiance of the authority of the British resulted in his loss of the strategic city of Rangoon. Meanwhile, Persian and Russian seafarers in the Persian Gulf began harassing the Company's ships while they were on passage for maritime trade. A strong fleet of the Indian Navy under Sir Henry Leeke wasrsent to deal with the pirates and captured Bushire (Basra) after defeating the Persian Fleet in 1853. Ships of the Indian Navy also assisted those of the Royal Navy in suppressing piracy during the war in the Chinese waters in 1860.

The two highest decorations ever to be awarded to the personnel of the Indian Navy before Independence were earned during the 1857 uprising and on shore. An Indian Naval Brigade comprising 78 officers and 1740 men were assigned shore service during the uprising. Mister Midshipman Mayo of the 4th Detachment was awarded the Victoria Cross for his bravery at Dacca. This VC was later presented to the Service and was on display with a photograph of the young officer in the RIM (later RIN) Officers Mess at Bombay. The other recipient of the VC was Mister Acting Master GB Chicken of the 3rd Detachment in recognition of his desperate single-handed defence against an attack by a party of 20 armed men, five of whom were killed by him.

In 1863, a Marine Survey Department, manned completely by naval officers, was started in India which during the next 120 years has developed into a full-fledged Hydrographic Survey Department under free India's Navy.

Before the formation of the Marine Survey Department, hydrographic survey was being carried out by the Bombay

Marine/Indian Navy itself. In fact, survey work was started in 1772 and officers of the Service surveyed the coastal waters of not only India and the neighbouring countries and islands but also the Persian Gulf, the Red Sea, the East African Coast, the East Indies, the Philippines, the Pelew Islands in the Pacific, the Chusan Archipelago in the East China Sea and Tasmania in the Far South East? Considering the primitive instruments, the limitations of the ships used by these officers and the dangers of venturing into the unknown, the feats of eminent hydrographers like Captains McCluer, Ross and Blair would be comparable to the great Arctic explorers.

NAVAL PROTECTION

In 1863 the Indian Navy was reorganised as a non-combatant force with two branches at Bombay and Calcutta which were renamed the Bombay Marine and the Bengal Marine, naval protection of Indian waters having been taken over by the Admiralty. Their new role was transport of troops and Government stores; maintenance of 'Station Ship' duties at Aden, the Andaman Islands (Port Blair), Burma and Persian Gulf; the maintenance of gun boats on the Irawaddy and Tigris; maintenance of all Government light craft employed for military duties and in the maintenance of light-ships and lighthouses around the Coasts of India and Burma and in the Southern portion of the Red Sea and the Marine Survey of India. The nomenclature was to change again in 1871 when an Indian Defence Force with two ships was constituted and yet again in 1877 when the Government restored the combatant status to the Service and called it His Majesty's Indian Marine with two divisions at Bombay and Calcutta. The Service underwent yet another change in name in 1892 when it was rechristened the Royal Indian Marine.

From 1892 to the outbreak of World War I, the RIM did not make any significant contribution to the maritime history of the country. Before the War, the main tasks assigned to the RIM were marine survey, maintenance of lighthouses and transportation of troops. During the War, however, there were notable exploits of the RIM in various theatres of naval operations. Its ships transported troops, arms, ammunition and stores to Egypt, Iraq and East Africa. While on patrol in the Suez Canal, RIM ship *Hardinge* fought against the Turks and thwarted their efforts to block the canal. She suffered severe damage and lost one of her funnels but succeeded in preventing the blocking of the canal. RIM ships landed troops in Mesopotamia and its smaller ships, designed for operations in inland waters, rendered excellent service in the Euphrates and Tigris rivers. Three other ships, the *Northbrooke, Minto* and *Dufferin,* carried out patrolling duties in the Red Sea. While carrying out these duties, the *Minto* called at Jeddah and transported some Haj pilgrims safely back to India. The RIM was once again reverted to its non-combatant role when the War ended in 1918.

The international situation at the end of World War I, shortage of funds and extensive retrenchment adversely affected the RIM. With the task of naval defence of India once again entrusted to the Royal Navy, the combattant status of the RIM was lost. For the services rendered by the Royal Navy, the Government of India had to pay a staggering sum of £ 100,000 annually to the British Government. The RIM had, therefore, to be reduced to a small force entrusted with minor coastal duties. Most of World War I veterans were demobilised and no reservists were left for calling up during emergencies. This led to the mobilisation of Indian public opinion against the wilful eradication of the country's naval and maritime traditions and a number of committees were appointed to examine the future role of the Service and to make recommendations for suitable changes or expansion to be implemented. The Rawlinson Committee, the last such committee to be appointed, recommended the formation of a small combatant force to suit the needs of the country which was to be controlled by an administrative authority operating from the major port.

Very few Indians joined the Royal Indian Marine at that time though recruitment was open both to the Indians and the British. The first Indian to join the RIM as an officer was Engineer Sub-Lieutenant D.N. Mukerji who was commissioned on January 6, 1928. He rose to the rank of Captain and took premature retirement from service in 1950 and emigrated to

England where he is still living. The frozen continent of Antarctica which straddles the South Pole and where the environment is, literally and metaphorically, as clean and pure as driven snow, had always attracted adventurers and explorers from all parts of the globe.

One of them was Lieutenant H.R. Bowers of the Royal Indian Marine who in 1910 had the distinction of being chosen to accompany the great explorer, Captain Scott, on his expedition to the Antarctic. Even though he was not an Indian, he was the first representative of this subcontinent to embark on an expedition to the South Pole. In the words of Commander G.E. Walker, RINVR, author of *The Historical Background of the Royal Indian Navy,* Lieutenant Bowers had the high honour of being selected as one of the party which made the last great journey to the South Pole itself. Scott wrote of him, "I believe he is the hardest traveller that ever undertook a Polar journey, as well as one of the most undaunted. Never was such a sturdy, active, undefeatable little man."

When only eleven miles from safety, the three survivors of that journey were compelled by a week-long blizzard and the exhaustion of their supplies to give up their march. Scott (one of the last acts of his life) wrote to Bowers' mother, "I write when we are very near the end of our journey, and I am finishing it in company with two gallant, noble gentlemen. One of them is your son. He had come to be one of my closest and soundest friends, and I appreciate his wonderful upright nature, his ability and energy. As the troubles have thickened, his dauntless spirit ever shone brighter, and he had remained cheerful, hopeful and indomitable to the end." Scott then wrote to his brother-in-law, "There is a piece of the Union Jack I put up at the South Pole in my private kit bag... send a small piece to the King and a small piece to Queen Alexandra.... A third piece is in the RIN Officers' Mess in Bombay, with the cups and spoons which Bowers carried with him on his journey, and which were found by his dead body in his last camp."

The cups and spoons of Lieutenant Bowers along with the piece of the Union Jack are now on display at the Naval Museum at Bombay. * By sheer coincidence, the first Indian to set foot on Antarctica was also a naval officer, Lieutenant Ram Charan, an officer of the Navy's Education branch and a specialist in meteorology, who accompanied an Australian expedition to the South Pole in 1960. Unfortunately, he died in a road accident in New Delhi in 1961.

The bulk of the personnel who took part in the first Indian expedition to Antarctica, Expedition Gangotri, in 1981 were also from the Indian Navy. Indian Navy also participated in the subsequent expeditions launched in 1982, 1983 and 1984.

The indomitable spirit of adventure of personnel of the Indian Navy has taken the Naval Ensign not only to the frozen continent of Antarctica but also to the top of the world's tallest mountain, the Everest. The intrepid and renowned mountaineer of the Indian Navy, Instructor Lieutenant Commander Manmohan Singh Kohli (later rose to the rank of Captain, Indian Navy) has had the distinction of not only climbing to the highest altitude without oxygen but also of putting nine men atop the peak and hoisting the Naval Ensign on it for the first time in its history.

With the reconstitution of the RIM as a combatant force in 1928, the White Ensign was hoisted for the first time in its history on November 11, 1928. The Indian Navy Discipline Bill, based on the recommendations of the Rawlinson Committee, was also taken up by the Legislative Assembly in the same year and, after six years of deliberations, the bill was passed by the Assembly and the Council of States on September 5, 1934.

When the Indian Navy Discipline Bill was presented to the Indian Legislative Assembly on February 21,1928, it was presented as a non-contentious measure, of which barely a fortnight's notice was given, as no more was thought necessary.

Mr. Mackworth Young, the Army Secretary, introducing the Bill, gave a brief history of the Service and pointed out that the intention was "to enable India to enter upon the first stage of her naval development and ultimately to undertake her own naval defence." He pointed out that Indians had always been eligible as officers of the RIM, but no qualified candidates had ever applied. One-third of the vacancies would be reserved for

Indians in future, provided that suitable candidates offered. (He was asked whether 'one-third' meant only one person—which in fact it did, as there were only three vacancies a year—and he replied, "There will be more than one." It is difficult to understand why he said this.)

Sir Shunmugham Chetty (later became finance minister in independent India) opened the opposition with brilliant speech saying:

"My reason for opposing the present motion is that, without the consent of this House, the Government of India have decided to create an Indian Navy; necessary legislation was passed by Parliament, and what we are asked to do today is simply to legislate for the discipline of this Indian Navy, which has been created without our consent and without our approval.

"The principles underlying the creation of a Navy are these: firstly, who will pay; secondly, who will officer the Navy; and thirdly what will be the control of the Legislature over the Navy.... The question, who will pay is very easily answered: the taxpayer in India will pay." He then pointed out that the "one-third of the vacancies" amounted to one officer per year, and after considering this in detail, went on, "We will-therefore have a Navy which for decades together will be·officered entirely by British officers; and I ask the House to consider whether they will be willing parties to the creation of Indian Navy, which, though Indians may not be technically and legally excluded, will take several years to be officered by Indians."

As regards control over the RIN, he said, "I would ask whether the people of India desire to create an Indian Navy over which their control will be exactly identical with the control which this House has over the Indian Army." At this point Mr. Jinnah (later the first Governor-General of independent Pakistan) commented, "Which means nil". "In time of emergency the Indian Navy can be taken over by the British Admiralty with the consent of the Governor-General in Council, not with the consent of the Indian Legis lature, not with the consent of the Indian people; and the Governor-General in Council is a subordinate branch of the British Government."

Sir Shunmugham then dealt with the question of control in an extremely able manner, and finished up: "Fortunately for us, we are placed in this situation now: that without the passing by the Indian Legislature of the measure that is now introduced, the Indian Navy cannot come into existence.... I am sorry to use strong words, but I would conclude by saying that I would not touch the present measure with a pair of tongs."

Many later speakers elaborated and restated the points made by Sir Shunmugham Chetty without adding anything to them; his speech, however, determined the course of the debate. Munshi Iswar Saran opposed the saddling of India with the cost of a Navy whose expansion they could not control, and ridiculed the argument that at present the Navy "was only a little one," which he said, was like the nursemaid's excuse for her bastard, in *Mr. Midshipman Easy.* Sir Henry Gidney ridiculed the one-third reservation for Indians, pointing out ironically that the next step would obviously be to apply the communal rota to the one officer a year to be recruited.

In replying for Government, Mr. Mackworth Young said that if Indian candidates were forthcoming in sufficient numbers, the proportion of the intake would be increased. He pointed out that even the old RIM could be taken over by the Admiralty in times of war—without even the consent of the Governor-General in Council. He said that it was absurd to suppose that H.M. Government would want to appropriate ships from the RIN in wartime and use them in the Atlantic (how oddly that reads, twenty-two years— and one world war—after it was said!) When the Bill came up again in 1934 Sir Shunmugham Chetty was the President ("Speaker") of the House; and although the question of Indianisation was again brought up, the Bill was passed without a division, everyone giving it his blessing at the "consideration" stage.

THE ROYAL INDIAN NAVY

The Royal Indian Navy thereafter came into being on October 2, 1934 with its separate Naval Headquarters at Bombay under the Flag Officer Commanding Royal Indian Navy (FOCRIN).

The Scindia Steam Navigation Company was formed in the early twenties but its maritime activities were virtually limited to coastal trade as overseas contracts granted to the Company were very few.

The training ship for cadets, *SS Dufferin,* was acquired by the Indian Mercantile Marine Department in 1926 and started training cadets for the Merchant Navy. A number of small shipping companies came into being during the early thirties which managed to capture a sizable chunk of coastal trade from foreign shipping companies but compared to the volume of exports and imports, the tonnage under the Indian shipping companies was virtually negligible.

Between 1934 and 1939, the Royal Indian Navy was developed into a small and efficient naval force and by the time World War II broke out, the RIN fleet comprised five sloops, a survey vessel, a patrol ship, a depot ship and a large number of small craft. Recommendations were made in 1939 for assigning greater responsibility for the naval defence of India to the RIN by the Chatfield Committee. In order to enable the RIN to carry out these duties, modernisation of the Service was also recommended.

The Chatfield Committee recommendations made in 1939 were based mainly on the proposals put forward by the RIN for the expansion of the Service which was to be completed in five years. The main features of the Committee's recommendations were the construction of four Bittern class escort minesweepers, development of depots and training establishments and acquisition of local naval defence equipment. Even though the recommendations were to be implemented over a period of five years, the outbreak of the War in 1939, greatly hastened the process of expansion. The annual subvention of £100,000 to be paid to the British Government along with miscellaneous other charges ranging between £15,000 and £20,000 was also discontinued on the condition that it would be utilised towards expanding the RIN fleet and maintaining a squadron of six escort vessels which would, besides assisting the Royal Navy, carry out local naval defence duties.

Formation of reserves for the RIN was also resorted to before the War. The Royal Indian Naval Reserve (RINR) comprised serving officers of the Indian Mercantile Marine and had two branches, Executive and Accountant, to which the Engineering branch was also added at the outbreak of the War. The Royal Indian Navy Volunteer Reserve (RINVR) was constituted by inducting qualified members of the general public as commissioned officers and giving them six months intensive training at Bombay. This was also done for sailors, called ratings at that time. In addition to the regular service ratings, special service ratings were recruited who served for five years before being transferred to the Fleet Reserve for 10 years. These ratings belonged to the cadre of Royal Indian Fleet Reserve (RIFR). Personnel from the merchant marine were also recruited as "Hostilities Only" ratings for service during the War. The personnel strength of the RIN on October 1, 1939 was 114 officers and 1,732 ratings with only 16 officers manning the Naval Headquarters which was located inside the Naval Dockyard at Bombay."

When World War II broke out, the Royal Navy undertook the task of building, commissioning and wording up fast sea-going motorboats for coastal patrol and corvettes and minesweepers which were suitably armed and equipped for carrying out anti-submarine and escort duties in the waters around India. Magnetic mines posed a major threat to the merchant marine at that time and hence 263 merchant and naval ships were fitted with degaussing cables made in India by June 1941.

The first Basset class trawler, *HMIS Travancore,* was built at Calcutta and commissioned into the RIN in July 1941 and was followed by five more within a year and another six soon thereafter. The first Bangor class minesweeper built in India joined the RIN in 1943. Six sloops built in Great Britain and named after Indian rivers, Jumna, Sutlej, Cauvery, Kistna, Godavarl and Narbada, also joined the RIN to reinforce its fleet. In order to maintain effective control over the operational and organisational aspects of the RIN at Bombay, the FOCRIN could pay only occasional visits to New Delhi, the focal point of command and control: This led to considerable delay in obtaining New Delhi's clearance on important matters as the bulk of the exchanges between the capital and Bombay had to be by correspondence or by signal. A Naval Liaison Officer was positioned at New Delhi in October 1939 to reduce the time taken in processing important papers but even this proved unsatisfactory and hence the Naval Headquarters was transferred from Bombay to New Delhi in March 1941.

At the time of the outbreak of the War, all training establishments of the RIN were concentrated inside the RIN Dockyard, Bombay. These were the Seamanship School, the Signal School, the Gunnery School, the Mechanical Training Establishment, the Boys' Training Establishment and the Antisubmarine School.

There were no schools for training in torpedo, radar and electrical disciplines. There were also no facilities for training officers who were perforce deputed to the Royal Naval Establishments in the United Kingdom for basic and advanced training in all disciplines.

As the size of the RIN fleet increased and the tasks assigned to it multiplied, several new naval establishments came up at Jamnagar, Cochin, Mandapam, Madras, Coconada (Kakinada), Vishakhapatnam and Calcutta.

To cope with the increased intake of sailors and requirements of equipping the fleet, the existing naval bases at Karachi and Bombay were expanded and modernised. The extremely rapid growth of the RIN in terms of the strength of the fleet and personnel posed grave problems of training personnel in the specialist and general tasks. For example, by June 1940 when Italy jumped into the fray, the RIN had doubled its strength and by 1942 it had expanded to nearly six times its pre-war strength.

The naval establishments also multiplied fast. To augment training %" boys at *HMIS Dalhousie* at Bombay, *HMIS Bahadur* was commissioned at Karachi. In addition, for training officers and ratings, two more establishments, *HMIS Himalaya,* the gunnery training establishment, and *HMIS Chamak,* the radar training establishment, where commissioned at Karachi. The other naval bases that came up about this time were *HMIS Shivaji,* the mechanical training establishment at Lonavla, *HMIS Akbar,* ratings' training establishment at Thane, *HMIS Talwar,* the Signal School at Bombay, and a mechanical training establishment at Pilani.

Merchant ships were armed for defence At Karachi, Bombay and Calcutta and inspection organisations were set up at Vishakhapatnam, Madras and Cochin.

In order to make up for the wartime losses of the merchant marine, the need was felt for a major merchant shipbuilding yard and accordingly a site was located at Vishakhapatnam by the Scindia Steam Navigation Company but the first major ship, a freighter, could only be launched well after the War in 1948.

The problem created by the inadequate supply of stores and supplies to the Allied forces owing to the United Kingdom's inability to send supplies in sufficient quantities was solved by the Indian mercantile marine who shouldered the responsibility of delivering stores to places as far as Malta and Hqngkong.

Under the overall command of the Commander-in-Chief, East Indies, sloops of the Royal Indian Navy took part in the operations in the Red Sea, Gulf of Aden and the Persian Gulf in 1940. *HMIS Jumna* and *HMIS Sutlej* took part in the Battle of the Atlantic in 1941.

In the same year, reoccupation of Berbera in the Gulf of Aden was made possible by the first combined operations, i.e. amphibious operations, by the Indian Army and the Royal Indian Navy. The RIN also played a vital role during the advance of the Allied Forces in Sudan. While *HMIS Clive* softened up the area between Port Sudan and Massawa with her armament and *HMIS Hindustan, Indus, Parvatiand Ratnagiri* led the attack, the minesweepers entered Massawa and annexed the port from the Italians.

HMIS Lawrence and *Lilavati* earned distinction in the operations in the Persian Gulf and two officers of the RIN were awarded the distinguished Service Cross. These were Lieutenant

N. Krishnan for his act of gallantry while boarding and overpowering the crew of an armed tug belonging to the Axis during Operation Countenance for the capture of Abadan in 1941 and Engineer Lieutenant D. Shankar (later rose to the rank of Rear Admiral and became the Controller General of Defence Production) who, while boarding an Italian vessel, *Cabote,* during the Persian Gulf operation in the same year, went through the blazing bridge-deck at considerable risk to his life and captured the crew.

One of the ships built by Australia during the War for the RIN was *HMIS Bengal* (733 tons), a Bathurst Class minesweeper. On November 5, 1942, she sailed from Fremantle as escort to *M.V. Ondina,* a Dutch tanker on passage to Diego Garcia. At 1145 hours on November 11, 1942, she sighted a vessel, about eight miles off, coming straight towards her. The newcomer could not be identified but, in any case, to adopt the safer course, Bengal sounded her action alarm, and the ship's company closed up at "Action Stations".

Bengal altered course to starboard, and instructed the tanker to take station on her starboard beam. At this time, another ship appeared over the horizon, coming up at *Bengal's* port bow. Both ships were larger than *Bengal,* whose armament comprised one 12-pounder gun and a few close-range, anti-aircraft guns. By this time both the ships had been identified as Japanese. The *Ondina* was, therefore, instructed to act independently and to rendezvous at a certain position the following day.

Bengal then increased to full speed, and turned to engage the first raider. She hoped, in this way, to allow the tanker time enough to get away, but the Master of *Ondina* would not leave her to face the two raiders alone. Instead, with his four-inch gunmounted aft, he returned the fire. The action that followed is best described in the words of the Commanding Officer Lieutenant Commander W.J. Wilson, RINR:

"The raider came up very fast and *Bengal* steamed straight ahead at her. The raider also increased speed, and opened fire at about 3500 yards with her forward guns. We retaliated, and hit first. At 3000 yards we must have hit the raider in the magazine because a great sheet of flame shot up astern, almost mast high. We then closed the range, and fought the action at about 2500 yards.

The second Japanese raider never came closer than 8000 yards. Both fired at us continuously. The first ship we engaged carried on firing until, in a great sheet of flame, she blew up and sank. She fired over 200 rounds at us. At 1246 hours our ammunition was running short. We had very few rounds left, and our vessel was damaged fore and aft. The ship that we sank was a large edition of the Kunikawa Maru class and was of approximately 10,000 tons. The second raider was slightly smaller, her tonnage being 8000. They were both firing 4-inch gun broadsides, and these appeared to be from 5.5 inch guns. We drew the enemy's fire, and acted as a screen, as long as possible, to allow the tanker to escape.

"The encounter lasted for over two hours, but really the first three minutes decided the issue. While shells were bursting all round them, the crew of, *Bengal kept* on firing one salvo after another. The sixth salvo made a direct hit on the first raider for, following a terrific explosion, flames leapt high in the air from her.

This greatly enthused the RIN crew, we kept on firing steadily. By that time, the second raider had come within range, and opened fire. Within a quarter of an hour of action, a fire broke out in *Bengal's* officers baggage room. She had also been damaged fore and aft, and had only five rounds of high explosives remaining. The Commanding Officer accordingly decided to break off the engagement, and started to make smoke—but not before the first raider had gone down by the stern and sunk.

"The *Ondina* had then opened the range at about seven miles, but the-second raider began to chase her and fire repeatedly. The tanker's ammunition was soon expended, and her Master, Captain H. Horsman was killed on the bridge. (He was posthumously awarded the Militair Willems Order-4-Dutch V.C.—by Queen Wilhelmina of the Netherlands.) The *Ondina* was then abandoned, whereupon the raider torpedoed her twice. The raider also machine-gunned the boat, killin the chief engineer and some of the Chinese crew. When the raider left the scene, volunteers boarded the vessel and, with some difficulty, got her under way. She eventually reached Fremantle, where she had been given up for lost.

"It was a matter of surprise, even to the ship's company, that the *Bengal* emerged from this action without serious damage. They had never been in action before, but when 'Action Stations' where sounded, everyone was perfectly calm, firm and disciplined, and all hands were, in fact, anxious to have a shot at the raider.

The Captain's example was highly inspiring, and the tribute he paid to his men was fully deserved. He said, 'No praise is great enough for their magnificent conduct in face of the greatest danger.' The FOCRIN Vice-Admiral Sir Herbert Fitzherbert spoke much in the same strain when in his message he said, 'We are all proud of you.'

"When *Bengal* reached Colombo, every ship in harbour gave her an official and spontaneous reception. A band played on the jetty, and as the ship's company descended the gangway of their ship, they were greeted with loud cheers. The acme of the crew's joy however, was when they steamed into Bombay. While still outside the harbour, RIN ships which happened to be in the vicinity, saluted them. The 75 officers and men received a public reception, and were honoured at a lunch in the Sir Cowasji Jehangir Hall.

"Besides the Commanding Officer of the ship, Lieutenant Commander W.J. Wilson, RINR, who was awarded the Distinguished Service Order, two Indian ratings were also decorated. Leading Seaman Ismail Mohammed, one of the 12-pounder gun's crew, was awarded the Indian Distinguished Service Medal for gallantry and devotion to duty. Petty Officer Mohammed Ibrahim, captain of the 12-pounder gun, was awarded the Indian Order of Merit Second Class for setting an excellent example of steadiness and resolution and using his weapon to the very best advantage even after the *Bengal* had been hit by enemy gun fire."

The writer well remembers decyphering the signals from *Bengal* in the Navy Office in Calcutta that night and passing the news to the then Naval Officer-in-Charge, Calcutta, Captain L. Sanderson, C.I.E., RIN.

Operating from Chittagong and Koronge Island, ships of the RIN carried ^put sustained attacks on the Arakan Coast of Burma. They also provided close support to troops that had been landed by the RIN landing craft for driving the Japanese away from the area. Despite its success in operations in various theatres of war around the globe, the losses suffered by the RIN were negligible and when VJ Day arrived, ships of the RIN and their men were still raring to go. Nix ships of the RIN were lost during the War: *HMIS Pathan* (Escort Patrol Ship) 23rd June, 1940 off Bombay by explosion; *HMIS Parvati* (Auxiliary) 30th April, 1941 mined off Massawa; *HMIS Parbhavati* (Auxiliary) 8th December, 1941 off *Goa; HMIS Sophie Marie* (Auxiliary) 1st March, 1942 mined in Macpherson Strait; *HMIS Indus* (Sloop) 6th April, 1942 air attack at Akyab; and *HMIS Lady Craddock* (Auxiliary) 16th October, 1942 Cyclone in river Hooghly. The end to World War II was hastened by the nuclear holocaust perpetrated on the innocent residents of Hiroshima and Nagasaki in Japan and on August 15, 1945, Emperor Hirohito surrendered.

At {he time of cessation of hostilities, the RIN fleet comprised seven sloops, four frigates, four corvettes, 14 minesweepers, 16 trawlers, two depot ships, 30 auxiliary vessels, 150 landing craft of various types, 200 harbour craft, several motor launches and harbour defence motor launches and over 25,000 officers and men.

As the guns fell silent on August 15, 1945, exactly two years before we were to gain Independence, the stage was set for carrying out the post-war tasks, such as sanitising—sweeping large areas for mines and other sunken hazards in and around Indian waters; preventing any further repetition of the traumatic experience; decommissioning or assigning peace-time roles to a large number of ships and craft with the RIN which had been rendered redundant and refurbishing the Navy to meet the post-World War II requirements.

The 1939-45 global conflict also brought in the growing realisation of the after-effects of man's merciless and persistent assault on ecology which began with the Industrial Revolution and which has assumed monstrous proportions today, the rapidly dwindling energy, food and mineral resources of the earth and the vast potential of the living and mineral wealth in the oceans, on the ocean bed and below the ocean bed.

International rivalry over sharing the marine resources considerably delayed the adoption and coming into force of the Law of Sea Convention. This is likely to inexorably shift the theatres of future tensions from land to sea. The clouds of portent are already discernible over the distant horizon and how far man will succeed in striking a happy balance between his increasing needs and available resources without affecting ecology, only the future can tell.

10

The Royal Indian Navy Mutiny

"During the Winter of 1945-46, the world picture was one of unrest and upheaval—international, national and domestic. The Indian scene, in addition to the worldwide economic and domestic upset, showed high political tension and widespread campaign for freedom from British control.

The IN A trials had also taken place in late 1945. And within the Indian scene was that of the Royal Indian Navy—a young over-expanded Service rapidly disintegrating in the rush to demobilise, with the inspiration and binding incentive of a common war unity and war effort gone, living in a supercharged political atmosphere with its own additional feelings of disappointment, apprehension, uncertainty and unredressed grievances." This is how the post-World War II scenario has been described just prior to the traumatic experience the Royal Indian Navy had of the mutiny in February 1946.

By the time the War ended in 1945, the Service had grown very rapidly. From a glorified flotilla with eight ships, some small craft and minimal shore facilities with a strength of about 1500 personnel prior to the War in 1939 into a Service virtually bursting at its seams with nearly 300 ships and craft, some designed and built as naval vessels and the rest commandeered from all possible sources and converted and suitably armed for the purpose, a large number of shore establishments and over 25,000 officers and men. The main task facing the naval authorities at that time was two-fold/-de-commissioning and assigning peacetime roles to a large number of ships and craft and, what was more important, the demobilisation, resettlement and rehabilitation of several officers and ratings belonging to a wide variety of ethnic, cultural, religious, educational, professional, linguistic and social background. The latter assumed grim and strident overtones with the winding up of the numerous organisations which had mushroomed in a most ad hoc manner all over the country during the War. This was further aggravated by the decision taken to reduce the Service to a much smaller force, based on the assessment of the time that the potential enemies of the Allied Forces in the region had already been totally annihilated!

SALIENT FEATURES OF THE MUTINY

Some of the broad features of the mutiny were: Bombay— processions taken out by the Naval ratings; the shouting of slogans; burning of the American Flag in the U.S. Information Office; hoisting the Congress, Muslim League and 'Jai Hind' flags; lowering of the Naval Ensign; and some acts of violence and exchange of fire in the Castle Barracks between the mutineers and military personnel who had been called in to quell the mutiny.

Karachi— acts of violence on *HMIS Bahadur* and *HMIS Himalaya* and a procession from there to *HMIS Chamak* (Radar School); and an exchange of fire between the military and the mutineers *of HMIS Hindustan,* a sloop. At other places, generally non-violent measures such as refusal to work and hunger strike were resorted to. With rare exceptions, the behaviour of the mutineers towards their officers was courteous with the usual marks of respect.

The casualties suffered by the mutineers and the others included one rating killed and six wounded, one RIN officer killed and one wounded, two British Other Ranks wounded in Bombay, and eight ratings killed and 33 wounded (including British soldiers) in Karachi. In response to appeals made by political leaders of eminence such as Shri Jawaharlal Nehru and Sardar Vallabhbhai Patel, the mutineers later surrendered. The mutiny, however, had wide repurcussions all over the country and the Central Legislative Assembly discussed it on February 22 and 23, 1946. When it was taken up at the Defence Consultative Committee Meeting held on March 8, 1946, Field Marshal Sir Claude Auchinleck, the then Commander-in-Chief of the three Services, recommended a Commission of Enquiry at the conclusion of the discussions. The Commission, as proposed by him, was to enquire into and report on "the causes and origin of the recent mutiny in the Royal Indian Navy."

The formal announcement on the appointment of a Commission of Enquiry was subsequently made by the War Department in April 1946. The Commission was to consist of: Chairman— The Honourable Sir Saiyed Fazl Ali, Chief Justice of Patna High Court; Judicial Members —Mr. Justice K.S. Krishnaswamy Iyengar, Chief Justice of the then Cochin State and Mr. Justice M.C. Mahajan, Judge of the Lahore High Court; Service Members—Vice Admiral W.R. Patterson, Flag Officer Commanding the Cruiser Squadron in the East Indies Fleet and Major General T.W. Rees, Commander of the Fourth Indian Division.

THE MUTINY

The Mutiny originated on February 18, 1946 on the then *HMIS Talwar,* the Navy's Wireless Communication Establishment in Bombay (even shore establishments are referred to as ships in naval parlance) and then spread to various naval ships and establishments all over the country and even beyond Indian shores. Only a few remained unaffected. Ten establishments and 45 ships, besides 11 miscellaneous ships and four flotillas, joined the mutiny. The major shore establishments and ships involved were:

BOMBAY : *The Royal Indian Navy Depot:* This comprised the Castle Barracks (now Naval Barracks) which housed about 900 ratings belonging to the ships in the Naval Dockyard and those awaiting appointment to other ships or to the release centres, the Fort Barracks which housed the H.O. (Hostilities Only) ratings, the Central Communication Office which handled all signal traffic for naval authorities in Bombay, the Colaba Receiving Station which was a wireless receiving station manned by about 80 ratings, the Mahul Wireless Station in Trombay Island, 14 miles away from Bombay, which housed the naval wireless transmitters and was staffed by about 50 ratings and the RIN Hospital at Sewri which had a bed strength of 300 and a 220 strong staff including nursing staff known as Sick Berth Attendants.

Other Establishments: HMIS Talwar which trained all visual and wireless communication ratings; *HMIS Machlimar* at Versova, 12 miles away from Bombay, which was manned by 300 ratings and which imparted training in anti-submarine operations; *HMIS Hamla* at Marve, 20 miles away from Bombay, which housed the Landing Craft Wing of the RIN with about 600 ratings; *HMIS Kakauri,* the demobilisation centre housing over 1400 ratings; *HMIS Cheetah,* the second demobilisation centre situated on Trombay Island; *HMIS Akbar* situated at Kolsett, 28 miles away from Bombay, and comprising a cookery school, a physical training centre, a few units to conduct some miscellaneous courses and a training school which undertook the basic training of 3000 recruits at a time for Spscial Service ratings (500 were there at the time of the mutiny); and *HMIS Feroze,* situated on Malabar Hill, Bombay which initially undertook training of Reserve Officers and later became the demobilisation centre for officers (it had 120 ratings at the time of the mutiny).

Ships: Sloops—*HMIS Narbada* and *Jumna;* Frigate—*HMIS Dhanush;* Corvettes—*HMIS Gondwana, Assam, Maharatta* and *Sind;* Fleet Minesweepers—*HMIS Kumaon, Kathiawar, Khyber, Punjab, Bombay, Madras, Orissa,* and *Oudh;* Old Sloops—*HMIS Clive* and *Lawrence;* Trawlers— *HMIS Agra, Cuttack, Karachi, Lahore, Madura, Nautilus, Nasik, Patna, Poona, Rampur, Berar, Amritsar* and *Cochin;* Ex-Persian Gunboats—*HMIS Nilam, Moti, Lai* and *Heera;* Auxiliary Vessels—*HMIS Kalavati, Ramdas, Dipavati* and *Bhadravati;* there were also a few Motor Minesweepers.

KARACHI: Shore Establishments: *HMIS Bahadur,* Boy's Training Establishment, *Chamak,* the Radar School and

Himalaya the Gunnery School. Ships: *HMIS Hindustan* and *Travancore;* Motor Launch 1262.

MADRAS: Shore Establishment: *HMIS Adyar.*

CALCUTTA: Shore Establishment: *HMIS Hooghly* (now *INS Netaji Subhash)..* Ship: *HMIS* Rajputana.

COCHIN : Shore Establishment: *HMIS Venduruthy.* Ships: *HMIS Baroda* and some launches, etc.

LONAVLA: Shore Establishment: *HMIS Shivaji,* the Navy's Mechanical Training Establishment, which trained artificers and stokers. It could accommodate 800 ratings.

JAMNAGAR: Shore Establishment: *HMIS Valsura,* the Electrical and Torpedo Training School, which accommodated about 300 ratings.

VISHAKH APATNAM: Shore Establishment: *HMIS Circars.*

Ships: *HMIS Sonavati, Ahmedabad* and *Shillong;* and certain flotillas.

MANDAPAM : Shore Establishment: *HMIS Tengra.*

ADEN : Shore Establishment: W/T Station.

BAHRAIN: Shore Establishment: W/T Station.

ANDAMAN & NICOBAR ISLANDS: Ships: *HMIS Rohilkhand, Hongkong, Deccan, Bengal, Bihar, Baluchistan* and *Kistna.*

NEW DELHI : Shore Establishment: *HMIS India.*

The following ships and establishments, however, did not mutiny:

HMIS Shamsher, a frigate—the solitary exception at Bombay; *HMIS Dilawar,* a Boys' Training Establishment, and Motor Launch 1261 at Karachi; a sloop, at Madras; *HMIS Barracuda,* a depot ship, at Calcutta; Motor Minesweeper 154, a launch at Cochin; *HMIS Tir,* a frigate at Vishakhapatnam; *HMIS Investigator,* a survey ship and *Llanstephen Castle,* a depot ship at Trincomalee; *HMIS Cauvery* and *HMIS Sutlej,* both sloops in the Pacific and *HMIS Calcutta,* which was at sea. Sub-Lieutenant R.K.S. Ghandhi (later Vice Admiral and Flag Officer Commanding-in-Chief ot the Western Naval Command) has the following to say with regard to *HMIS Shamsher,* the only ship which did not participate in the Mutiny at Bombay :

"After completing my Sub-Lieutenant Courses in England, I arrived back in India in October 1945 and joined *HMIS Shamsher. Shamsher was* a river class frigate which we had recently acquired from the Royal Navy and I was part of its first commission. The officers at that time were, Commanding Officer Lieutenant Krishnan, Executive Officer Lieutenant Gautam Singh, Engineer Officer Lieutenant Commander Bhushan, Senior Engineer Lieutenant Zahid Hassain, Surgeon Lieutenant Mohinder Singh, Supply Officer Lieutenant E.L. Pinto, Communication Officer Lieutenant Ameer Aslam and Sub-Lieutenant Anthony Pillai. There were a couple of Britishers also; one was Lieutenant Hammond and the other was a Sub-Lieutenant whose name I forgot. When I joined, I was the Navigating Officer, Gunnery Officer and incharge of the mess and wines.

"At that time *Shamsher* was a test ship and probably the Britishers were trying it as an experiment, in that it was practically, *in toto,* a ship manned by Indian officers. This period was one of great confusion and speculation amongst the reserve officers of the Indian Navy.

The British Government had decided that the post-War strength of the Indian Navy was to be an induction of only 100 reserve officers to the permanent cadre of which 66 would be Indians and 34 would be British.

Therefore, a great deal of time and energy was spent by reserve officers sitting at the Coffee House discussing their future employment. I well remember at that time that I was shocked to see officers spending so much of their working hours away from their ships and in the evening also there would hardly be any officer on board to look after the men. "By and large, *Shamsher* was a happy ship, an efficient ship, and as we did a great deal of sea time, we were away from the flesh pots of Bombay, which all helped. Krishnan was a great leader and even those days he always called himself Captain.

"In February 1946 (the exact date I do not remember), we were at sea on passage Northwards to Bombay. During the dog watches, (evening duty hours), we received a message from Bombay W/T that the Royal Indian Navy sailors mutinied and that the leader had requested all ships to do likewise. On the heels of the first signal, we received another signal giving the list of the ships that had mutinied.

Ameer Aslam was the Communication Officer who dashed up to the bridge and showed me this signal, having informed me that he had given a copy to the Captain. As soon as I saw this signal, I rushed downstairs and told the Captain that it was our duty— and I proposed to him—that we enter Bombay Harbour and bombard the Royal Bombay Yacht Club.

It must be remembered that before Independence the Royal Bombay Yacht Club did not admit any Indians and this was a very sore point with me. When I told Lieutenant Krishnan that we should bombard the Yacht Club he was quite shocked and taken aback and turned round to me and said 'thank you. Please go up to the bridge, and keep watch'—or words to this effect and he made me feel that this was not a very mature thing to do. I pleaded with him and told him once again that we must open fire on the Yacht Ccib at Bombay. He once again told me to go us to the bridge which I did. Whilst I was on the bridge, Ameer Aslamand I were discussing the news and he having come up through the lower deck, a communication sailor, knew some of the men whose names were being mentioned as leaders of the mutiny. Aslam shortly thereafter went downstairs, came back again to tell me that there was a conference going on in the Commanding Officer's cabin with all the senior officers, including Lieutenant Hammona.

"By this time, the lower deck (sailors quarters) had already got the information that a mutiny had taken place and from the bridge I could see small knots of sailors talking and gossiping. "At about 8.00 p.m. we received a message from the Flag Officer, Bombay, informing us that an aircraft had ditched about 200 miles west of Bombay and that we were to proceed there and carry out a search. The Captain came up to the bridge and asked me to lay out the course to the ditched aircraft and thereafter we altered course north-westward for this position.

The sailors of course knew at once that instead of entering Bombay harbour and joining their shipmates in mutiny, we had altered the course of the ship and feelings began to get hot on the lower deck. "After night rounds, Gautam Singh informed the Captain that the men were impatient and that we should clear lower deck and explain the situation to them.

Lieutenant Krishnan, knowing my views and presuming quite rightly that I was a hot head, directed that I go up to the bridge and keep watch while he addressed the lower deck and the officers. Therefore, I was not actually present to hear Krishnan's famous speech but Aslam came up immediately after and told me of the very good theatrical performance of the Commanding Officer.

He explained to the men what mutiny was. He further explained to them that he was as much an Indian as any one else. He tore open his shirt and exclaimed that if his body was cut, black Indian blood would flow out of it. He managed to calm down the sailors and told them that we were on a task of mercy to search for a ditched aircraft.

"About 48 hours later we entered Bombay harbour to find the entire Indian Navy at anchor with black flags flying from the mastheads. Of course before that we had heard on the All India Radio that Gorkha soldiers had boarded our ring leaders' ship at Karachi and that for all intents and purpose the mutiny was over and the ring leaders behind bars.

As we entered Bombay harbour, it was such a sad sight to see soldiers in Khaki uniform with guns on the upper deck of our ships. We were also asked to hoist the black flag but this the Captain refused to do as all of us had told him that we would not do it when we are the only ship which never mutinied. "As soon as we entered and the gangway was lowered, a boat came alongside and a fair-haired officer of the rank of Lieutenant stepped on board and I overheard him telling Lieutenant Krishnan that he wanted the firing pin mechanisms from my guns, rifles and revolvers. I told the Captain that I refuse to give the firing pins to this Britisher whereupon both officers laughed and Lieutenant Krishnan introduced me to Lieutenant Mukat Kaul whom I have known ever since. At that time Kaul had absolute blonde hair, and looked like an Englishman ! Thus ended the saga of Indian Mutiny as seen from *Shamsher* the only ship which did not mutiny.

"Many years after the event, Krishnan told me that he had engineered with Aslam the diversionary signal for the ditched aircraft!"

Lieutenant Krishnan, who won the Distinguished Service Cross in action in the Persian Gulf in 1941, rose to the rank of Vice Admiral and was the Flag Officer Commanding-in-Chief of the Eastern Naval Command before retirement. He was present at the time of Pakistani General Niazi's surrender to our forces in December 1971 at Dhaka after the Indo-Pak conflict. He died in 1981.

DISCIPLINE DURING THE WAR

During World War II, the discipline in the RIN appeared to have been satisfactory on the whole. Many senior officers and others even described it as excellent! The Commission, however, stated: "one cannot overlook the numerous mutinies which have occurred in Navy's ships and Establishments during the War."

There were nine mutinies between 1942 and 1945 and the Commission recorded that "the manner in which the mutinies originated show that many of the ratings were prone to indiscipline and had exaggerated notions about their rights which reacted unfavourably on their sense of duty and loyalty to the Service.

The investigation which followed some of the mutinies has further disclosed that there were faults in the administration and that there was considerable room for improvement in the conditions of Service." After the mutiny in March 1942 in the

Mechanical Training Establishment at Bombay, the then Flag Officer Commanding Royal Indian Navy, Vice Admiral Sir Herbert Fitzherbert came to the conclusion that "Had the officers maintained proper contact with the apprentices and had the general discipline of the Establishment been in a satisfactory state, the outbreak of indiscipline could not have occurred."

In January 1943 Admiral Fitzherbert was so alarmed at the state of indiscipline in the Navy that he found it necessary to circulate the following note to the Commanding Officers of all the ships and Establishments:

"I am disturbed over the number of cases of insubordination which have occurred recently in His Majesty's Indian Ships. The frequency with which these cases have occurred points to the fact that there is something inherently wrong with the way Ships' Companies have been handled by their officers.

"I have given the fullest consideration to the recent causes and am convinced that in nearly all cases, the root cause was the mishandling of the situation by the officers, usually at a very early stage.

"Napoleon said 'There are not bad men, there are only bad officers.' The truth of this statement is amply borne out by recent happenings. It is necessary for me to enunciate certain truths concerning the handling of the men which should be known but are apparently not appreciated by all officers.

".The first and most important of all activities indulged in by any officer should be the achievement of complete trust between the men and their officers. This can only be achieved by close and intimate contact and the exercise of tact coupled with firmness when this is called for.

"It must be remembered that no two men are alike. All have different personalities and characteristics and the same treatment for the same offence is rarely justified. In this connection, I would once again stress the importance of the Divisional Officer not only knowing the name of every man in his division but also the details of his family. "It is a truism to say that all men will respond to decent treatment. Of course, they will. The fact that all men are human seems to be forgotten frequently. "The fact that a case should be dealt with completely at the very beginning is an important one.

Several cases have occurred recently in which, it is obvious, that trouble was allowed to boil up through inadequate steps being taken at the outset. "No request should ever be put to one side but should be fully enquired into and if the request cannot be approved, the fullest possible explanation should be given as to the reason for the request not being approved.

"It will be evident to all who study our men that a definite 'fear complex' exists which puts younger and weaker ratings at the mercy of an unscrupulous rating with a stronger character. The possibility of this difficulty occur ring must be constantly borne in mind and immediate steps must be taken to deal with it. "The object which all officers should endeavour to achieve is the full realisation by every man in the Ship's Company that the officers have the welfare of the men at heart. This can only be achieved by personal example, close and understanding contact and intelligent propaganda. "I wish to impress on all officers the vital necessity for intelligent and tactful handling of their men at all times. Firmness is essential in many cases but this should not be mistaken for bullying even by the most critical.

"The practice of officers always taking the first opportunity of leaving their ships on arrival in harbour is to cease. Any officer is only entitled to leave his ship when he is fully satisfied that there is not the slightest need for his presence on board and that no man in his division has any need of his advice or assistance.

"If officers do their work properly, there should not be slightest reason if why the Ship's Companies of our little ships should not be very happy *i* families.

"This letter is to be brought to the notice of all officers and Commanding Officers are to discuss it with all officers under their command."

The Commission records that notwithstanding Admiral Fitzherbert's warning and directive, the relations between the officers and men remained unhappy and the diagnosis made nearly three years earlier that much of the discontent among the men was due to the indifference and unsympathetic attitude of a large number of officers still holds good.

The previous mutinies, in the Commission's opinion, undoubtedly had a bearing on the mutiny of February 1946 insofar as they showed that there was discontent and dissatisfaction in the Service and some of the grievances required immediate redressal.

They should have served as warnings to the naval authorities and compelled them to examine the conditions in the Service as a whole and also those in the Ships and Establishments which were not involved in them with a view to finding out whether there was any danger lurking around the corner.

The Commission adds that another aspect of these mutinies that required to be stressed was that while those who took part in the mutinies had received their justifiable punishment, the manner in which some of them had been dealt with seemed to have contributed, to some extent, to the prevalent discontent in the Service.

Lieutenant Commander B.S. Soman (later Admiral and Chief of the Naval Staff, 1962-66) appearing before the Commission as a witness, while setting forth the causes" of the Mutiny, mentioned "that the higher authorities took no notice of the warning given as early as September 1942." Evidently, he was referring to the mutiny which took place on *HMIS Orissa* in September 1942, which was found on investigation to be due to bad discipline and to the fact that there was little contact and no sympathy between the officers and men.

Recognition of freedom fighters

In 1972, the Government of India addressed the Chief Secretaries of State Governments and Union Territories stating that ex-personnel of the Royal Indian Navy who had participated in the RIN mutiny would also be considered for the grant of freedom fighters pension. The conditions stipulated for the grant of freedom fighters pension was that "only those who lost their jobs or means of livelihood due to participation in the national movement would be brought under this scheme." A list of 457 sailors of the RIN who were discharged/dismissed/ released from service as a result of the RIN Mutiny was prepared and subsequently 19 more sailors were added to this list making a total of 476.

It was decided that only those sailors who were either "dismissed from the service" or "discharged SNLR" (Service no longer required) should be eligible for the grant of freedom fighters pension. This decision was based on the appreciation that these categories of ex-sailors of RIN lost their jobs/livelihood as a result of their participation in the RIN Mutiny. This was approved by the Government for implementation on June 19, 1973.

11

Navy Grows Wings

BIRTH OF THE FLEET AIR ARM

Until the time Britain ruled over this subcontinent the British grand naval strategy dictated monopolistic maritime hegemony over the Indian Ocean, with its own bluewater navy operating from three *Royal Navy* bases in Asia, at Trincomalee in Sri Lanka, rated as one of the best natural harbours in the world, Singapore, the most strategically positioned port for the control of the Far Eastern waters, and at Bahrain in the Gulf, which would have a direct bearing on the stretch of the ocean area between India's west coast and the African east coast.

Since Britain was responsible for the maritime defence of India and all other British possessions in the east, the navies of the British-occupied ritories in South Asia were assigned the responsibility of conducting coastal defence operations only. For this purpose the minuscule fleet that the combined navy of India and Pakistan-the *Royal Indian Navy*-was allowed to develop until the outbreak of World War II, comprised five sloops, one survey vessel, one patrol ship, one depot ship and a number of smaller craft.

But by the time the War ended, the strength of this flotilla, mainly because of its involvement in various theatres of operation in Asia and beyond, had risen to that of an impressive fleet of seven sloops, four frigates, four corvettes, 14 minesweepers, 16 trawlers, two depot ships, 30 auxiliary vessels,

150 landing craft of various types, 200 harbour craft and several motor launches and harbour defence motor launches. However, this unwieldy *Royal Indian Navy* fleet was soon whittled down to a much smaller flotilla, and by the time the subcontinent was partitioned on August 15,1947, it had only six sloops, four frigates, one corvette, 16 minesweepers, one survey vessel, six trawlers, six motor mineweepers, one motor launch, eight harbour defence motor launches and a squadron oflanding craft.

When the assets of the *Royal Indian Navy* were divided between India and Pakistan in 1947, as mentioned in the previous chapters, only about two-thirds of these ships and craft came to India. With a coastline extending to beyond 6,000 kilometres, it was then felt necessary, that the small Indian flotilla should be immediately expanded to a full-fledged navy. For this purpose, along with the other platforms for operating weapons at sea, an air wing or a fleet air arm was considered an essential attribute of the future navy for India, even at that time, because the effectiveness of an aircraft as a weapon system in naval warfare had been convincingly demonstrated by the British, Japanese and US navies during World War II.

Post-Independence Plan for Aircraft Carriers

Within six months of Independence a 10-year expansion plan for the Navy was drawn up at Naval Headquarters, based on the concept of two fleets for the Navy, one for the Bay of Bengal and the other for the Arabian Sea. The nucleus of each fleet was to be formed by a light fleet carrier which would be replaced by two fleet carriers, and these carriers were to be protected against enemy surface ships for which cruisers were considered essential. This expansion plan, prepared in 1948, was based on the concept of the Royal Navy undertaking the blue water responsibilities and the 'dominion' navies ensuring the naval defence of their coasts, their fleets comprising ships of all types in use mother navies of the time, including aircraft carriers. It read:

Lessons of the last war have proved abundantly the value of aircraft carriers. The hard fighting core of a balanced fleet consists no longer of battleships but aircraft carriers. Battle fleets have given place to a much more powerful fighting force-the carrier task force whose striking power is provided by aircraft carriers. Fleet carriers of the type envisaged are large and powerful vessels requiring much technical skill and experience for efficient running. It is, therefore, proposed that the Royal Indian Navy starts its naval aviation by the acquisition of two light fleet carriers which are smaller vessels with half the complement of aircraft, in the first instance. These two light fleet carriers would be given up when the first two fleet carriers are acquired.

The peace complement of aircraft in each of these light fleet carriers is one fighter squadron and one strike squadron of 16 aircraft each. The peace complement of aircraft for a fleet carrier is four squadrons of 16 aircraft each. Two of these should be fighter squadrons and two strike squadrons, making a total of eight fighter and eight strike squadrons for the four carriers. Aircraft will also be required at naval bases where ships are likely to be stationed and also at the site of the Gunnery and Navigation Schools (at Cochin) for training purposes. It is considered that two such units, oneon each coast, will be required.

The Fleet Requirement Unit for the training schools (on the west coast) should have 14 aircraft and the second Fleet Requirement Unit on the other coast need have only 10 aircraft, making a total of 24 aircraft. Thus during the 10-year acquisition plan, the Navy proposed to acquire two light fleet carriers, which were to belater replaced by four fleet carriers and a total of 280 aircraft (16 squadrons of 16 aircraft each and two Fleet Requirement Units with 24 aircraft), out of which one light fleet carrier and 154 aircraft (32 fighter aircraft, 16 strike aircraft, 24 second-line aircraft and 82 training aircraft) were to be acquired during the first phase by 1954, the capital expenditure during the period being Rs 13.13 crore and the recurring expenditure Rs 8.69 crore. The second light fleet carrier was to be acquired in 1956, the four fleet carriers in 1958, I960, 1962 and 1963 and another 134 aircraft between 1955 and 1963.

Shore Support

The Paper also proposed to set up naval air stations. It said: A number of naval air stations will be required for basing the Fleet Aircraft Requirement Units, Transport Squadron, Air Sea Rescue Squadron, Communication Squadron and the First Line Squadron when not actually embarked on carriers, when these ships are undergoing refit. In addition to these, air stations will be required for basing training squadrons.

One air station will be required for the Operational Flying Training School. The College of Naval Air Warfare, with its several wings (Advanced Training Wing, School for Naval Air Gunners and School for Naval Observers), will need another air station. One airfield will be required to provide a base for the Communication Squadron.

The need for a Fleet Air Arm was accepted by the Defence Ministers' Committee (Navy) at its meeting held on October 26,1949, and the proposal for its formation was passed by the Standing Committee for Parliament on November 13,1950.

The acquisition of two light fleet carriers and four fleet carriers was, however, considered' too expensive for present resources' by the Defence Ministers Committee (Navy) and hence the requirement was soon reduced to two light fleet carriers, each carrying one fighter squadron of 16 aircraft, one strike squadron of 16 aircraft and two amphibious aircraft, with the shore support of 10 aircraft for basic flying training, 18 aircraft for operational training, 8 aircraft for observer training and 13 aircraft for the Fleet Aircraft Requirement Unit making up a total of 117 aircraft.

The capital cost of aircraft carriers as well as the aircraft was thus reduced to Rs 5.55 crore. The two carriers are now proposed to be acquired in 1956 and 1959.

There was another reappraisal of the nation's finances at this stage leading to the imposition of extreme budgetary stringency which immediately affected the Navy's plan for acquiring an Air Arm. The Navy's expansion programme had consequently to be drastically slashed down and the proposed fleet strength reduced to a small carrier force, to be developed around only one small aircraft carrier.

PLANS APPROVED FOR TWO CARRIERS

The proposal received due support from the Governor General of India, Earl Mountbatten of Burma, and was approved by Shri Jawaharlal Nehru, the Prime Minister of India. It also received the, blessings of the Nobel laureate, Professor P.M.S. Blackett, the British Defence Scientific Adviser, who visited this country at the invitation of the Government of India.

He concurred with the plans for the expansion of India's navy on the lines recommended by the 10-year expansion plan, according to which it was proposed to acquire a light fleet carrier from Britain in 1955 to be followed, if funds could be made available, by a similar carrier in 1957. The services of an experienced officer from the Royal Navy's Fleet Air Arm, Captain H.C.Ranald, were loaned to the Indian Navy from the British Admiralty and a Directorate of Naval Aviation was set up at Naval Headquarters in 1948 with Ranald as the Navy' s first Chief of Naval Aviation (CON A).

Infrastructure of Operational and Technical Personnel

Recalls Captain Balbir Law, one of the aviation pioneers and the first Commanding Officer of the fighter squadron.

Those were heady and exciting days and the decisions were implemented at a fair pace. A small team of Royal Navy Officers were loaned to the Indian Navy to create the infrastructure, ashore and afloat. This team led by Captain Ranald, began the task of recruitment and training of aircrew and technical personnel in 1948, to meet the planned requirement for the Indian Navy to acquire two light fleet carriers by 1957. It was decided to train quickly, a small nucleus, using *the Royal Navy's* training establishments in the UK and, thereafter, to feed the additional requirements through the existing facilities of the Indian Air Force. The over all aim was that the nucleus trained with the Fleet Air Arm would not only retain the personnel in specialised skills for maintaining and operating aircraft from carriers but also lay the foundations for building the Navy's own aviation training establishments in India.

Volunteers were asked for the fledgling aviation wing and in 1948, out of the officers who had volunteered, thirteen were selected and deputed to the Indian Air Force's flying training academy at Jodhpur for a four-week flying course on Tiger Moths. These were Lieutenant (later Commodore) G.M. Shea' Lieutenant (later Commander) J.N. Vats, Lieutenant (later Commander) B.S. Ranjit, Lieutenant (later Commander) A.S. Bathena, Lieutenant (later Commander) H.K. Mukherji, Lieutenant M.M. Bakshi, Lieutenant (later Captain) T. Chakraverti, Lieutenant (later Commander) K. Cockburn, Lieutenant (later Commander) R.S. Sokhi, Lieutenant (later Commander) P.N. Parasher, Lieutenant (later Commodore) P.C. Rajkhowa, Lieutenant (later Lieutenant Commander) G.C.D'Cruz and Lieutenant (later Captain) B.D. Law. Out of these volunteers, ten officers qualified in the flying aptitude testsandwere sent forbasic flying training to the Royal Naval Air Station, Donibristle, in Scotland, in March 1949, three-Shea, Vats and Ranjit-having failed to make the grade. Out of these ten, seven qualified at Donibristle (Cockbum, Bathena, and Rajkhowa did not qualify) and were transferred to the Royal Air Force Station, Syerston, for the next phase of training, where five earned their 'wings' and two officers failed to qualify, Mukherji on Prentice and D'Cruz on Harvard aircraft. In August 1950 these five officers were sent to the Royal Naval Air Station, Lossiemouth for operational training (Bakshi, Chakraverti and Sokhi for antisubmarine operations and Law and Parashar in fighter operations) whereafter two years' rigorous training, four officers-Lieutenant P.N. Parashar, Lieutenant B.D. Law, Lieutenant T. Chakraverti and Lieutenant R.S.Sokhi-qualified in 1952 and returned to India. The fifth, Lieutenant M.M. Bakshi, died tragically in a flying accident during his operational training.

During their training in England, two out of these four officers had completed the fighter course on Seafires (the naval version of Spitfires) and the other two had been trained in the strike role in Fireflies. Parashar and Law were then attached to the 781 Communication Squadron and Sokhi and Chakraverti to the 771 Fleet Requirement Squadron at Lee-on-Solent for consolidating their flying experience and for conversion to twinengine and amphibian aircraft and a brief course on helicopters. They flew a wide variety of aircraft including the Anson, Oxford, Martinet, Firefly, the amphibian biplane Sea Otter, the twin-engined biplane Dominie and the front-line antisubmarine and fighter aircraft Seafury.

Y.N Singh, the Navy's First Aviator

Wellbefore the partitionof India, an Indian officer of the Royal Indian Navy, Lieutenant {later Commodore) Y.N. Singh, had been trained in flying in the UK and had become a qualified pilot in 1944, when he earned his wings at the Elementary Flying School, St Eugene, and served in the British 804 Squadron as a fighter pilot. In fact he was the first Indian ever to fly from the deck of an aircraft carrier at sea.

Besides these five officers, four other officers, Lieutenant (later Commander) N. Pavamana, Lieutenant {later Commander) Joginder Singh, Lieutenant (later Commander) C.R. Menon and Lieutenant (later Commodore) B.R. Acharya were soon selected for the Navy's air arm and received their basic training from the IAF and were awarded wings in 1953. Because of the absence of technical staff required for aircraft maintenance, two officers of the Engineering Branch of the Navy, Lieutenant (later Commander) P.V. George and Lieutenant Commander (later Rear Admiral) H.D. Kapadia, were sent to the UK for specialisation in air engineering. Two engineer officers of he Indian Air Force, Lieutenant (later Commander) *MS*. Shrikhande and Lieutenant (later Commander) V.S.P. Mudaliar were transferred to the aviation wing of the Navy to strengthen its technical base.

The Navy at this time also required officers to serve as observers-officers who fly in naval aircraft and are assigned the tasks of reconnaissance, antisubmarine warfare, aerial photography, photo intelligence, tactical coordination, radar control, communication, air navigation, etc., and hence a batch of five officers-Lieutenant (later Vice Admiral) M.K. Roy,

Lieutenant (later Commander) M.N. Gupta, Lieutenant (later Lieutenant Commander) J.V. Nazareth, Lieutenant (later Commander) V. Chakravarthy and Lieutenant C.P. Ramachandran-was sent to the UK for training in 1951.

The Birth Pangs

The Defence budget for 1949-50 had provided for adequate funds for the acquisition of carrier aircraft so that these aircraft could be used to impart adequate training to the naval pilots in preparation for the acquisition of the first aircraft carrier in 1955 from the UK but no naval aircraft could be sparedat this time by the Royal Navy for transfer to India.

Besides political pressures within the country, the war in Korea slowed down the pace of development of the Fleet Air Arm for the Indian Navy. This was because the aircraft and aircraft carriers which India had proposed to acquire were no longer available as they were fully committed to the Korean War. The pressures on the Indian borders also necessitated attaching greater priority for developing the other two Services and the resultant slackening of pace also meant a change in the role of the proposed Fleet Air Arm.

Whereas the original plans would have provided real teeth and considerable punch to the Service as a whole, the new role assigned to the Air Arm was the secondary task of providing the Fleet with aircraft to enable the surface ships to practice and develop their anti-aircraft defence systems and, to a limited extent, for air-to-surface communication and reconnaissance. The change in the role implied a change in the type of aircraft required. The main role of the aircraft-cooperation with the Fleet at sea, reconnaissance and communication-dictated an aircraft which could fly singly over the sea with some degree of safety and ability to alight on the water, sufficient endurance, long-range communication and navigation facility, and the ability to carry a small load of equipment and additional personnel. The *Royal Navy* had operated two amphibian aircraft, Walrus and Sea Otter, for reconnaissance by catapulting them off most of its capital ships, but these had by now become too old for acquisition.

Naval Headquarters had in the mean while decided to recommend the acquisition of a non-carrier aircraft for pre-carrier acquisition training. The aircraft chosen was the *Sea Fury FBI!* and it was proposed to set up a shore based strike squadron with 40 such non-carrier aircraft to be acquired by the end of 1950.

However, this proposal too fell through as the Defence budget had to be severaly curtailed owing to stringent austerity measures adopted by the Government of India and naval aviation became one of the targets of these measures, reducing the number of aircraft carriers to be acquired, to only one, shelving the *Sea Fury* acquisition programme and severely trun cating the projected requirement of other ships, craft, weapon systems and equipment. At one time the Government was even contemplating the withdrawal of all personnel training in aviation and giving them the option to revert to general service or to consider a transfer to the Air Force, if acceptable to them. Ultimately, against very stiff opposition from the IAF, the Navy succeeded in obtaining Government approval for keeping naval aviation going, even though on a very restricted scale.

THE FLEET REQUIREMENT UNIT

Eventually, it was in June 1951, that the for mauonota Heet Requirement Unit for providing aircraft to be used for maritime reconnaissance, training of pilots and observers, evaluation and calibration of radar and communication equipment, support of the fleet in anti-submarine exercises and as air targets for anti-aircraft gunnery practice and training in tracking, with a complement of one squadron commander, eight pilots, four observers, one air engineer officer, one air electrical officer and 31 sailors was finally approved by the Government of India.

The change in the role did not deter Naval Headquarters from going ahead with recruiting and training personnel in all the trades and professions of naval aviation to ensure that the new arm would be completely self-sufficient. A new and highly skilled cadre emerged; it comprised pilots, observers, engineers, electrical and radio specialists, armament and ordnance specialists, safety equipment and aircraft handlers, stores men and medical officers specialising in aviation medicine. Some of these aviation personnel sub specialised to prepare for the day when the tide would turn and the navy would man its first aircraft carrier.

The Sealand

The first aircraft eventually selected, mainly because it was the only acceptable aircraft available at that time for acquisition for the Fleet requirement Unit, was the *Sealand Mark 1L* twin-engine amphibian aircraft, manufactured by Short Brothers at Belfast, North Ireland, and it was decided to acquire ten such aircraft in the first lot. This was a simple, slow and relatively very cheap aircraft which could carry two pilots, an observer, communication and direction-finding equipment, a chart table, a dome for taking navigational sights of the sun, moon or stars, and four passengers, it had an endurance of over five hours and had the luxury of a loo! Whilst it may be difficult to justify the choice of this aircraft, it must be appreciated that the deterioration in the international situation leading to the Berlin blockade, and the requirements of the Korean War and war resources, appeared to have precluded the release of suitable combat aircraft for the Indian Navy. According to Commander P.N. Parashar, one of the intrepid pioneering pilots of the Indian Navy, 'Cochin being surrounded by water and the need to find an aircraft which could fulfil multiple non-combat roles for the Fleet, aided by the personal flying experiences of Captain H.C. Ranald, must have influenced the choice of this aircraft.

The first Sealand aircraft, numbered IN 101, was formally handed over to Shri P.V.R. Rao, Deputy High Commissioner at the Indian High Commission in London (Shri Rao was to later become the Defence Secretary), By Rear Admiral M5.Slattery, Chairman, Short Brothers & Harland Ltd., at a colourful ceremony at Rochester, Kent on January 13,1953. Later, between February 4 and October 23,1953, all ten aircraft were ferried to Cochin by some of the Indian pilots trained in the UK and a British firm undertaking aircraft ferrying service.

During one of these ferrying trips, Lieutenant P.N. Parashar and Lieutenant T. Chakraverti distinguished themselves by flying in formation from Lee-on-Solent in England to Malta in a single-seater Seafury aircraft in three hours and 11 minutes, setting a new speed record for the distance. This feat provided considerable laudatory publicity in the British and Maltese press and journals.

Naval Air Station

Meanwhile negotiations had been going on for some time for the transfer of the Cochin airfield to the Navy for providing a home to the Navy's aviation wing and setting up the Fleet Requirement Unit with all necessary facilities. It had been used to a limited extent during World War II as was its nearest neighbour-Sulur in Coimbatore.

The vital task of developing the air station at Cochin, adjacent to the naval base, *Venduruthy,* was given to Commander George Douglas who had served in the Royal Navy's Fleet Air Arm with distinction, had been awarded the Distinguished Flying Cross for valour, was demobilised after World War II and permitted, by special dispensation, to join the Indian Navy. The first Indian pilot to land a Sealand aircraft on water was Lieutenant B.D. Law, who successfully touched down on the Ernakulam Channel at Cochin on April 9, 1953.

From the beginning, this new clan of aviators acquired a sense of identity and enthusiasm which surpassed all expectations. Every person, senior or junior, was full of vigour, competitiveness and comradeship, whether in achieving the number of flying hours or in the highest standards of aircraft maintenance, and this spirit asserted itself even more strongly on the sports grounds of the entire naval base. On May 11, 1953, the day the first Indian Naval Air Station, *Garuda* was commissioned, the formation of four Sealand aircraft which took part in a fly-past was led by lieutenant Commander P.N. Parashar, the other three pilots being lieutenant Commander B.D. Law, Lieutenant Commander T. Chalaaverti and Squadron Leader L.C. Dart of the IAF.

CEREMONIAL FLY-PAST AND TARGET-TOWING

On October 10, 1953, the President, Dr Rajendra Prasad reviewed the Indian Fleet at Bombay when six Sealand aircraft took part in a fly-past over the Fleet and dipped their wings in salute to the Supreme Commander, and one Sealand aircraft, piloted by Lieutenant Commander Y.N. Singh with Lieutenant M.K. Roy as crew, successfully carried out a landing on water. On November 17, 1953 four Sealand aircraft took part in a flypast in honour of the First Sea Lord of the British Admiralty, Admiral Sir Rhoderik McGregor, at Cochin. These Sealand aircraft also provided a ceremonial antisubmarine patrol in April 1954 for Queen Elizabeth II of Brita in, whose ship, *SS Gothic,* which also had the Duke of Edinou Vghon board, was on passage from Aden to Colombo. Lieutenant P.N. Parashar was the leader of the flight which ceremonially escorted the yacht of the President of Yugoslavia, Marshal Tito, when it left Cochin harbour in December 1954 after a formal visit.

The Fleet Requirement Unit was formally visited by the President of India, Dr Rajendra Prasad, in February 1956; by the British First Sea Lord, Admiral of the Fleet, Lord Lotus Mountbatten of Burma and Lady Edwina Mountbatten in March 1956, arid by His Imperial Majesty Haile Selassie, Emperor of Ethiopia, in October 1956. In August 1954, the unit began providing aircraft as aerial targets for ships of the Commonwealth Navies taking part in the annual Joint Exercises of Trincomalee GET) along with Sunderland flying boats and Shackleton Maritime Reconnaissance aircraft of the Royal Nayy operating from China Bay, near Trincomalee. Flying for the Commonwealth Navies continued for 11 years, for JET exercises continued to be held till 1957, when the frequency of the participation by the Indian Navy was reduced and eventually discontinued in 1965.

The Firefly

At this time the necessity of acquiring an aircraft capable of towing a drogue or sleeve target was felt and the Sealand aircraft was found to be considerably underpowered for withstanding the drag produced by such a towed target.

Accordingly, two Firefly Mark I single-engine carrier-borne strike aircraft, which were being operated from the aircraft carriers of the Royal Navy and had been used during the Korean War, were fitted with target-towing equipment for towing drogue and sleeve targets and acquired for the Fleet Requirement Unit in February 1955.

Three months later, three more Firefly Mark I aircraft were acquired. Between September and December 1958, another five Firefly Mark IV aircraft, fitted with 20-millimetre cannon and also capable of carrying bombs and rockets, were acquired, raising the Firefly strength to ten, and adding offensive punch to Indian naval aviation.

Reminisces Balbir Law, We remained shore-based and second line from the operational point of view but whether operating as a squad ronoras a detachment, the flying operations provided each and every one of us invaluable experience and self-confidence. Maintenance, repair and overhaul facilities were developed to achieve remarkable standards.

Above all, even these limited facilities ingrained in the minds of the Service as a whole, the importance of developing a Navy in which aircraft and helicopters would play a vital role.

The Air Arm began to attract and draw intelligent, young and highly enthusiastic volunteers from the Executive and technical branches of the Service. We also recruited short-service officers from the universities and the two merged very successfully, and their high professional standards truly formed the backbone of the new branch and contributed greatly towards its future successes.

The Hindustan Trainer 2

Meanwhile, it had been decided to supplement the basic flying training imparted by the Indian Air Force, with flying training at Cochin, and hence three Hindustan Trainer 2 (HT2) aircraft had been acquired by the Fleet Requirement Unit from the Hindustan Aircraft Limited (HAL), Bangalore and ferried to Cochin by Lieutenant Commander D.D. Law and Lieutenant R.A.J. Anderson on October 7,1956.

Air Squadrons

Since the Fleet Requirement Unit had by now acquired adequate aircraft to justify the setting up of a Naval Air Squadron, it was rechristened and commissioned as the Indian Naval Air Squadron 550 (INAS 550) with ten amphibian Sealand aircraft, ten Firefly target-towing aircraft and three HT2 trainer aircraft on June 17, 1959 and placed under the command of Lieutenant F.K.K. Menon.

Advent of Jet Aircraft-The Vampire

It was now decided to acquire some jet aircraft for *INAS 550* as the deal for acquiring an aircraft carrier hadbeen gone through in 1957, the light fleet carrier *Hercules,* to be renamed and commissioned as *Vikrant,* had been purchased and it hadbeen decided to provide India's first aircraft carrier with jet-powered fighter aircraft.

Since the Cochin airfield was not long enough to operate jet aircraft, it was decided to acquire the IAF storage depot at Sulur near Coimbatore as it had a suitable runway which was not being used by the Air Force any longer. The Gunnery School at Cochin had a small establishment manned by a naval detachment at Coimbatore which provided all the facilities to personnel using the shooting range there, and therefore could provide all facilities to the air squadron. Soon three Vampire FB-52 aircraft were acquired from the Hindustan Aircraft Limited, Bangalore and a trainer Vampire T-55 aircraft was transferred to the Navy from the Indian Air Force. And with that a Naval Jet Flight came into beingat Sulur on September 2, 1957 with Lieutenant Commander B.D. Law as its first Commanding Officer and with a complement of four officers and 56 sailors.

A few naval pilots were soon sent to the IAF Flying Instructors' School at Tambaram and the first naval pilot to qualify as a flying instructor was Lieutenant B.R.Acharya followed by Lieutenant (later Vice Admiral) S.C. Chopra, Lieutenant (later Commander) R.S. Grewal and Lieutenant (later Commander) K.K. Punchhi, all of them topping in their courses.

In 1960 the nomenclature of the Naval Jet Flight at Sulur was changed to *Indian Naval Air Squadron 550 'A' Flight* and that of the Fleet Requirement Unitat Cochin to *Indian Naval Air Squadron 550 'B'Flight,* with the task of training pilots for the two squadrons of fighter and antisubmarine aircraft for the *Vikrant,* assigned to the former. In March 1961 a further change was implemented with the *INAS 550 'A'* Flight and the Naval detachment at Sulur merging to become the Naval Contingent, Within six months, i.e., on September 5,1961, the Naval Contingent, Coimbatore was commissioned as a full-fledged naval base, *Hansa,* with Commander T. Chakraverti as its first Commanding Officer; and the squadron of aircraft at Coimbatore was commissioned as *INAS 551* on September 1 the same year, with Lieutenant R.S. Grewal as its first Commanding Officer. With the incréase in the requirement of personnel to occupy aviation billets onboard *the Vikrant* as well as the shore aviation establishments and with the growingnecessity of phasing out the obsolescent Sealand aircraft, JNAS 550, which originally was the Fleet Requirement Unit, was wound up on March 1,1962 and a Station Flight, *Gantda* wasformed with two Sealand aircraft. *INAS 550* was reformed and started using the new Alizes of the 310 Squadron and the Seahawks of the 300 Squadron for providing flying practice to its pilots.

The Soviet MI-4 Helicopter

It was in 1964, that five naval pilots, Lieutenant (later Vice Admiral) H. Johnson, Lieutenant (later Commodore) M.P. Wadhawan, Lieutenant (later Commodore) V. Ravindranath, Lieutenant (later Commander) S.R. Debgupta and Lieutenant (late Commander) P. Jha, started flying a Soviet-gifted MI-4 helicopter for the Thumba rocket-launching range. This helicopter was assigned the task of carrying out surveillance of the sea areas off Thumba in Kerala, prior to the launching of rockets.

Dove, HT2 and Kiran

During the year 1965, two Dove aircraft, three Hindustan Trainer 2 aircraft and one Kiran, a jet trainer aircraft built by the Hindustan Aircraft Limited, Bangalore, were acquired for the *INAS 550.* The officers who commanded the Fleet Requirement Unit (FRU) from 1950 to 1959, and their dates of assuming command were Lieutenant Commander Y.N. Singh (March 11,1953), Lieutenant R.S. Sokhi (January 3, 1954), Lieutenant Commander T. Chakraverti (February 5,1954), Lieutenant M.K. Roy (Februay 1, 1955), Lieutenant M.N. Gupta (February 2, 1957), Lieutenant Joginder Singh (September 17, 1957) and Lieutenant N. Pavamana (February 3,1958); and the Commanding Officers of *INAS 550* from 1959 to 1965 were Lieutenant P.K.K. Menon (June 18,1959), lieutenant (later Commodore) J.C. Puri (November 18,1959), Lieutenant (later Rear Admiral) A. Ghosh (December 1, 1960), Lieutenant R.S. Grewal Qanuary 16, 1961), Lieutenant V. Ravindranath (September 12, 1961), Lieutenant (later Commander) Arun Rao (November 1, 1962), Lieutenant (later Captain) R.D. Dhir (April 9,1964) and Lieutenant V. Ravindranath (April 10,1965).

Rear Admiral H.D. Kapadia

The person who had the longest association with naval aviation and made a significant contribution to the development of material support and maintenance facilities was Captain (later Rear Admiral) H.D. Kapadia, a specialist in Air Engineering. To quote Commander P.N. Parashar, this officer, in his various appointments in the UK and as Director of Air Maintenance and Repair at Naval Headquarters: played a very important part in all planning stages of naval aviation. Infact, out of all the "backroom boys", Homi Kapadia made the maximum contribution to the creation and expansion of naval aviation.'

In June 1964 *INAS 551* was shifted to *Hansa* at Dabolim, Goa and the jet flight and ancillary aviation units at Combatore were wound up.

Aircraft for the Vikrant-The Seahawk

As regards fighter, reconnaissance, antisubmarine and rescue aircraft for the *Vikrant,* the primary requirement for the aircraft to be chosen for the carrierborne fighter squadron of the Navy was an appropriate level of sophistication, reliability, versatility and ease of maintenance e, in a Service that was still learning to operate aircraft at sea. Taking all these vital aspects into account, the Indian Navy chose the British Seahawk jet aircraft, designated as a fighter ground attack carrier bome aircraft and manufactured by Messrs. Hawker Siddley, which had been in operation in the Royal Navy since 1953 and which was the cutting edge of the British naval task force during the 1956 Suez operations, when it operated six squadrons of this aircraft from carriers along with the French forces. Powered by a Rolls Royce Nene engine, the Seahawk had thus already proved itself and was already in operation with two other navies-the Dutch and the German. In 1959, an order was placed for 24 Sea hawk FGA Mark VI aircraft to be mainly used as fighter-bombers and the first aircraft was handed over to the Indian Navy on January 22, 1960. Soon three more Sea hawks were received and a four-aircraft Seahawk Flight was established at the Royal Naval Air Station, Lossie mouth for training Indian pilots. The Commanding Officer-designate of the squadron, Lieutenant Commander Balbir Law, and the Senior Pilot-designate, Lieutenant Commander B.R. Acharya, soon converted to Sea hawks and the Air Weapon Instructor-designate, Lieutenant R.N. Ghosh, was deputed to the Gunnery School at *Excellent,* Whale maximum speed and the tanks containing just enough fuel to reach Santa Cruz airport, it should be possible to execute a free take-off. It would otherwise mean the locking up of the Alizes on board for almost eight months, till the catapult was rectified for the summer exercises in 1963.1 assured Captain Mahindroo, Commanding Officer, that it was an acceptable risk.

When quizzed on the merits of the Seahawk and the Alize vis-a-vis similar aircraft in operation in other navies of the world at that time, Admiral Sir John Treacher, who was the *Vikrant's Work*-Up Officer after her commissioning, said: I could not fault the choice of aircraft. The Seahawk was an obvious natural for any service wishing to establish an Air Arm. It had the performance required to do the job, it was small enough to be manageable and forgiving enough for the essential confidence to be built up rapidly. The Alize was obviously the right size, with perhaps the most reliable turboprop engine the world has ever seen and although its ASW (antisubmarine warfare) capability was relatively modest, it was, again, the right aircraft at the time.

The Alouette III (Chetak)

An important component of carrier operations is a helicopter which can be used for various purposes such as search-and-rescue operations when a plane-guard ship is not available, reconnaissance, antisubmarine warfare, and antiship operations using torpedoes and short-range missiles. With the finalisation of the acquisition of the *Vikrant,* the requirement of helicopters for the Fleet Air Arm was projected to the French naval authorities and, after the conversion of Lieutenant Commander P.K.K. Menon to helicopter-flying at IAF Station, Palam, two pilots, Lieutenant M.P. Wadhawan and Lieutenant (later Commander) *AS.* Dhillon were deputed to base Ecole at La Beurgedu-lac in France, in January 1961, for conversion to Alouette n, Bell G2 and BellG3 helicopters, these helicopters having been found to be superior to the British Dragonfly he licopters which had been offered by the Admiralty. The Alouette II was more reliable than the Dragonfly, was cheaper and had been fitted with gas turbine engines which would obviate the necessity of storing petrol on board, as was required for the Dragonfly.

Two Alouette II helicopters were obtained on loan from the French Navy after the Indian pilots had been trained in search-and-rescue operations and embarked on the *Vikrant* for plane-guard duties off Malta during the carrier's work-up. On expiry of the contract period of three months, the helicopters were returned to the French Navy.

A Sikorsky S-55 helicopter was obtained on loan from the Indian Air Force in 1962 and embarked on the *Vikrant* with its IAF crew but soon Lieutenants Menon and Wadhawan converted to Sikorsky S-55 helicopters and before long another Sikorsky S-55 helicopter joined the Vikrant, both being operated by Naval pilots. One of those helicopters was lost in 1964 when it sank in the Emakulam channel in Cochin and the other returned to the IAF in the same year.

Meanwhile, it had been decided to acquire the latest version of the Alouette helicopter, the Aloutte III, from Sud Aviation, France and the first two helicopters arrived in mid-1964 in crates. These were assembled by the Navy's air engineers with the assistance of a French technician at Cochin and embarked on the *Vikrant* in July 1964.

It was the Alouette III helicopter which was later converted to its new *avatar,* Chetak, the Medium-range Antisubmarine Torpedo Carrying Helicopter (MATCH). This helicopter was equipped with antisubmarine weapons comprising two depth-charges or two antisubmarine torpedoes or a mix of the two and was indigenously manufactured by the Hindustan Aircraft limited, Bangalore for operating off the deck of carriers as well as smaller ships such as tankers, frigates, destroyers and even survey ships. Equipped with folding blades, this helicopter was powered by a 8,700-shaft-horse-power turbine and had an endurance of 25 hours, with a maximum speed of 113 knots. It had a crew of three-pilot, copilot and an aircrew in rescue operations at sea.

The three-aircraft air element chosen for the *Vikrant*-the Seahawk fighter-bomber, the Alize antisubmarine aircraft and the Alouette helicopter-had to operate in all the roles of carrier-borne aircraft such as fighter defence of the fleet and merchant shipping, maritime reconnaissance and anti-ship strike, antisubmarine defence and a variety of miscellanous tasks such as search and rescue, minelaying, ground attack, support of ground forces, aerial photography and transfer of stores and personnel. A fresh batch of 22 refurbished seahawk FGAMark IV and Mark VI aircraft were acquired from the Royal Navy during the early 1960s. The Fireflies and HT-2 trainer aircraft were paid off in 1964 and the few obsolescent Sealand amphibian aircraft, disposed of in 1965. Air Stations for the Fleet Air Arm Following the fall of Singapore and the Japanese assault on Sri Lanka in 1942, several Royal Naval Air Stations and Royal Air Force airfields were setup in India for providing training and maintenance support to British aircraft carriers operating in the Eastern waters. At Cochin, the Royal Air Forcehad set up an Air Ministry Experimental Station on Willingdon Island, in

1941 which was followed by a maintenance unit, an operations room and an advanced Flying Boat base.

Nearly eleven years before the commissioning of *Garuda* at Cochin, a Royal Naval Aircraft Repair Yard, *HMS Garuda,* had been commissioned at Peelamedu, Coimbatoreon October 1,1942, and was in operation for over three years. *HMS Vairi,* commissioned at Sulur, Coimbatore on February 1, 1945, was a depot establishment for 500 aircraft and operated Hurricane IIC and other aircraft from its airfield from November 1943 until the end of the War. On July 1,1944 *HMS Vallum* was commissioned at Tambaram, Madras which had the dual function of an aircraft repair yard and a frontline air station, operating aircraft of a Fleet Requirement Unit until March 1945. In 1943, the Royal Navy established the Royal Naval Air Station at Cochin which had an Aircraft Erection Depot for assembling carrier aircraft, transported by sea for use in the naval theatres of war in the east, at the rate of 130 aircraft per month. This section was commissioned as *HMS Kalugu on* February 1, 1945, which was later decomissioned on August 1,1946. Consequent on the acquisition of Sealand aircraft for the Fleet requirement Unit in January 1953, the requirement of setting up a Naval Air Station with an airfield and other facilities for operating and maintaining aircraft, was projected to the Government. The choice fell on Cochin for the already existing naval base at this place, *Venduruthy,* which had already become the premier training establishment of the Navy, was continuous to the airfield used by the Director General of Civil Aviation to operate the domestic air service. In fact, the airfield and the various facilities had already been taken over by the Navy on January 1,1953 and commissioned as *Venduruthy II,* an adjunct of the main training establishment. The first Sealand aircraft touched down at the newly acquired airfield at Cochin, on February 4,1953.

The first such facility to be established was the School for Aircraft Handling and Fire-Fighting, later renamed the School for Naval Airmen (SFNA), which was set up on August 17,1956, with Lieutenant Commander *BS.* Ranjit as its first Officer-in-Charge, for training non-technical personnel in such disciplines as airmanships, aircraft-handling, fire-righting, specialised transport, air photo, air traffic control, safety equipment and aircraft recognition. On June 3,1957, the Naval Air Technical School (NATS) was set up with Lieutenant Commander V.V.Narayan as its first Officer-in-Charge for the training of all naval aviation technical personnel as well as the technical training of pilots, observers and flight engineers.

The Observer School was established in March 1960, with Lieutenant H.C. Bhandari as its first Officer-in-Charge for indigenising the training of Observers who had hitherto been trained in the UK.

Until 1956, maintenance of all naval aircraft had been entrusted to the Hindustan Aircraft Limited (HAL), Bangalore, but in July 1956, a HAL repair unit was set up in Cochin. It was, however, felt that the Navy itself should be able to undertake the maintenance of all naval aircraft and hence a Naval Aircraft Repair Organisation (NARO) was established at Cochin in February 1960 with Lieutenant Commander V.S.P. Mudaliar as its first Superintendent. This organisation was also entrusted with the testing and tuning of all new systems and equipment.

In November 1960, was established the Naval Aircraft Inspection Service with Lieutenant J.Stephen as its first Chief Inspection Officer for ensuring an effective quality control of all equipment fitted in naval aircraft. While *Hansa,* at Sulur, Coimbatore, continued to function as the mother establishment of all jet aircraft, its location was not considered satisfactory. The Navy had been seeking to transfer this air station to a suitable site on India's eastern or western seaboard but none of the existing ports met the requirements of a naval air station. The fortuitous liberation of Goa in 1961 presented a golden opportunity to Naval planners as Dabolim in Goa, situated halfway between Cochin and Bombay, has a fully developed airfield which had been used by the Portuguese for several decades. This airfield was soon handed over to the Navy to set up its second naval air station, the existing 4,500-foot runway extended to 8,000 feet and other facilities created. On June 18,1964 Hansa and *INAS 551* were transferred from Sulur,

Coimbatore, to Dabolim, to be followed by the stationing of *INAS 300* at this air station in September 1964, after its disembarkation from *Vikrant.*

In order to ensure the availability of Alouette helicopters at Bombay for operations from ships and for search-and rescue purposes, a small unit for the maintenance of helicopters was set up at *Kunjali in* the same year.

India's First Aircraft Carrier

In 1943, the hulls of six aircraft carriers of the Majestic light fleet class were laid down in British yards and launched during the years 1944 and 1945. The carriers were expected to be commissioned for the Royal Navy for operations during World War II but the cessation of hostilities in 1945 led to the stoppage of work on their construction. However, only one out of the six carriers, the *Leviathan,* was never completed and was finally broken up in 1968 but the other five were eventually completed and operated by three navies. The Hercw/es was acquired by the Government of India and commissioned as *Vikrant* in 1961, the *Magnificent* was completed and acquired by the Royal Canadian Navy in 1948 (and disposed of in 1965), the *Terrible* was completed in 1949 and transferred to the Royal Australian Navyin 1949 as *Sydney, the Majestic was* completed in 1955 and transferred to the Royal Australian Navy as *Melbourne;* and the *Powerful* was completed in 1957 and acquired by the Royal Canadian Navy as *Bonaventure.* To quote Balbir Law: Naval Headquarters had continued to press for acquisition of an aircraft carrier and serious negotiations had begun with the Admiralty. In 1956, a new Chief of Naval Aviation was appointed-Captain R.HJP. Carver, RN. The Air Arm owes much to this CONA during whose term of office all the detailed planning for acquiring and manning the aircraft carrier was undertaken. He was an officer with a distinguished war record and quickly moulded his team in New Delhi with determination, skill and affection, to move forward. Even socially, the Air Branch became more conspicuous in the military and Government circles. The Carvers did much to build new bridges between the Air Branch, the Air Force and the Army.

A new training programme was launched to prepare for the manning of the carrier and her operational squadrons. A small Naval flying unit was established at Sulur, Coimbatore, to refamiliarises aircrew and maintenance personnel with operating jet aircraft (Vampires). We had one empty hangar and four empty wartime barracks at Coimbatore-the two separated by a distance of almost fifteen miles, and for which we were provided one three-ton truck and a jeep, to start with. The lack of essential facilities and comforts bound us together, made us improvise, and every one found the challenge of achieving the assigned tasks exhilarating. We ferried in our own Vampires, and made do with' furniture' from empty crates and within days the flying task began. We established friendly ties with the local Air Force and the Army contingents. Almost all the officers and men, who were at Coimbatore during the early stages, later rejoined me to form the 300 Seahawk Fighter Squadron. Naval Headquarters was also concerned about providing adequate shore facilities for the new carrier and her operational aircraft. The airfield at Cochin was too small with no room for suitable expansion. Furthermore, it was surrounded byrapidly developing commercial centres which demanded expansion of the commercial ports and ancillary facilities. Alternative sites and disused airfields, along the coast but within easy reach of the sea, were being looked at.

At about this time, Captain Carver's period of secondment to the Indian Navy came to its end and the Admiralty deputed another distinguished officer who remained at Naval Headquarters until after the new carrier had arrived in India. The appointment of CONA had also been upgraded to the rank of Commodore. The new CONA, Commodore (later Rear Admiral) D.W. Kirke, had already acquired a reputation in his own service as a 'go-getter' and had earlier helped in the development of the Australian Naval Air Arm. He was a man with a strong personality, boundless energy and a strong sense of humour and could be at ease with anyone from the peon to the Minister. He knew that unless detailed target dates were established, it would not be possible to man and commission the carrier within a predictable period of time. The overall plan existed but its implementation required quick and responsible decisions. It was a critical phase in which charm, tact and bluntness were needed to achieve the immediate objective. Commodore Kirke felt very comfortable in his new driving seat with in a couple of days of his arrival at Naval Headquarters and soon went into action. As a couple, the Kirkes were very affectionate and sincere and, within a remarkably short time, became an important part of the small, busy social circle of New Delhi.

The CONA and his staff faced a complex organisational task involving three countries. Selection of all the different categories of personnel, their training schedules at different establishments and manufacturers of ships, aircraft and equipment, the delivery, acceptance and the positioning of aircraft at different air stations, work-up of squadrons ashore, the trials and commissioning of the carrier, and, finally, the work-up of the ship and her squadrons, was a mammoth task to complete from a distance of 4,000 miles. It required skilful planning, co-ordination and leadership. It was all brilliantly executed by Commodore Kirke who later became the Flag Officer Flying Training in the Royal Navy as a Rear Admiral.

At this stage it was also clear that in the absence of an alternative site having been found, the existing facilities at Cochin and Sulur would have to be improved to receive the frontline squadrons. Support facilities for the Alize's were established, and more importantly, repair and overhaul facilities were extended to include the Sea hawks. A small extension and the strengthening of the runways was undertaken, and provision made for the storage of weapons and ordnance, i.e., bombs, rockets, etc. Much credit is owed to two 'salt-horse' (non-specialist) Captains of *Garuda* during this period, Captain *NS.* Tyabji and Captain (later Commodore) K.K. Sanjana. The former took command of the air station at the critical point when there was a sudden burst of activity on all fronts, training (aircrews and technical personnel), development of the airfield and planning for the future development. His boundless enthusiasm and tenacity-got him thoroughly involved with the Air Branch and most young members of the branch were influenced by his qualities of leadership. Iamreminded of anaccident in which the aircraft, a Firefly had caught fire and the pilot had received severe burns to his face, hands and back. The young officer was in a critical condition and in intensive care. After two or three days, when barely able to whisper through bandages, he asked Captain Tyabji to sit beside him and promise that if he was, in due course, found to be medically fit, he would be permitted to continue to fly. Long before the accident, the Captain had already assessed the character and potential of this bright, handsome young officer, and their determination matched each other's. He kept his promise and Sub-Lieutenant Arindam Ghosh, after months of skin-grafting, joined the frontline antisubmarine 310 Alize squadron. Ghosh regrettably died, when a Rear Admiral, in 1985.

Towards the end of 1959 and early in 1960, our aircrew and maintenance personnel began to assemble at naval air stations in the UK and France and commenced operational flying training on their newly acquired aircraft. Most of the aircrew had no previous experience of operational flying. It was an enormous task to make each individual pilot fully proficient in the skills of using his aircraft as a weapon system, and also to mould the squadron and crews to fulfil the varying roles of naval air warfare. The latter is most important, as naval aircraft do not operate in isolation but are part of a naval task force of which the carrier is a mobile air base. The limitations of size and, therefore, the number of aircraft that can be carried also dictate that aircrews and their aircraft perform a multiplicity of roles.

The frontline squadrons made excellent progress and achieved high standards in all aspects of air training and work-up ashore. They received all the support from the officers and men of their Britishand French parent stations who in turn drew much credit from the achievement of the Indian Naval Air Squadrons. The stations involved were *Lossie mouth* and *Brazody* and French Naval Air Station *Hyeres, Toulon.'*

The Vikrant-Commissioning and Work-up

The keel of the *Hercules,* which was acquired by the Government of India in 1957, had been laid down at High

Walker, Newcastle-upon-Tyne on October 14, 1943. The construction work was undertaken by the renowned shipbuilding concern Vickers-Armstrong and the hull was launched on September 22,1945 by Lady Cripps, wife of the British Chancellor of the Exchequer, Sir Stafford Cripps and the ship was formally named *Hercules*. Further construction was, however, stopped in 1946 because World War II had ended in 1945 and the hull was mothballed. But when it was acquired for the Indian Navy in 1957, the hull was towed to Belfast and its refit was entrusted to another renowned shipbuilding concern, Harland and Wolff at Belfast, Northern Ireland. On completion of refit the ship was commissioned as *Vikrant* on March 4,1961.

During the period from 1957 to 1961, extensive reconstruction and modernisation of the hull and equipment was undertaken and the ship virtually emerged as a new ship. The ship was fitted with state-of-the-art innovations in carrier design such as an angled deck/a mirror landing sight and a steam catapult. The carrier was also tropicalised, additional accommodation provided for the Flag Officer of the Fleet and his staff and certain areas partially air-conditioned, the latest electrical and electronic equipment installed and modem weapons and weapon control systems fitted.

During the early 1950s the Government had continued to be hesitant to commit it self to the creation of a full-fledged Fleet Air Armby acquiring an aircraft carrier. Sir Gopalaswami Ayyangar, the then Defence Minister, had stated in 1952 that no specific time-frame had been set for acquiring a carrier and Shri K.N. Katju the incumbent of the portfolio after Sir Ayyangar, had stated in the *Lok Sabha* in April 1955 that the decision on the camer was yet to be taken. The Defence Committee of the Cabinet finally approved the proposal at its meeting on April 30,1956 (the author then serving in the Military Wing of the Cabinet Secretariat, recorded this historic decision of the Defence Committee of the Cabinet presided by Prime Minister Jawaharlal Nehru), and in 1957 a group of officers and technical staff numbering about 150 arrived at Belfast to supervise the modernisation and completion of the carrier. The flow of officers and sailors continued and early in 1961 larger batches started arriving and by February almost the entire ship's company had arrived.

The ship officially became a unit of the Indian Navy when she was informally commissioned at 1000 hours on February 16,1961 with the Commanding Officer-designate, Captain (later Rear Admiral) P.S. Mahindroo, reading out the commissioning warrant at a simple ceremony at Mustergrave Channel, Belfast. This was done to enable the large complement of officers and sailors, who were staying ashore, to move on board.

The officers and sailors earmarked for the *Vikrant* had been staying ashore in Belfast for a long time and had endeared themselves to the local residents. The Chairman of the Bangor branch of the local Royal Navy Association, Commander T.R. Eames, expressing his appreciation of the high standard of behaviour maintained by the Indians, said: During the three years that the ship was undergoing modernisation, Captain Mahindroo's men had behaved in a most exemplary manner which reflected great credit on the Indian Navy, the ship and the country.

Many homes would indeed miss their cheerful and courteous presence.' Added the *Belfast Telegraph on* February 17, 1961: 'Yesterday the crew accommodation (on board the *Hercules)* became available and early in the morning more than 800 bluejackets of the Indian Navy, carrying heavy kitbags, began streaming on board and settling into their new quarters.

More than 400 of them said farewell to landladies in Belfast and Bangor with whom they have been staying for several months while the carrier was still in the hands of the civilian workers. The remaining 400 arrived in drafts during the past few days and were accommodated temporarily at the Royal Navy Reserve headquarters in Belfast, HMS *Caroline*'. Commenting on her stay in Ulster while her husband, an officer of the *Vikrant,* was busy supervising the carrier's completion, an Indian wife said, Even if Ulster people are not so well versed in foreign news, they have made the greatest impression on us by their warm welcome, and their uninhibited friendliness.

On February 20, 1961 Commodore R.L.H. Marsh of the Royal Navy accepted the ship from Harland and Wolff and informally handed it over to Captain Mahindroo at the ship's berth at Musgrave Channel. On March 4, 1961, Shrimati Viyaja Lakshmi Pandit, the then High Commissioner for India in the UK, renamed her *Vikrant* and formally accepted the ship on behalf of the Government of India fromMrOrr-Ewing, the Civil Lord of the Admiralty, while a formation of Seahawk aircraft flew past dipping their wings in salute to the ship. Present at the ceremony were the 1100 officers and men of the ship, the fourth Sea Land, representatives of Canada, Australia, the USA and Pakistan, the Lord Mayor of Belfast, the General Officer Commanding-in-Chief of Northern Ireland and a large number of Civilian and Service dignitaries.

In its report on the carrier's commissioning ceremony, the *Belfastlelegraph* said A hymn composed in 3,000 B.C. to *Aditi,* the Indian God of Eternity, figured in the commissioning ceremony of the Indian Navy's aircraft carrier *Vikrant.* The four verses of the hymn were recited by the resplendent figure of Captain P.S. Mahindroo. He spoke in Sanskrit, the language in which the hymn was originally written. The ceremony formally commissioning the ship was a mixture of east and west. The drill and marching of a guard of honour and the playing of the ship's small band was of a standard which could not have been bettered by the Royal Navy. But the commands were given in both English and Indian (sic).

The ceremony took place in the giant aircraft hangar of the carrier which is one of the most modern of her kind in the world today. Watching were the officers and men who will man the *Vikrant* and hundreds of guests, including members of the Indian community in Northern Ireland and wives of the crew in colourful saris.

Mr Ian Orr-Ewing, the Civil Lord of the Admiralty, said that the *Vikrant was the* first modern capital ship of the Indian Navy. He had seen the 300 squadron which would operate from the ship and had been greatly impressed with its discipline and operational qualities. Stating that Mrs Pandit, and the *Vikrant* had much in common, Mr Orr-Ewing said they were both dedicated to duty; they were living examples of commonwealth unity; they both made a powerful contribution to the preservation of peace throughout the free world and they both had calm and dignity.

In accepting the ship on behalf of the Indian Government, Mrs Pandit said that the commissioning ceremony represented a major milestone in the naval history of India. Their maritime history went back into the distant past and it was true to say that much of India's new naval traditions, discipline and training methods owed a great deal to the close association they had with the Royal Navy. India's defence policy was based on the principles of peaceful coexistence and they were proud of the growing strength of their naval air arm which was making a valuable contribution to the country's defence.

She read the message from the Indian Minister of Defence, Mr Krishna Menon, in which he described the ceremony as a step forward in the development of the Indian Navy. He wished the ship a creditable tour of duty in the service and defence of their country and said a hearty welcome would await the *Vikrant* when she arrived in Indian waters.

Mrs Pandit added that the Commonwealth could only be kept together by the little people of every country getting to know and understand each other, and not at the top or at meetings of great people. As these little links forged they would have more effect than everything these meetings achieved. The High Commissioner mentioned that two local girls would shortly be marrying members of the crew of the *Vikrant,* and she stressed the importance of people of different countries being able to understand each other and knowing their weaknesses and strength. Mrs Pandit said that this was vital in the cause of world peace. On the following day, March 5, 1961, the *Vikrant* left Belfast and proceeded to Portsmouth and then to Portland for sea trials with Captain *YS.* Mahindroo in command, Commander Y.N. Singh as Commander (Air), Commander (later Rear Admiral) Gautam Singh as the Executive Officer and Lieutenant Commander B.D. Law as Lieutenant Commander (Flying). For about a month, the *Vikrant* conducted the trials of all her flight-deck and other shipboard equipment and returned to Belfast for rectification of defects and the final testing and tuning of all equipment. A momentous event that occurred on May 18, 1961 was the landing and arresting of the first jet aircraft, a Seahawk, on board the carrier by Lieutenant Commander R.H. Tahiliani, who later rose to the rank of Admiral as the Chief of the Naval Staff. The first deck-landing of an Alize antisubmarine aircraft took place on May 23,1961.

By June 1961 the *Vikrant* had been readied for proceeding to India and towards the end of the month the carrier sailed from Belfast and embarked the aircraft of her jet fighter squadron, the Sea hawks comprising the new 300 Squadron, in the English Channel on August 4, 1961 after a few day's work-up off Portsmouth. During the carrier's brief stay at Portsmouth Admiral Mountbatten came on board to enquire about the performance of the ship's radar which was not providing a 360-degree coverage of aircraft flying around the ship, particularly those behind the stem. He soon took it up with the manufacturers of the radar system and the defect was removed before the carrier proceeded to Plymouth for gun trials and returned to Portsmouth. Meanwhile the carrier had sailed for Toulon in France where she had embarked the aircraft of her antisubmarine and reconnaissance aircraft, the Alize"s comprising the 310 Squadron, on May 23,1961. Also embarked on the same day were two Alouette Helicopters for the *Vikrant's* 321 Flight loaned from the French Navy for search-and-rescue duties at sea and for carrying out 'plane-guard' tasks, i.e., standing by to rescue the crew of ditched aircraft during flying operations. She then sailed for Malta for an intensive six-week work up during which *Rajput* joined her to carry out plane-guard duties as the helicopters on board the carrier could not operate at night.

The Guru

It had been decided that a very small team led by an experienced naval aviator should guide the work-up and submit an independent report on the standards achieved at the end of the period. Treacher, who led this team, had recently completed his tenure as Commander (Air) of the Fleet Carrier, *Victorious.* His own very high standards of professional ability, tact and qualities of leadership, inspired everyone. The entire ship's company rose to meet the challenge and demands of a very intensive period of training for the next three months. Treacher's total commitment to the task and close involvement with every aspect of the work-up brought him in close contact with practically the entire ship's company. Most of the sailors and, in particular, those of the Supply and Secretariat (logistic support) Branch found it easier to call him Commander 'Teacher'. Towards the end of the Work-up, when most people had smiles achievement on their faces, they affectionately called him Commander 'Guru'.

The task of working up the carrier began with the initial deck-landing qualifications of the frontline squadrons off the South Coast of England, then off Toulon, France and finally off Malta. This was a most exciting period and could well be described as the point were Indian Naval Aviation came of age. Operational work-up involves moulding the ship, aircraft and crews to undertake all operations, offensive and defensive, by day and by night, with live weapons, conducted with efficiency and in as short a time as possible. Every one displayed the same spirit of enthusiasm and confidence as during those early days at Cochin, and the work-up was a total success.

The Commanding Officer received kudos from the C-in-C, Mediterranean FIeet and a number of other senior naval observers and was congratulated on the carrier's excellent performance which was particularly noteworthy because Captain Mahindroo was not an aviator hi self but had imbibed all the fine points of flying safety and carrier operations during his short attachment to the Royal Navy's aviation establishments and carriers. Recalls Mahindroo: During the work-up we had to make sure that all pilots were adequately trained in night-flying at Malta because once we left Malta we would not have these facilities at sea or in India. Our plane-guard ship, the *Rajput,* had a number of breakdowns and hence could not always accompany us.

The *Vikrant* sailed from Malta on October 6, 1961 proceeded to Toulon to return the two helicopters borrowed from the French Navy and then set course for India and reached Bombay on November 3,1961 after calling at Alexandria, Port Said and Aden and after disembarking the 300 Squadron and the 310 Squadron at sea off Bombay, these squadrons proceeding respectively to Sulur and Cochin.

Vikrant's Homecoming

A day before her arrival, the carrier had been joined by *Beas* and had proceeded towards Bombay with two escorts, the *Rajput* and the *Beas,* and as she entered the home waters on November 3, she was given a rousing reception by the flagship, *Mysore,* with aircraft of the Indian Air Force taking part in a flying welcome to the carrier. The carrier majestically sailed into Bombay harbour and secured alongside at Ballard Pier at 1702 hours on that momentous day and received a tumultuous welcome. A large number of senior dignitaries including the Prime Minister of India, Pandit Jawaharlal Nehru, and the Chief of the Naval Staff, Admiral R.D. Katari, were present at Ballard Pier to welcome her home.

Rear Admiral P.S. Mahindroo reminisces on watershed in India's naval history and records his impressions of his stay in England prior to the carrier's commissioning and of her work-up and shake-down cruise thus: Everyone on board was full of pride on the commissioning day. Pride not merely due to the fact that they formed the complement of the largest ship of the Navy, but also because they were entrusted with the task of making India's first aircraft carrier a first class fighting unit. Today, thirty years later, probably very little is remembered of the efforts put in by the advance party of the Indian Navy who, with the help of the Admiralty Overseeing Team, supervised the refit and modernisation of the *Vikrant* Hundreds of workers of Harland and Wolff shipyard also worked hard for three years to make the ship operational.

Naval Headquarters, in consultation with the Admiralty, had decided which machinery and equipment onboard the Hercules were to be changed and which were to be overhauled and refitted. After obtaining Naval Headquarters' approval on major work to be carried out, the shipyard began modernising the ship. At first our officers and the Overseeing Team members would meet the manager of the shipyar data conference once a month to check the progress. Towards the end, this was changed to once a week. During March 1960, Admial R.D. Katari, and given the good news that had been selected to command the Indian Navy's first aircraft carrier. He had asked me howlfelt.

Towards the end of 1960 the Indian Chief of the Naval Staff came to England. Hevisited Belfast and saw the carrier under refit and was fully satisfied wit h the progress. There was, however, one point that had been worrying him. The first Sea Lord had suggested to Admiral Katari that as the Indian Navy had no previous experience of carrier operations it might be a good idea if a Royal Navy Captain trained us during the work-up and until our arrival in India, the Royal Navy Captain and take over the ship after its arrival. Admiral Katari asked for my reaction. But we could not have two captains on the ship. The Naval Chief assured me that he had full confidence in our officers and men and was certain that we would fulfil the task entrusted to us.

The carrier was to be commissioned as *Hercules* on February 16, 1961, when the ship's company of about 50 officers and 800 sailors would start living on board. The responsibility of looking after the ship would then be taken over from the shipbuilding yard by our officers and sailors. At this stage, the highest priority was given to living accommodation, mess-decks, galleys, pantries etc. Harbour trials of machinery and equipment were also carried out. The ship then went out to sea on a couple of occasions to test her machinery but the main sea trials were to be held after the commissioning. Thereafter trials and acceptance of flight-deck machinery, gunnery equipment, radar system, flying control systems, etc., were to be held at Portsmouth and Plym outh. A batch of about 400 sailors was due to arrive from India two or three days before the commissioning. It was impossible to find accommodation for such a large number in hotels and guest houses. *Caroline,* the headquarters of the Royal Naval Reserve at Belfast, came to our rescue. With the kind courtesy of the Commanding Officer we managed to accommodate this large number of sailors in the twin decks of that ship On the morning of February 16, on board and after inspecting a guard of honour, addressed the ship's company. After the commissioning the momentum of the work on board increased. Both the civilian workers of the Yard and the ship's company got busy in getting the ship ready for the final take-over and eventual departure from Belfast.

Our first priority now was preparing for the naming ceremony to be held on March 4, 1961. Even though the ship was thronged by Yard workers, she had to be got ready to receive important dignitaries and other guests. After the *Herculeshad* been renamed the *Vikrant on Match 4, sea* trials and work continued at Belfast until the carrier was ready to sail for Ports mouth towards the end of June. By this time, some officers and men had been away from home for more than three years. A few had even got married to Irish beauties. More than 700 well-wishers were on the jetty to give the *Vikrant* a splendid send-off on the day of departure. We could see waving scarves for a long time. On arrival at Portsmouth and after an exchange of normal courtesy calls, we got down to the main task of testing the equipment. We were assisted by experts of the Royal Navy, manufacturers of the various equipment, RN Dockyards and experts from various RN specialist schools. This phase was gone through with a lot of care as it was known that after completion of trials and acceptance of equipment, the responsibility for the machinery would rest entirely on officers and men of the carrier.

Our pilots had now completed their training. They had flown from airfields but had no experience of landing and taking off from a narrow and restricted deck of a moving ship, in this training we were assisted by a very experienced and able officer of the Royal Naval Fleet Air Arm, Commander J. Treacher. He helped ensure that all flight-deck machinery and equipment were tested to provide 100 per cent efficiency and safety. Healso supervised the procedures adopted for flying control and flight-deck operations. He stayed with us during our work-up at Malta until we finally sailed for India.

After the acceptance of the equipment, the *Vikrant* went out to sea and worked up off the Isle of Wight. This gave us the feel of the ship. Any defects that came to light and were beyond the capacity of the ship's company were rectified by the Royal Naval Dockyard. During this month pilots also got their initial practice of 'rolling' (touching down and taking off) on the deck and eventually landing and taking off from the ship. It was during the six weeks at Malta that the ship worked up to her operational efficiency to enable her to launch and recover our aircraft. The work up at Malta was indeed an experience. The ship spent normally five days at sea and returned to harbour for replenishment on week-ends. The tempo of flying training during the work-up period could be gauged from the fact that the *Vikrant* completed 1000th deck-landings by the end of September 1961, berely six weeks after her arrival at Malta. A 'well-done' message was received from Naval Headquarters, New Delhi. Malta offered excellent facilities for training our pilots in night-flying. Again Plane-guard was a problem. But a friendly approach to the local Royal Air Force enabled us to get their sea-rescue launch for three to four hours every night, and we managed to qualify some of our senior pilots in night-flying.

We had achieved a high degree of efficiency. Drills in flying control, on the flight-deck, aircraft direction room and operations room were perfected. There was complete coordination and understanding between the bridge and the engine room. On October 6, 1961 we sailed from Malta. Eight Sea hawks flew over Malta to bid farewell to our hosts for two months. On our return journey to India we paid courtesy calls at Alexandria, Port Said and Aden. Flying practice was carried out throughout the passage. *Vikrant* entered home waters on the morning of November 3, 1961. Demonstrations of rocket firing, strafing and bombing were carried out by twelve Sea hawks and four Alizes. These demonstrations were witnessed by dignitaries embarked on the *Mysore.* These aircraft also flew over Worli, Dadar, Byculla and the Gateway of India. Jet aircraft and maritime reconnaissance Liberators took part in a flying welcome accorded by the Indian Air Force. In the afternoon we berthed at Ballard Pier.

Bibliography

Ajey Lele: *Strategic Technologies for the Military : Breaking New Frontiers*, Sage, Delhi, 2009.

Arend, A.: *International Law and the Use of Military*, London, Routledge, 1993.

Armacost, Michael H.: *The Politics of Weapons Innovation: The Thor-Jupiter Controversy*. New York: Columbia University Press, 1969.

Baldeo Sahai: *Indian Navy - A Perspective : From the Earliest Period to Modern Times*, Publications Division, Ministry of Information and Broadcasting, 2006.

Betts, Richard K.: *Cruise Missiles: Technology, Strategy, Politics*. Washington, D.C.: The Brookings Institution, 1981.

Binkin, Martin: *Military Technology and Defense Manpower*. Washington, D.C.: The Brookings Institution, 1986.

Blackwell, James: *Thunder in the Desert: The Strategy and Tactics of the Persian Gulf War*. New York: Bantam, 1991.

Bracken, Paul: *The Command and Control of Nuclear Forces*. New Haven, Conn.: Yale University Press, 1983.

Brodie, Bernard: *The Absolute Weapon*. New York: Harcourt, Brace, 1946.

Carver, Michael: *Twentieth-Century Warriors*. New York: Weidenfeld & Nicolson, 1987.

Chandra, R.: *Judicial System in Mechanical Warfare*, Lucknow, Print House (India), 1992.

Deitchman, Seymour J.: *Military Power and the Advance of Technology: General Purpose Military Forces for the 1980s and Beyond*. Boulder, Colo.: Westview Press, 1983.

Din, Allan M.: *Arms and Artificial Intelligence: Weapons and Arms Control Applications of Advanced Computing*. New York: Oxford University Press, 1987.

Fallows, James: *National Defense*. New York: Random House, 1981.

G.M. Hiranandani: *Transition to Eminence : The Indian Navy 1976-1990*, Lancer Pub, Delhi, 2005.

G.M. Hiranandani: *Transition to Triumph : History of the Indian Navy 1965 - 1975*, Lancer, Delhi, 2000.

H.B. Kala: *Demystifying Military Leadership*, Manas Pub, Delhi, 2003.

Jones, W.H.: *The Government and Politics of Indian Military*, London, Hutchinson, 1971.

Mary, W.: *Military Space Force: the Cultural Dimensions of Authority*, Cambridge, Belknap Press, 1985

Posen, B.R.: *The Sources of Military Doctrine*, Ithaca, 1984, Cornell Univ. Press.

Radhakrishna: *Handbook of Military and Defence Services*, Sumit Enterprises, Delhi, 2009.

Ralph, Robert: *Probabilistic Risk Assessment in the Nuclear Power Industry: Fundamentals and Applications*. New York: Pergamon Press, 1988.

Rosen, P.: *Societies and Military Power: India and its Armies*, Ithaca, Cornell University Press, 1996.

S. Ram and R. Kumar: *Role of I.N.A. and Indian Navy*, Commonwealth Pub, Delhi, 2008.

Vadm MK Roy: *War in the Indian Ocean*, New Delhi, Lancer, 1995.

Index

□□□